Moosa Salim Jabir Al Azri

Foreign Investment in the Sultanate of Oman

Moosa Salim Jabir Al Azri

Foreign Investment in the Sultanate of Oman Legal Guarantees and Weaknesses in Providing Investment Protection

KS
KLAUS SCHWARZ VERLAG • BERLIN

Bibliographic information published by the Deutsche Nationalbibliothek
The Deutsche Nationalbibliothek lists this publication in the Deutsche Nationalbibliografie; detailed bibliographic data are available on the Internet at *http://dnb.dnb.de*

British Library Cataloguing in Publication data
A catalogue record for this book is available from the British Library
http://www.bl.uk

Library of congress control number available
http://www.loc.gov

First edition
Layout & Cover: Joachim Trapp, Berlin
Printed in Germany

www.klaus-schwarz-verlag.com

ISBN 978-3-87997-462-7

Acknowledgements

I would like to express my sincere thanks to my supervisor, Professor Surya Subedi, for all the guidance and tremendous support he has given me in the completion of this work and his valuable advice and wisdom that have proved so inspiring.

I also wish to offer my gratitude to HE Shaikh Mohammed bin Abdullah Al Hinai, Advisor of the State in Oman (the former Minister of Justice), for his support in obtaining my PhD scholarship. My thanks also to Kathryn Spry and Anne White for their proofreading, and to all my family and friends who have given me much needed encouragement and emotional support over the last four years.

Abstract

As a developing country, the Sultanate of Oman finds it relatively challenging to balance foreign investment protection whilst safeguarding its national sovereignty and interests; however, it recognizes the importance of providing the necessary legal protection for foreign investors. This is the first study to examine foreign investment protection in Oman. It identifies existing guarantees and weaknesses in protecting foreign investment within the Omani legal system and establishes how this level of protection could be enhanced from a legal perspective. It examines the extent of Oman's existing legal obligations under the terms of the multilateral and bilateral investment agreements to which it is a signatory, to examine the role they play in safeguarding foreign investors' rights.

It also investigates the effectiveness of Oman's dispute settlement mechanisms for resolving foreign investment disputes. Oman's administrative policies and practices relating to foreign investment are analysed in order to pinpoint any shortcomings in the current system for enforcing foreign investment legislation. Based on these findings, policy recommendations are made which are intended to improve the protection offered to foreign investment in Oman whilst allowing Oman the necessary degree of protection to its own public policy space.

This study concludes that Oman have taken the approach to provide adequate legal protection for foreign investment. In addition, in the context of the development of international investment law, the *Al-Tamimi* case in particular illustrates the need for Omani legislation and legal practice to strike a balance between protecting foreign investors' rights and safeguarding national interests. Moreover, Oman cannot reduce any guarantees in its international agreements, particularly with regard to seeking international dispute resolution, unless it can guarantee an efficient national legal system and dispute resolution mechanism.

Whilst improved legal protection plays an important role in attracting foreign investment, this needs to be part of a broader strategy aimed at making the Sultanate a desirable destination for overseas investors. Thus, this study recommends that in order to enhance protection for current foreign investors and attract future investment Oman needs to establish a specialised investment council with a unified policy, making it easy to do business in the Sultanate. This initiative needs to be supported by a new national arbitration centre in Oman and training to upskill the Omani judges and workforce.

Chapter 2:

Overview on Foreign Investment Related Laws and Policy in Oman

Chapter 3:

Legal Guarantees and Weaknesses under Oman's International and Regional Obligations

Chapter 5:

Guarantees and Weaknesses in the Omani Dispute Settlement Mechanism with regard to Foreign Investment Disputes

Chapter 6:

Findings, Recommendations and Conclusion

Bibliography

I dedicate this book to my father,
who passed away while I was working on it.

0.1 Introduction

A new era started in Oman in 1970 when Sultan Qaboos bin Said al Said became its new ruler but the country was not able to focus on developing foreign investment until the war in the south of the country ended in 1975.[1] At that time, Omani policies and practices concerning foreign investment were a real concern for overseas investors and needed to be evaluated. As Subedi notes, the need to balance providing protection for foreign investors with the regulatory powers of states poses particular challenges for those dealing with the Law of Foreign Investment.[2]

However, since the beginning of the 1990s, the Sultanate of Oman has considerably changed its position toward foreign investment and has developed a new policy to attract Foreign Direct Investment (FDI) that relies on four key elements. These are: devising a new legal framework, facilitating business for foreign investors, liberalizing its economy, and promoting the country as a suitable destination for foreign investment.[3] Omani decision makers adopted this attitude as a result of the widespread notion among developing countries that FDI would enhance the national economy, provide jobs for their nationals and help with the transfer of the latest technology and knowledge, taking into consideration the sharp fall in oil prices, which in 1998 caused the problem of a national deficit of 122 million Omani Riyals (OMR). Consequently, the Omani government was convinced that the only way to attract FDI was by providing the right conditions for foreign investors.[4]

It is clear that the new legal business framework forms the cornerstone of this development that is intended to support FDI by modernizing Oman's investment-related framework to make it more liberal and open.[5] This governmental approach is reflected in the provisions of a number of laws and amendments to these since the early 1990s. The most relevant legislation includes the Foreign Capital Investment Law (FCIL), issued in

1 The Dhofar war was in the south part of Oman (1970-1975) during the Sultan Qaboos era. See Calvin Allen and W Lynn Rigsbee, *Oman Under Qaboos: From Coup to Constitution, 1970-1996* (Frank Cass 2000).

2 Surya P Subedi, 'The Challenge of Reconciling the Competing Principles within the Law of Foreign Investment with Special Reference to the Recent Trend in the Interpretation of the Term „Expropriation"'(2006) 40 Intl Law 121,125.

3 K Mellahi, C Guermat, J G Frynas and H Al-Bortmani, 'Motives for Foreign Direct Investment in Oman' (2003) 45 Thunderbird Intl Bus Rev 431, 433.

4 Ibid 433.

5 Ibid.

1994 by Royal Decree 102/94 and then followed by several amendments; the new Income Tax Law, promulgated in 2009 by Royal Decree 28/2009, and the new Omani Labour Law by Royal Decree 35/2003, amended in 2011 by Royal Decree 113/2011.

Oman has also signed many multilateral and bilateral agreements focusing mainly or partly on foreign investment, the most significant being the World Trade Organisation (WTO) Agreement signed in 2001 and the Free Trade Agreement (FTA) with the United States which entered into force on January 1, 2009.[6] The principle underpinning the protection of foreign investment in customary international law is the classic notion of diplomatic protection and the treatment of aliens.[7] Bilateral treaties have played a significant role in the creation of customary principles of international law[8] concerning the protection of foreign investment, but whether the absence of a comprehensive international treaty has had a negative impact on the development and protection of foreign investment remains a controversial issue.

In terms of attracting foreign investment, Oman still appears to be lagging behind its regional neighbours, despite its strategic location. In 2012, for example, the number of FDI projects in the UAE was 328, whereas Oman had succeeded in attracting just 48 in total.[9] Taking into account the anticipated depletion of the Sultanate's relatively modest oil reserves, attracting and protecting FDI needs to be a priority for Oman.

Since there is an undeniable need for both developing and developed countries to attract foreign investment, the legal aspects of foreign investment cannot be ignored or underestimated.[10] Therefore, the title of this book is 'Foreign Investment in the Sultanate of Oman: The Legal Guarantees and Weaknesses of Providing Investment Protection' and it

6 Office of the US Trade Representative (USTR), 'Oman Free Trade Agreement' <www.ustr.gov/trade-agreements/free-trade-agreements/oman-fta> accessed 25 April 2016.

7 Surya P Subedi, *International Investment Law: Reconciling Policy and Principle* (3rd edn, Hart Publishing 2016) 78.

8 M Sornarajah, The International Law on Foreign Investment (3rd edn, CUP 2011) 232-233.

9 FTB, *The FDI Report 2012: Global Greenfield Investment Trends* <http://ftbsitessvr01 ft.com/forms/fDi/report2012/files/The_fDi_Report_2012.pdf> accessed 25 April 2016.

10 Richard J Hunter, Robert E Shapiro and Leo V Ryan, 'Legal Considerations in Foreign Direct Investment' (2003) 28 Oklahoma City ULRev 851, 872.

represents the first comprehensive legal study to examine the current weaknesses in Omani legislation regarding foreign investment and to review these laws in the context of international law. It aims to determine whether these new legal developments will be effective at achieving the goal of attracting foreign investment to Oman and protecting it.

0.2 Research Aim and Objectives

The main aim of this research is to identify the guarantees and weaknesses in the existing Omani legal system regarding the protection of foreign investment and to establish how the level of protection offered to foreign investors could be enhanced from a legal perspective. Appropriate national legal instruments play a crucial role in ensuring that a safe and well-regulated environment is provided for all investment partners, including foreign investors. Therefore, all Omani legislation addressing the issue of foreign investment, especially its FCIL, will be scrutinised.

Attention will also be paid to assessing the functions of some key multilateral and bilateral investment agreements to which Oman is a party, in order to determine the extent of its obligations under these treaties and the role that they play in safeguarding the rights of foreign investors. Therefore, Oman's commitments under international agreements, such as the terms of the multilateral WTO agreements, The Cooperation Council for the Arab States of the Gulf (GCC) Economic Agreement, Oman's bilateral investment treaties (BITs) and its FTA with the United States, will be examined.

In addition, Oman's administrative policies and practices relating to foreign investment will also be investigated in order to pinpoint any shortcomings in the current system and any failures in enforcing foreign investment legislation in Oman.

The dispute settlement mechanism that currently operates in Oman for dealing with foreign investment cases will be investigated by analysing the approach taken towards foreign investment cases by both the Omani courts and independent dispute settlement bodies. This analysis will provide a clear picture of the legal guarantees that are currently in place for foreign investors in Oman and the challenges that remain to be tackled.

Finally, legal findings and policy recommendations where it is neccceasry will be made which are intended to boast foreign investors' confidence and improve the legal protection of foreign investment in Oman. The current legal system governing foreign investment in Oman will be analysed in order to identify any policy reforms needed in existing regulations and practices.

0.3 Research Questions

In order to pursue the main aim of identifying the strengths and weaknesses in the current Omani legal framework regarding the protection of foreign investment in order to establish how the level of protection offered to foreign investors could be enhanced from a legal perspective, this book addresses the following research questions:

1. What are the recent trends in international investment law and what degree of protection does this law afford foreign investment?
2. How did Oman's foreign investment law and policies evolve?
3. What international and regional obligations does Oman have to protect foreign investment and do these provide adequate safeguards?
4. What are the strengths and weaknesses of the current Omani legal framework?
5. To what extent can Oman's dispute settlement mechanism be relied upon for resolving foreign investment disputes?
6. How can Oman protect its public policy space while extending protection to foreign investors? In other words, what policy can and should Oman undertake to improve the country's economic development by attracting and protecting foreign investment whilest simultaneously enhancing its sovereignty?

0.4 Research Methodology

In order to achieve the aims and objectives of this study and to address the research questions concerning protection for foreign investment in Oman, the main approach involved conducting a thorough documentary research, including literature review and analysis of relevant cases. In addition, interviews with various concerned parties were used to gather data on the perceived strengths and weaknesses of the current legislation on foreign investment and existing practices in this area.

0.4.1 Documentary Research

There is currently an absence of literature dealing with foreign investment in Oman from a legal point of view, with studies to date having tackled this issue solely from an economic perspective. A number of different areas of literature were examined to provide the background for a theoretical analysis of the questions posed by the research. Both primary sources and secondary sources were scrutinized, beginning with existing Omani legislation including the FCIL, the Companies Law, Labour Law, and other related legislation.

In addition, the potential role of general international law and the treatment of aliens and the principles of international minimum standards of customary law including the concept of fair and equitable treatment are considered in relation to the case of Oman.

The regional and international agreements (bilateral and multilateral) and conventions to which the Sultanate is party are also scrutinized in accordance with the rules and principles of general international law.

An analytical approach will be adopted to investigating Omani dispute settlement mechanisms and the procedures and approaches applied in the litigation and arbitration systems in Oman, regarding foreign investment issues.

The practices applied by related organisations are identified and evaluated and information relating to the legal challenges faced by foreign investors gathered from reports issued by the Omani government and by other corporate bodies in order to gain an insight into difficulties created by current practices and policies.

Secondary sources used include texts, specialist journal articles, national and regional newspapers, business magazines and relevant literature. Material was collected mainly from the Brotherton Library, University of Leeds, the Edward Boyle Library, University of Leeds, the Laidlaw Library, University of Leeds, the Omani Public Authority for Investment Promotion and Export Development (PAIPED), Omani Ministry of Commerce and Industry (MoCI), Omani Ministry of National Economy, Omani Chamber of Commerce and Industry.

Relevant cases which were ruled on by the Omani Courts, international courts and arbitral cases are considered in order to examine the practice in national and international courts and tribunals in issues related to foreign investment. The cases issued by Omani courts are in Arabic, and mainly come from two judicial organs: the Omani Administrative Court and the Commercial circuit of the Omani courts. *Adel A Hamadi Al-Tamimi v Sultanate of Oman (Al-Tamimi)* is an example of the arbitral award to which Oman is a party. The case is subject to the rules of the Oman-USA FTA and was taken to the International Centre for Settlement of Investment Disputes (ICSID).[11] It is analysed in order to examine the effectiveness and compatibility of the Omani judicial and legal system. This involves a comparative analysis of the key issues involved in this case. It is relevant because it is a recent case as the award was issued on 27 October 2015. The rulings of the Tribunal in this case are extensively referred to throughout the book, since it raises a number of different important issues related to the foreign investment environment in Oman.

Finally, it is important to mention that although this research is not essentially comparative, limited comparative analysis is undertaken in the final chapter for legal and policy recommendations. This comparative perspective involves comparison with Singapore and the United Arab Emirates (UAE), whose experiences may provide lessons for the Omani legal system on foreign investment. The relevance of both countries is explained in Chapter Six.

0.4.2 Interviews

In order to understand the actual situation on the ground and address the objectives of the study, it is important to gather a variety of perspectives on the legal issues from concerned parties. In order to provide explanations and insights into the guarantees and weaknesses of the protection of foreign investment in Oman, a number of interviews were conducted with relevant professionals.

0.4.2.1 Choice of Participants

Purposive sampling was adopted with regard to the identification and choice of participants. In purposive sampling, participants are selected on the assumption that they have the experience and knowledge needed to answer the questions.[12]

---

11 *Adel A Hamadi Al-Tamimi v Sultanate of Oman* (Award) 27 October 2015 ICSID Case No ARB/11/33.

12 Uwe Flick, *An Introduction to Qualitative Research* (4th edn, SAGE 2009) 122.

The researcher's priority was the relevance of the selected sample group and their potential contributions to answering the book's questions.[13] The group of participants and the number of interviewees (16) were chosen for two reasons: first, the number of professionals dealing with foreign investment issues in Oman is limited; second, the analysis in the research relies largely on the documentary study.

Following the above, the choice of interviewees was based on the roles played by them. Participants were selected from four groups engaged in foreign investment matters: foreign investors; lawyers representing foreign investors (lawyers); government agencies engaged in policy formulations and legal drafting (policymakers) and judges dealing with foreign investment cases (judges). They included four foreign investors, five policymakers (one minister, two from MoCI and two from PAIPED), four lawyers specialised in representing foreign investors before Omani courts and authorities, and three judges.

0.4.2.2 Conduct of Interviews

Qualitative interviews took place from July to September 2014. Participants mainly were contacted by phone inviting them to participate in the interviews. Some of them were identified before the fieldwork and others were referred to by others. Prior to the interview, participants received the research questions, information about the study and the consent form. Most participants communicated their willingness to participate in the interviews by contacting the researcher by telephone. All the interviews were carried out in Oman, in the workplace or offices of the participants or in a place they chose, such as their home.

While some interview questions covered broad issues relevant to all participants, a few specific questions were developed for each group, i.e., foreign investors, lawyers, judges or policymakers. The aim of so doing was to elicit as much information as possible from the targeted group. The questions were framed in open-ended language in order to allow participants freedom in their responses. In addition, the format contained no leading questions, to avoid pre-empting answers from the participants.

13 S Sarantakos, *Social Research* (2nd edn, Palgrave 2005) 152.

0.5 Research Ethics – Informed Consent and Data Protection

Based on the University's code of ethical conduct, ethical approval was sought and obtained before the commencement of the fieldwork. The Faculty of Education, Social Sciences and Law, Environment and LUBS (AREA) Faculty Research Ethics Committee evaluated and approved the application, which contained a summary of the research, the letters to be sent to the participants, an information sheet and the consent form.[14]

All participants were above 18 years old and not related to any vulnerable individuals. All participants were able to give their consent voluntarily by signing the consent form. In addition, the researcher informed all participants about the interview process and their right to withdraw.

No risk was identified of mental or psychological distress to any of the participants. No conflicts of personal, financial or professional interests were anticipated, and nor accrued. The participants, in their professional capacity, provided information of their own free will without any financial or other inducements. They were told that if they so wished, transcripts of their respective interviews would be made available to them.

All personal and identifying information elicited during the interviews was kept in accordance with the Data Protection Act and the University of Leeds Code of Conduct on Data Protection. Interview transcripts and related notes were kept securely in a locked drawer. In writing up the results, all data was anonymised and information by which participants' might be identified was removed. The collected data will be destroyed after the completion of this research.

0.6 Data Analysis

Typed transcripts of the recorded interviews were prepared. Before proceeding to analysis, familiarity with the data was gained by repeatedly listening to the recordings and reading the transcripts. In order to label words, statements or paragraphs with their assigned meanings, and to generate interpretations of the data, thematic analysis was applied. Thematic analysis was selected because it is a flexible approach, and one

14 The application was approved on 25 April 2014, Ethics reference: AREA 13-058.

which is relatively quick and easy to learn.[15] Moreover, the relatively small volume of data involved, and the purpose of using interviews in this research (to illustrate and support the theoretical analysis, rather than as a boss for theory greater in itself) rendered certain more complex data analysis procedures such as inductive analysis[16] or grounded theory[17] less appropriate for this research. The analysis involved three main steps. First, the data were labelled with keywords in order to label the interview data. This procedure employed both deductive and inductive coding. Deductive is a top-down process whereby codes are decided in advance, based in the research questions or the literature, while inductive coding is botton-up, with codes derived from the data.[18] Secondly, codes and categories were further analysed for differences and similarities. The final stage of the analysis involved identifying concepts and ideas from the common themes. This process, known as theoretical coding, entails interpretation of the data by connecting codes or core categories to the literature, in order to gain deeper insight into the theoretical significance of the data. For example, in the light of the research question, two broad themes of strengths and weaknesses were established, and within each, a number a priori codes (e.g. Judiciary, administrative procedures, Omanisation, taxes, money transfer) were assigned based on prior literature on FDI. At the same time, to maintain openness to the data, flexibility was retained to remove or combine codes. The codes were subsequently graped into categories, reflecting the themes of individual chapters of the the book, such as FDI policy, international obligations, dispute settlement and so on.

In order to eliminate bias from prior assumptions or personal opinions, the researcher treated data consistently and uniformly. The researcher was aware of his responsibility to address the interpretation and analysis of the data provided by the interviewees in an objective manner, and to keep an open mind on the findings.[19] In order to provide better understanding of the data, the findings from the interviews are integrated into various chapters, instead of being discussed in a separate chapter.

---

15 Braun, V. and Clarke, V. (2006), Using thematic analysis in psychology. Qualitative Research in Psychology, 3 (2) 77-101. <http://eprints.uwe.ac.uk/11735> accessed 16 June 2016.

16 See Flick (n 12) 406.

17 K. Charmaz, *Constructing Grounded Theory: A Practical Guide Through Qualitative Analysis* (SAGE, 2006).

18 Braun and Clarke (n 15).

19 Flick (n 12) 318.

0.7 Originality of the Work and Expected Contribution to Knowledge

Whilst researching the topic of this research, no detailed study was found that defines the legal strengths or weaknesses involved in providing investment protection in the Sultanate of Oman, although a small number of papers and articles discuss the issue from the economic and commercial points of view. This study is therefore the first comprehensive scholarly analysis to present the problem of guarantees and weaknesses in providing foreign investment protection in Oman from the legal perspective.

Several studies of the legislation of Arab countries exist, but none relate to the Sultanate specifically, making this research an innovative legal study. It follows that it will be the first that considers the legal guarantees and weaknesses in providing foreign investment protection in Oman. This appraisal also is the first one which presents an analysis of the *Al-Tamimi* case decided by an ICSID tribunal which has wide ramifications for the investment law and policy in Oman. This is the first case against Oman that was referred to ICSID.

In addition, this study is expected to be very valuable for Omani policymakers since it will enable the Omani government as the host country to address the weaknesses in their legal system. It will also help foreign investors to clearly understand the legal guarantees available and challenges they may face in Oman.

Overall, this study will contribute to the area of international investment law by conducting a comprehensive study of the legal framework governing foreign investment in the Sultanate of Oman, filling the current gap in knowledge in this field.

0.8 Outline of the Study

To address the research questions, the book is divided into six chapters, in addition to this introduction.

Chapter 1: The Protection of Foreign Investment in International Law

This chapter is divided into four sections. The first of these analyses the evolution of international investment law, taking into account how laws have responded to changes in the political and economic context and examines four eras of legislative developments: the pre-colonial, the colonial, the post-colonial and the global.

This is followed by a discussion of the important role of customary international law in protecting foreign investment. The idea that there should be legal protection of foreign investors under customary international law has always been controversial[20] since the enforcement of the protection provided by this law has always relied largely on diplomatic and military action by the home country of the investor.[21] Attention is also paid to the key principle of an international minimum standard of treatment, which has been developed to provide protection for foreign investors.[22]

The third section of this chapter analyses the protection of foreign investment under BITs. Although BITs are intended to encourage and protect investment between contracting states, it has been argued that such agreements may have a detrimental effect on economic development in those countries. This section attempts to determine the exact nature of the role of BITs in the development of foreign investment, in particular, the impact of BITs on the development of customary international law in this area, the relationship between BITs and the attraction of foreign investment among signatory countries and the role of BITs in protecting foreign investment.

The absence of comprehensive international treaties dealing with all issues of foreign investment law has meant that international courts and tribunals have different understandings and interpretations of international customary law.[23] Thus, the final section of Chapter 1 assesses the extent to which the absence of a comprehensive international treaty in the protection of foreign investment has led to uncertainty and confusion in this area.

---

20 Patrick Dumberry, 'Are BITs Representing the "New" Customary International Law in International Investment Law?' (2010) 28 PSILR 675, 676.

21 Jan Wouters, Philip de Man and Leen Chanet, 'The Long and Winding Road of International Investment Agreements: Toward a Coherent Framework for Reconciling the Interests of Developed and Developing Countries?' (2009) 3 Hum Rts & Intl Legal Discourse 263, 264-265.

22 Subedi (n 7) 79.

23 See Subedi (n 7) 122; Stephan W Schill, 'Enhancing International Investment Law's Legitimacy: Conceptual and Methodological Foundations of a New Public Law Approach' (2011) 52 Vancouver J Intl L 57, 90-91.

Chapter 2: Foreign Investment Law and Policy in Oman

This chapter focuses on presenting the evolvement of foreign investment laws and policies in the Sultanate of Oman and begins by tracing the development of the Omani legal system since 1970 in order to facilitate understanding of the general legal environment in Oman. It shows how Omani foreign investment law has evolved with the aim of providing better protection for foreign investment, and begins by discussing the previous foreign investment regime, especially the 1974 Law and its subsequent amendments. Finally, the new features of the 1994 FCIL are analysed.

Chapter 3: Legal Guarantees and Weaknesses under Oman's International and Regional Obligations

This chapter provides an analysis of Oman's international investment and investment-related agreements, including those with the GCC, the WTO Agreements, its FTA with the USA, Oman's BITs and GCC-Singapore FTA. In addition, it investigates the obligations provided by international treatment standards included in Oman's agreements, particularly three kinds of treatment standards: national treatment, most favoured nation (MFN) treatment, and minimum standards treatment. Then, the risk of expropriation in Oman's treaties is examined. Furthermore, Oman's international obligations with regard to three issues; taxes, custom duties and money transfer are analysed. The guarantees and weaknesses of dispute settlement under these treaties are investigated, including the Dispute Settlement Body (DSB) of the WTO, the International Court of Justice (ICJ), Oman's BITs, the Oman-USA FTA dispute settlement provisions, and ICSID. In addition, the impact of the *Al-Tamimi* case on Oman's foreign investment law and policy is analysed.

Chapter 4: Guarantees and Weaknesses in the Omani Legal Framework

This chapter focuses on four key areas. It analyses the Omani national legal system that deals with the foreign investment risk of expropriation, focusing on the following issues: the legal protection from expropriation provided under the Omani system, concerns caused by indirect expropriation, the value of the guarantee, guarantees of compensation in Omani legislation on property and intellectual property rights protection, the role of consumer protection, and the associated challenges.

The second part analyses guarantees of non-discriminatory treatment. This done by examining the legal basis for non-discriminatory treatment in Omani law, the incentive of taxation and customs duties, the role of tax incentives, the guarantees provided by Free Zones (FZs), Duqm Special Economic Zone (DSEZ) and Knowledge Oasis Muscat (KOM), the guarantees of transferring money and finally activities in which investors cannot invest.

The third part examines the laws relating to industrial regulations. It considers trade union regulations in Oman, the guarantees for companies wishing to bring workers to Oman, the challenge to employment regulations and the challenges posed by the Omanisation policy and the minimum salary for Omanis.

Finally, the guarantees of political stability are analysed by examining the basis of political stability associated with the concerns behind the handover of power in the Sultanate.

Chapter 5: Guarantees and Weaknesses in the Omani Dispute Settlement Mechanism with regard to Foreign Investment Disputes

Dispute Settlement is an important consideration for any country intending to create an attractive environment for foreign investment. The chapter begins, therefore, by examining the Omani litigation system covering foreign investment. It investigates the reform of the Omani judiciary, the basis for its independence, Omani court practice and the levels of confidence in the Omani national court system.

Then, the chapter analyses whether the Arbitration Law and mechanism in Oman provide an appropriate environment for the resolution of disputes concerning foreign investment. Therefore, it analyses the following issues: the extent to which arbitration is supported by the Omani courts, how arbitral awards are enforced in Oman, and finally, whether the interpretation of public policy in arbitration cases adopted by Omani courts is a narrow or broad one.

Chapter 6: Findings, Recommendations and Conclusion

This chapter presents the research findings and a series of policy recommendations which are intended to enhance legal protection for foreign investment in Oman. The main arguments and findings in the analysis that underpin the overall argument are reiterated. These include the steadiness and consistency in greater foreign investment protection, the contribution of Omani law and practice to the development of international investment law, and the importance of the efficiency of national regulations and practice. The chapter concludes with specific recommendations for providing a better environment to protect and attract foreign investment, drawing on a comparison between Oman's experience and those of Singapore and UAE, especially the Emirate of Dubai. They include a specialised investment council with a unified policy, making it easy to do business in Oman, the need for training and the need for a national arbitration centre in Oman.

Chapter 1:
The Protection of Foreign Investment in International Law

1.1 Introduction

The objective of this chapter is to assess and evaluate the legal basis for the protection of foreign investment under international law. A clear understanding of the actual legal protection offered by international law is needed before investigating the protection available at the Oman national level. In the context of foreign investment it should be clarified that international law is mainly concerned with three issues: (1) the host country's treatment of the foreign investor's property; (2) the state's responsibility when a state act violates international law; and (3) the practice of diplomatic protection by the investor's home country.[24] Therefore, the issue of protecting foreign investment can be approached from two perspectives: that of the exporting countries and that of the host states. The former focus mainly on the interests of their nationals in securing and protecting their investment, whilst the latter are more interested in maintaining their sovereignty over their national territory and economy.[25]

It has been observed that the current international investment framework is the result of "a long and complicated process"[26] and this chapter traces the evolution of international investment law over the course of four historical periods: the pre-colonial era, the colonial era, the post-colonial era and, finally, the global era. It then considers the extent to which customary international law provides protection for foreign investment, by examining two fundamental principles of customary law, which apply to international investment law. The first of these is the availability of the protection offered to aliens under customary international law and the second, the principle of international minimum standards.

In addition, the chapter investigates the role of BITs, which were developed for the purposes of regulating investment and have come to dominate the development of international investment law. Three areas

24 Rafael Leal-Arcas, 'The Multilateralization of International Investment Law' (2009) 35 NCJ Intl L & Com Reg 33, 52-53.

25 See Gerhard Loibl and Malcolm D Evans (eds), *International Law* (3rd edn, OUP 2010) 742.

26 Wouters, de Man and Chanet (n 21) 263.

are investigated in this context: (1) the impact of BITs on the development of customary international law in foreign investment; (2) the role which BITs play in protecting foreign investment; and (3) the role of BITs in attracting foreign investment.

Finally, the impact of the current lack of comprehensive global treaties on the protection offered to foreign investors is explored in order to provide further insights into the area of protection of foreign investment under international law.

1.2 Overview of the Evolution of International Investment Law

This section traces the evolution of international investment law, taking into consideration how it has responded to changes in political and economic circumstances, since it has been observed that the political context from which international investment law emerged has "determined its core character".[27] On this basis, the development of this law can be divided into four eras.

1.2.1 The Pre-colonial Era

Various forms of foreign investment between nations began long before international law was codified. Evidence of this has been found in Asia, Europe, the Middle East, Africa and other parts of the world.[28] Hundreds of years ago, European manufacturers and traders went to Asia, Africa and Latin America to trade with and later invest in local communities.[29] Chinese, Indian and Arab traders all invested abroad together with Europeans as foreign investors in some parts of the world. For example, in the fifteenth century, the Portuguese traded and invested in some parts of East Asia, such as Singapore.[30] Similar cases of foreign investment can be found in various locations in East Asia, China, India, Latin America, Europe and the Middle East.

27 Kate Miles, 'International Investment Law: Origins, Imperialism and Conceptualizing the Environment' (2010) 21 Colo J Intl Envtl L& Policy 1, 1.

28 Sornarajah (n 8) 19.

29 Subedi (n 7) 22.

30 Helen Hughes and You Poh Seng, *Foreign Investment and Industrialisation in Singapore* (University of Wisconsin Press 1969) 1.

Some of the current principles applied in international investment law were already in existence among nations hundreds of years ago. For example, the principle of Most-Favoured-Nation (MFN) treatment can be found in a treaty concluded in 1417 between King Henry IV of England and Duke John of Burgundy in Amiens, which granted English vessels the right to use the harbours of Flanders in the same way as "French, Dutch, Sealanders and Scots".[31] Nevertheless, although during this era there was a practice of foreign investment and emergence of the MFN principle, foreign investment law was still far from emerging.

1.2.2 The Colonial Era

From the late eighteenth century until the end of the Second World War, European colonial powers controlled large parts of Asia, Africa and Latin America.[32] As a result, European investors in these colonies were in less need of protection from international law governing foreign investment.[33] International investment law can be seen as the product of the worldwide growth of European trade and investment during the seventeenth to the early twentieth centuries.[34] It was established as part of the international legal system and was intended to serve as an instrument for protecting the interests of capital-exporting countries.[35] Its principal aim was to prevent the risk of the property of European traders being expropriated or nationalised by the host country, where as imperial powers they applied the legal systems of their home countries.[36] The mid-nineteenth century witnessed the widespread application of international investment principles, which were largely supportive of protection of foreign investment and obliged capital-importing countries to ease trade and investment restrictions.[37]

During this era, the issue of FDI continued to be subject to national law. International law was applied to foreign investment issues in exceptional cases, because the original focus of classical international law, when it evolved in the nineteenth century, was solely on "allocating jurisdiction

31 Subedi (n 7) 91.
32 Kenneth J Vandevelde, 'A Brief History of International Investment Agreements' (2005) 12 UC Davis J Intl L & Policy157, 158.
33 Subedi (n 7) 7; Sornarajah (n 8) 19.
34 Miles (n 27) 1.
35 Ibid 2.
36 Subedi (n 7) 22.
37 Ibid 2.

among States".[38] Therefore, cases involving the host country and foreign investors were dealt with under national law or colonialist power's national law.

In this era there were no known special treaties covering foreign investment. However, most international trade agreements between countries included some provisions dealing with the protection of assets of nationals of one party in the territory of the other. For example, the United States started to "conclude bilateral treaties of "Friendship, Commerce and Navigation" (FCN)" in the early eighteenth century.[39] Another example can be found in the agreement concluded in 1861 between the British Government and the Sheikhdom of Bahrain,[40] which stated in Article 4, that:

> The British subjects and dependants in Bahrain shall receive the treatment and consideration of the most favoured people. [...] All offences which they may commit or which may be committed against them shall be reserved for the decision of the British Resident, provided the British agent of Bahrain shall fail to adjust them satisfactorily.[41]

During this era and before the principle of diplomatic protection was applied, the main trading countries in Europe tended to respond to complaints from influential citizens and companies about trading issues by sending a small fleet of warships to blockade the coast of the host country until compensation had been made for damage incurred by foreign investors. For example, in 1902, the governments of Great Britain, Germany and Italy sent warships to the Venezuelan coast demanding compensation for the losses incurred by their nationals as a result of Venezuela's failure to pay its sovereign debt. Some scholars refer to this period as the Era of Gunboat Diplomacy.[42]

Two legal doctrines played an important role in shaping developments in international investment law in this era. The first of these was the Calvo

38 Leal-Arcas (n 24) 52-53.
39 Vandevelde (n 32) 158.
40 Subedi (n 7) 23.
41 Cited in S D Sutton, '*Emilio Augustin Maffezin v Kingdom of Spain* and the ICSID Secretary-General's Screening Power' (2005) 21 Arbitration Intl 113, 119.
42 Subedi (n 7) 27.

Doctrine,[43] which originated in the nineteenth century, and influenced the constitutions, treaties and investment pacts of several Latin American countries. The Calvo Doctrine consisted of four key elements. First, it argued that in accordance with the principle of sovereignty of states, no foreign investor had the right to permanent ownership of land in the host country. Second, foreign investors were required to bring any disputes arising in a particular state before that state's national courts prior to referring them to any international tribunal.[44] Third, foreign investors should not receive better treatment than that available to citizens of the host state. Finally, the rights enjoyed by foreigners were to be determined by host state laws.[45]

The other influential doctrine which emerged during this period was the Hull Formula,[46] widely regarded as one of the most significant developments in international investment law during this era. The Hull Formula can be said to represent the view of the United States and of other Western countries concerning the rights and obligations of host nations in general and, more specifically, regarding the approach to compensation under international law in the case of expropriation.[47] Hull stated:

> The taking of property without compensation is not expropriation. It is confiscation. It is no less confiscation because there may be an expressed intent to pay at some time in the future. If it were permissible for a government to take the private property of the citizens of other countries and pay for it as and when, in the judgment of the government, its economic circumstances and local legislation may perhaps permit, the safeguards which the constitutions of most

43 Carlos Calvo was an Argentinian jurist who argued as „early as 1868 against the exercise of diplomatic protection and the existence of the minimum standard of treatment". See Andrew Newcombe and Lluis Paradell, *Law and Practice of Investment Treaties, Standards of Treatment* (Kluwer Law International 2009) 13.

44 Subedi (n 7) 29, 30.

45 Newcombe and Paradell (n 43) 13.

46 Cordell Hull was US Secretary of State during 1938. See Tuomas Kuokkanen, *International Law and the Environment: Variations on a Theme* (Kluwer Law International 2002) 180.

47 Subedi (n 7) 32.

countries and established international law have sought to provide would be illusory.[48]

1.2.3 The Post-colonial Era

The post-colonial era began as the Second World War ended and is generally deemed to have continued until the 1990s, when a new period of globalisation commenced.[49] The analysis of the evolution of foreign investment during this era will start by establishing the broader general political and economic situation, before moving onto the actual legal development regarding foreign investment issues.

It can be argued that the political situation during this era was shaped by three trends. First, the developed countries engaged in a programme of massive nationalisation of industries that were deemed to be of strategic importance. At the same time, in the developing world, there was a growing movement against colonisation, which led to an increase in the number of cases involving the taking of foreign investors' property. In addition, newly independent countries regained national control over their own natural resources and economy.[50]

Following the Second World War there was a general fear among countries that had newly achieved their independence that a foreign presence within their economy might serve to weaken their sovereignty.[51] This led to conflicting viewpoints between the capital-exporting developed countries and the capital-importing developing countries concerning the protection of foreign investment. On the one hand, the capital-exporting states placed greater emphasis on protecting and securing the investments of their nationals. On the other, capital-importing states were anxious to retain a certain amount of control over the important parts of their economies.[52]

The period from 1945 to 1990 witnessed the gradual development of a legal regime governing the treatment of international foreign investment but at the same time, there was widespread disagreement within the

48 See Green Haywood Hackworth, *Digest of International Law* (vol 3, US Dept of State 1942) 655-661. The complete correspondence, in English and Spanish, was published under the title *Compensation for American-Owned Lands Expropriated in Mexico* (US Dept of State 1939).

49 Vandevelde (n 32) 158.

50 Leal-Arcas (n 24) 55- 56.

51 Ibid 56.

52 Loibl and Evans (n 25) 742.

legal system concerning the treatment of foreign investors.[53] The ICJ commented on what it saw as an unsatisfactory situation in the early development of international investment law:

> Considering the important developments of the last half century, the growth of foreign investments and the expansion of the international activities of corporations, in particular of holding companies, which are often multinational, and considering the way in which the economic interests of States have proliferated, it may at first sight appear surprising that the evolution of law has not gone further and that no generally accepted rules in the matter have crystallised on the international plane.
>
> Nevertheless, a more thorough examination of the facts shows that the law on the subject has been formed in a period characterised by an intense conflict of systems and interests [...] Here as elsewhere, a body of rules could only have developed with the consent of those concerned. The difficulties encountered have been reflected in the evolution of the law on the subject.[54]

The favouring of a liberal approach to trade by the victorious Allies in the aftermath of the Second World War was one of the most important factors which affected the structure of international law on foreign investment, which can be seen as a reaction against the protectionist policies that had previously been applied during the 1920s and 1930s. This led in 1947 to the establishment of the General Agreement on Tariffs and Trade (GATT), which opened the door for the creation of multilateral agreements by changing the primary legal framework of trade relations agreements from bilateral to multilateral. Although investment issues needed to be addressed outside the GATT framework, there is no doubt that the liberal approach towards trade adopted by the ratifying countries affected international foreign investment law positively.[55]

---

53 Christopher M Ryan, 'Meeting Expectations: Assessing the Long-Term Legitimacy and Stability of International Investment Law' (2007) 29 U Penn J Intl L 726, 726.

54 *Barcelona Traction Light and Power Company Limited (Belgium v Spain)* (Judgment) 5 February 1970 (ICJ Reports 1970,4) paras 46–47.

55 Vandevelde (n 32) 161, 162.

A number of developments in international foreign investment law occurred during the post-colonial era. International foreign investment law started to form as an independent body of law. Moreover, as a further step towards recognising the rights of developing countries, it became acceptable in international law for the host country to expropriate the assets of foreign investors under certain conditions. Nevertheless, according to the Hull Formula, this expropriation had to be accompanied by "prompt, adequate and effective compensation".[56] This era also witnessed the drafting by the Organization for Economic Cooperation and Development (OECD) of the 1967 Convention on the Protection of Foreign Property, as a result of the keenness of its founding members to promote and protect foreign investment. This convention has since been used as a model for many bilateral investment protection agreements. Following this development, the International Chamber of Commerce (ICC) adopted its own Guidelines for International Investments in 1972.[57]

It can be argued that, from the point of view of those wishing to invest overseas during the years immediately following the Second World War, international investment law presented a number of serious deficiencies. First, it offered inadequate coverage of the issues concerning foreign investors at that time, being unable to address the investment practices of the time or to provide legal solutions to issues that concerned investors. For example, one obvious shortcoming was its failure to address the foreign investor's right to make financial transfers from the host state to elsewhere.[58]

Another major problem was related to the ambiguity of the principles being applied, leading to significant differences in interpretations. Moreover, international foreign investment law did not provide any effective enforcement mechanisms to enable foreign investors to claim their contractual rights when these were violated by the host state. In addition to these specific shortcomings, there was the more general difficulty that the content of international investment law was the subject of serious disputes between the developed and the developing countries, which was part of a broader ideological debate in which the

56 Subedi (n 7) 34.

57 Palitha T B Kohona, 'Some Major Provisions in Modern Investment Protection Agreements' (1987) Third World Legal Stud, 151.

58 Jeswald W Salacuse, 'TheTreatification of International Investment Law' (2007) 8 *Stud Intl Fin Econ & Tech L*, 241.

latter demanded a new international economic order that would take their needs into consideration.[59]

As a result, a significant change occurred during the 1970s due to the pressures exerted by investors from developed countries and consequently, the international community began to rely on treaties instead of international customary law, which was doubted in protecting foreign investment and faced difficulties in dealing with various foreign investment issues. Another important reason why customary international law was mistrusted during this era was that it did not grant foreign investors a direct right of action against the government of the host nation.[60] Hence, unlike the colonial era, when the tendency had been for developed countries to rely on themselves to protect the investment of their nationals, in the post-colonial era they began to enter into bilateral agreements with less developed countries, newly industrialised nations, Socialist states and other developed countries.[61]

1.2.4 The Global Era

The current era of globalisation began in the 1990s.[62] Generally speaking, over the last 50 years, and especially since the start of the 1990s, there has been an effort to create a global regime of codified international investment law led by the ever-increasing integration of the world economy.[63] Despite the fact that the investment law dimension of the 1947 Havana Charter[64] was unsuccessful, major efforts continued toward evolving a global system of investment law via a range of instruments, including the 1992 Foreign Investment Guidelines issued by the World Bank.[65] During this era, states generally became reliant on foreign investment and in order to compete with each other, most countries have made significant attempts to provide a favourable and attractive environment for overseas investors, reflected in the incorporation of investor-state arbitration clauses into BITs. As a result

59 Ibid 241-242.
60 Ryan (n 53) 730-731.
61 Kohona (n 57) 152.
62 Vandevelde (n 32) 158.
63 Thomas Waelde, 'International law of foreign investment: toward regulation by multilateral treaties' (1999) *Bus L Intl* 50, 50.
64 The United Nations Conference on Trade and Employment, held in Havana, Cuba, in 1947.
65 Waelde (n 63) 50.

of their awareness of the growing competitiveness of this environment, states now rarely fail to enforce arbitral awards.[66]

Under the international customary law, the host state defines the conditions under which foreigners may establish their investment on its territory. However, legal outcomes that were viewed as unsatisfactory led to the general feeling that there was a need for new legal tools that would facilitate investment movements between states. Consequently, a number of instruments have been created to achieve a positive environment for investment under the terms of public international law.[67] These include BITs, investment insurance schemes, investment dispute settlement mechanisms, and multilateral instruments, such as the WTO Agreements. The current global era has witnessed positive changes in the context of international agreements, a development which is clearly reflected in the merger of trade and investment provisions in these agreements.[68]

Therefore, a noticeable feature which has emerged during this era is the liberalisation of government policies toward FDI. This was largely due to the increasing interest that government policymakers in potential host nations, especially those in developing countries, showed in attracting FDI.[69] As a result of the massive increase in FDI[70] and concern about the implications for the competitiveness of national companies and technology transfer, some developed countries, such as the USA, adopted less liberal attitudes toward FDI, unlike the developing countries. This situation led to the development of international institutional initiatives designed to benefit from the liberal policy in developing countries and create pressure against the position of the USA.[71] Despite efforts by host country governments in recent years to liberalise their FDI policies, there is still concern about finding the appropriate balance between rights and obligations in reference to both foreign investors and host governments within a new international investment law system.[72]

---

66 Guiguo Wang, 'International Investment Law: An Appraisal from the Perspective of the New Haven School of International Law' (2010) *18 Asia Pac L Rev* 19,19.

67 Loibl and Evans (n 25) 711.

68 Vandevelde (n 32) 175.

69 Thomas L Brewer, 'International Investment Dispute Settlement Procedure: The Evolving Regime for Foreign Direct Investment' (1994) 26 L & Policy Intl Bus 633, 639.

70 For example, the total international FDI flows increased from US$88 billion in 1986 to US$234 billion in 1990. See Ibid 633.

71 Ibid 639.

72 Ibid 640.

After 1990 there have also been comprehensive developments in the rule-making instruments which operate at bilateral, regional, interregional or multilateral levels, whether in the form of binding treaties or voluntary instruments.[73] Foreign investors' rights around the world are now protected largely by international treaties, which have become the principal source of international investment law.[74] In particular, this era has witnessed an "explosion in the number of BITs".[75] This situation led one arbitral tribunal in 2003 to suggest that hundreds of BITs had effectively formed customary international law with regard to the rights of investors.[76]

There is no doubt that one of the most important developments which occurred during the current era has been the creation in 1 January 1995 of the WTO[77] which addresses investment issues through its agreements, including the General Agreement on Trade in Services (GATS), the Agreement on Trade Related Investment Measures (TRIMS) and the Agreement on Trade-Related Aspects of Intellectual Property Rights (TRIPS). Of these three, TRIMS is the most relevant to this research since it expanded the jurisdiction of the WTO with respect to investment matters beyond the service sector.[78] The imposition on foreign investment of certain trade-distorting performance requirements is banned by this agreement.

However, it is argued that the international investment system should be considered as more flexible than the WTO system and international environmental and human rights law. This is because in comparison with the former, international investment law includes the non-governmental actors directly in investment disputes, and it is stronger than the soft enforcement mechanism or soft-law regime of the latter.[79]

All these developments have led some authors to assert that the current era is witnessing the emergence of a "common law of international

73 E C Schlemmer, 'A New International Law on Foreign Investment' (2005) J S Afr L 531, 532.

74 Jeswald W Salacuse, 'The Emerging Global Regime for Investment' (2010) 51 Harv Intl LJ 427, 429.

75 Vandevelde (n 32) 176. For example, by the end of 2008 there were 2608 BITs in effect, see Salacuse 428.

76 Salacuse (n 74) 429.

77 World Trade Organization, 'Understanding the WTO: Who we are' <www.wto.org/english/thewto_e/whatis_e/who_we_are_e.htm> accessed 3 May 2016

78 Vandevelde (n 32) 175.

79 Anna de Luca, 'Note on the Yearbook on International Investment Law & Policy 2008–2009: Foreign Investment Promotion and Protection vs Host States' Regulatory Powers (2010) 11 J World Investment & Trade 1115, 1118.

investment".[80] It is argued that this trend toward bilateral and multilateral agreements on investment issues runs contrary to the liberalisation approach of the international investment system.[81] The international investment law system has reached a crossroads, and the scope of this system is broader today than at any other time in history. The increasing number of investment agreements is causing problems for both foreign investors and host countries as each party brings unique expectations and demands to the system. International investment law has developed rapidly in recent years to meet the needs of both capital-exporting and capital-importing countries as a result of all interested parties bringing their own demands and needs to the system.[82] International investment law has faced continual criticism and currently faces challenges from those who call into question its ability to meet the needs of all parties "in a sustainable and predictable manner".[83]

1.3 Protection of Foreign Investment under Customary International Law

Over the course of history, international customary law has played an important role in providing protection for foreign investment through a number of fundamental principles. For example, it is clear that throughout the colonial era and for part of the post-colonial era, customary international law was the primary source of norms for the protection of international investment frameworks.[84] However, the norms of customary international law in the field of foreign investment, like any other customary international rules, are created and applied both together with and independently from treaty rules.[85]

According to the ICJ, customary international rules are the result of extensive, uniform and representative state practice accepted as law. This includes executive acts, legislation and regulations, judicial decisions, international treaties, and verbal acts. Rules enacted in national

80 Anna de Luca 1115, 1118.
81 Schlemmer (n 73) 532.
82 Ryan (n 53) 726.
83 Ibid.
84 Vandevelde (n 32) 160.
85 Tarcisio Gazzini, 'The Role of Customary International Law in the Field of Foreign Investment' (2007) 8 J World Investment & Trade 691, 714.

legislation may reflect customary international rules, provided that they are widespread among states, uniform in their content and coupled with a general sense of legal obligation under international law. The resolutions adopted by the UN General Assembly provide evidence of customary international law.[86] Moreover, because of the horizontal nature of the international law system and the large number of different countries composing the international community, the creation of customary international norms may take place over a considerable period of time.[87]

Regardless of the thousands of investment-related treaties which now exist, it is believed that customary international law still plays an important role in protecting foreign investment.[88] This section will analyse the extent of the protection which international customary law offers to aliens and the principle of international minimum standards. This will be followed by a comprehensive investigation of the extent to which customary international law provides protection specifically for foreign investment.

1.3.1 International Customary Law Protection for Aliens

The weak legal protection offered to aliens during the era of Roman law and the Middle Ages changed with the development of the national state and migration.[89] This protection was expressed clearly, for example, in Article 2 (3) of the 1850 treaty between Switzerland and the United States:

> [I]n case of [...] expropriation for purposes of public utility, the citizens of one of the two countries, residing or established in the other, shall be placed on an equal footing with the citizens of the country in which they reside in respect to indemnities for damages they may have sustained.[90]

Nonetheless, before the Russian Revolution in 1917, international law commentators had no reason to believe that rules were necessary

86 Ibid 692-693.

87 Ibid 695.

88 Ibid 691.

89 Edwin Borchardt, The 'Minimum Standard' of The Treatment of Aliens (1939–1940) 38 *Mich L Rev* 445, 449.

90 Cited in Robert Wilson, *United States Commercial Treaties and International Law* (Hauser Press 1960) 111.

to protect foreign investment, since it was already considered to be safeguarded by the national law of the host country. The assumption was that this national legal framework would guarantee satisfactory protection for alien investors.[91]

The question concerning the protection of aliens in international law is greatly affected by the international relations between developing and developed countries.[92] The former place greater emphasis on the independence and sovereignty of states and reject the economic influence of Western countries, arguing that domestic, not international, law should be the basis of aliens' rights.[93] On the other hand, the latter argue in favour of foreign investors' rights to protect and secure their property.[94]

This difference of attitude among countries seems to have contributed to difficulty in establishing international agreement in this regard. Among early efforts to create a multilateral legal framework to protect aliens and their property were a number of non-governmental initiatives, such as the International Law Association's Draft Statutes of the Arbitral Tribunal for Foreign Investment and the Foreign Investment Court (ILA Statute),[95] and the ICC proposal for an International Code of Fair Treatment for Foreign Investment (ICC Code) in 1949. The Draft Convention on the International Responsibility of States for Injuries to Aliens (1961 Harvard Draft) was prepared by Louis Sohn and Richard Baxter at the request of the UN Secretariat. Although the ILA Statute and the ICC Code were not adopted, both initiatives were important in shifting the main concern from being solely the traditional concept of state responsibility for injuries to aliens and their property, to protection of foreign investment with the aim of promoting economic development.[96]

In addition, the position among scholars and tribunals on the level of protection to aliens is varied accordingly. For example, Nwogugu has pointed out that international law allows the taking of an alien's property without imposing on the host state a corresponding obligation

91 This attitude changed after the Revolution as a result of the expropriations of national enterprises without compensation by the newly formed Soviet Union. See Rudolf Dolzer and Christoph Schreuer *Principles of International Investment Law*, (1st, OUP 2008) 11-13.

92 Malcolm N Shaw, *International Law* (6th edn, Cambridge University Press, 2008) 823.

93 Borchardt (n 89) 447.

94 Shaw (n 92) 823.

95 The Draft Statutes were published in 1948.

96 Newcombe and Paradell (n 43) 21.

to pay compensation except in restricted circumstances.[97] However, one can argue that the agreed rules in international customary law put the responsibility for compensation on states, meaning that they have limited alternatives not to pay reparations.

In the other hand, John Bassett Moore noted in his brief in the *Constancia Sugar* case before the Spanish Treaty Claims Commission, that unlike nationals, aliens do not have the advantage of exercising political rights.[98] Furthermore, the tribunal in the *Hopkins (US) v Mexico* case before the United States-Mexico General Claims Commission of 1923 concluded that "by virtue of their diplomatic and arbitral appeal, aliens may on occasion receive "broader and more liberal treatment' than nationals under municipal law".[99]

In the *Roberts (US) v Mexico* case, the tribunal remarked:

> Roberts was accorded the same treatment as that given to all other persons [...]. Facts with respect to equality of treatment of aliens and nationals may be important in determining the merits of a complaint of mistreatment of an alien. But such equality is not the ultimate test of the propriety of the acts of authorities in the light of international law. That test is, broadly speaking, whether aliens are treated in accordance with ordinary standards of civilization.[100]

The availability of customary international law protection to aliens, including foreign investors, the international law of state responsibility, the concept of diplomatic protection and international human rights law are considered to be the main principles of modern foreign investment law.[101] The treatment of alien property in international law has moved from the position that the alien has submitted to the application of local jurisdiction by entering and carrying on business in the host country, to the principle of diplomatic protection, which incorporates the protection of international minimum standards of treatment.[102]

97 E Nwogugu, *The Legal Problems of Foreign Investment in Developing Countries* (Manchester University Press 1965) 22.

98 Borchardt (n 89) 455.

99 *Hopkins (US) v Mexico* (Award) March 1926, Mexican-US General Claims Commission IV RIAA 41, 42 at 50-51 (1927).

100 *Roberts (US) v Mexico*, I Op COMM 100 at 105 (2 November 1926).

101 Subedi (n 7) 79.

102 Miles (n 27) 15.

Importantly, state responsibility arises when an act of state violates the rights guaranteed to aliens, either under customary international law or under a treaty.[103] The ICJ insisted on host states' obligation to provide protection for aliens and their property under international law. This is clearly reflected in *Belgium v Spain - Barcelona Traction, Light & Power Company, Ltd* where it stated:

> [W]hen a State admits into its territory foreign investment or foreign nationals it is [...] bound to extend to them the protection of the law. However, it does not thereby become an insurer of that part of another State's wealth which these investments represent [...]. The real question is whether a right has been violated, which right could only be the right of the State to have its nationals enjoy a certain treatment guaranteed by general international law, in the absence of a treaty applicable to the particular case.[104]

However, in 2006, the International Law Commission (ILC) issued its Draft Articles on Diplomatic Protection, stating:

> Diplomatic protection belongs to the subject of 'Treatment of Aliens'. No attempt is made, however, to deal with the primary rules on this subject—that is, the rules governing the treatment of the person and property of aliens, breach of which gives rise to responsibility to the State of nationality of the injured person. Instead the present draft articles are confined to secondary rules only—that is, the rules that relate to the conditions that must be met for the bringing of a claim for diplomatic protection.[105]

Jiménez argued that the contents of the standard in the ILC's Draft Articles are not clear. Nor is the nature of the standard clear, either as a general principle of law or of customary international law.[106]

---

103 Subedi (n 7) 79.

104 *Belgium v Spain* (n 54) para 87.

105 Draft Articles on Diplomatic Protection with Commentaries 2006, para 2.

106 Alberto Alvarez-Jiménez, 'Minimum Standard of Treatment of Aliens, Fair and Equitable Treatment of Foreign Investors, Customary International Law and the Diallo Case before the International Court of Justice' (2008) 9 J World Investment

1.3.2 The Principle of International Minimum Standards

Customary international law prescribes certain minimum standards of treatment of foreign investment.[107] Both capital-importing and capital-exporting states have an interest in enhancing the flow of foreign investment. To this end, not only must economic concerns be considered, but also the treatment of foreign investors in the host state.[108] The principle of international minimum standards is the most important legal principle which has been developed to offer protection to foreign investors.[109] The issue which needs to be addressed in this context is how the historical debate between developing countries, which support the national treatment standard, and their developed counterparts, which defend the notion of international minimum standards, can be resolved.

Developing countries, especially those in Latin America, argue for national standard treatment relying mostly on the concept of sovereignty and sovereign equality, and contend that placing an alien in a better position legally than the citizens of the host state is a violation of territorial sovereignty.[110] Furthermore, they assert that every foreigner who resides within the national borders of the state is subject to the law of the territory.[111] Article 9 of the Montevideo Convention on the Rights and Duties of States 1933 supports the notion of the standard of national treatment by stating that:

The jurisdiction of states within the limits of national territory applies to all the inhabitants. Nationals and foreigners are under the same protection of the law and the national authorities and the foreigners may not claim rights other or more extensive than those of the nationals.

On the other hand, developed countries, including the US, the UK and the European states, adopted the position in the early twentieth century that foreign nationals and their property were entitled, under customary international law, to a minimum standard of treatment.[112] Those countries that support international minimum standards argue that states must bring their domestic laws up to the minimum standards

& Trade 51, 57.

107 Subedi (n 7) 78.

108 J Menalco and R Solifs 'Creation and Enforcement of a Minimum Standard of Treatment Applicable to Foreign and Domestic Juristic Persons' (1962) 37 *Tul L Rev* 205, 210- 211.

109 Subedi (n 7) 79.

110 Miles (n 27) 17.

111 Subedi (n 7) 23.

112 Newcombe and Paradell (n 43) 12.

provided by international law.[113] They counter the argument regarding state sovereignty by arguing that states have the right not to admit aliens to their territory, but once admitted, they are entitled to receive a certain standard of civilised treatment. Moreover, they maintain that the national standard of the host state may not provide sufficient protection for foreign investors, if both nationals and foreigners are treated equally badly[114] and the national laws of individual states may not reflect international legal obligations.[115] In such cases, therefore, the notion of national treatment would not provide sufficient protection for foreign investors.

In 1910, Root argued that the standard of justice shaped a part of international law and any national law had to conform to this general international standard in the case of the treatment of aliens. He stated:

> If any country's system of law and administration does not conform to that standard of justice, although the people of the country may be content or compelled to live under it, no other country can be compelled to accept it as furnishing a satisfactory measure of treatment to its citizens.[116]

As Miles has observed, the argument that the host state treats its nationals in like manner was regarded as an inadequate response to the accusation of violation of the minimum standard.[117] As a result, the view that the standard of national treatment applicable to foreigners should not fall below the minimum standard recognised in international law is supported by many scholars in Western countries.[118]

Given the growth in development of international foreign investment, for full implementation of the principle, it is vital whether developing countries accept the application of the international minimum standards of treatment in their territory as an international law principle. Despite early disagreements concerning the principle of international minimum standards, the obligation on the host country to provide foreign investors

---

113 Subedi (n 7) 24.

114 Ibid.

115 Miles (n 27) 17.

116 Elihu Root, 'The Basis of Protection to Citizens Residing Abroad' (1910) 4 AJIL 517, 521–22 cited in Subedi (n 7) 24.

117 Miles (n 27) 17.

118 A F M Maniruzzaman, 'Expropriation of Alien Property and the Principle of non-Discrimination in International Law of Foreign Investment: an Overview' (1998-1999) 8 J Transnatl L & Policy 57, 73.

with the international minimum standard of treatment has become a norm of international customary law.[119] Arbitral tribunal awards have asserted the existence and the application of international minimum standards of treatment.[120] Even as early as 1955, some scholars like Shea announced the death of the Calvo Doctrine because it had failed "to receive recognition as a principle of international law."[121]

Furthermore, as BITs and other bilateral treaties proliferated, the principle of the international minimum standard was expanded to include "full protection and security" of foreign investment by the host states, "fair and equitable treatment" and payment of fair or just compensation against expropriation.[122] Clear support for the principle of international minimum standards can be found in Article 31 of the Articles on State Responsibility which states:

> 1. The responsible State is under an obligation to make full reparation for the injury caused by the internationally wrongful act.
>
> 2. Injury includes any damage, whether material or moral, caused by the internationally wrongful act of a State. The obligation to make reparation is governed in all its aspects by international law, irrespective of domestic law provisions.

With regard to possible shortcomings of the system of protection offered by this principle, Subedi noted that although the principle of an international minimum standard of treatment is broadly settled, its scope and meaning is still the subject of dispute. Exactly what is covered by the international minimum standard remains unclear, for example.[123] This degree of vagueness led Sornarajah to observe that there is no truly international standard relating to the treatment of foreign investors, owing to the disagreement between developed and developing countries on these

119 Dumberry (n 20) 680.
120 Soranrajah (n 8) 334.
121 Wenhua Shan, 'Is Calvo Dead?' (2007) 55 Am J Comp L 123, 123.
122 Subedi (n 7) 80.
123 Ibid.

standards and the collective position of developing countries supporting the instruments linked with the New International Economic Order.[124]

However, one may argue that tribunal practice may be helpful to some extent in clarifying the scope and meaning of the minimum standard that host countries are obliged to provide to all foreign investors under customary international law. In the *Neer v Mexico* case, which is considered to be an influential decision on what state actions are regarded as failing to achieve the minimum standard of treatment,[125] the Tribunal found that:

> [T]he treatment of an alien, in order to constitute an international delinquency, should amount to an outrage, to bad faith, to wilful neglect of duty, or to an insufficiency of governmental action so far short of international standards that every reasonable and impartial man would readily recognize its insufficiency.[126]

It is clear that this case produced an early definition of the international minimum standards by indicating that "the propriety of governmental acts should be put to the test of international standards".[127] A violation of international minimum standards, as explained in the *Neer* case, needs the availability of "an insufficiency of governmental action so far short of international standards that every reasonable and impartial man would readily recognize its insufficiency".[128] One can argue that notwithstanding this explanation by *Neer*, it could not be said that it removed the vagueness. This is because what can be regarded reasonable and impartial by one country might be not to another. In addition, what can be recognised as insufficient by a man from a developed country might not be by another from a developing country.

---

124 Soranrajah (n 8) 334.

125 Thomas J Westcott, 'International Investment Dispute Settlement Procedure: The Evolving Regime for Foreign Direct Investment' Recent Practice on Fair and Equitable Treatment (2007) 8 J World Investment & Trade 409, 411.

126 *Neer v Mexico (Neer)*, Opinion, United States-Mexico General Claims Commission, 15 October 1926, AJIL 555, 1927.

127 Ibid para 4 cited in Barnali Choudhury, 'Evolution or Devolution? Defining Fair and Equitable Treatment in International Investment Law' (2005) 6 J World Investment & Trade 297, 298.

128 Ibid cited in Astha Mishra and Anand Mishra, 'Fair and Equitable Treatment Standard in International Investment Law: an Analysis vis-a-vis Public International Law' (2012) 11–12 Kor ULRev 107, 119.

In 1989 the ICJ reflected the change in the international community since the *Neer* case in the 1920s, in an explanation of the principle of international minimum standards in the *ELSI* case.[129] The Court said state arbitrariness requires "a wilful disregard of due process of law, an act which shocks, or at least surprises, a sense of judicial propriety".[130]

It has been argued that the weak point of the principle of international minimum standard of treatment is the lack of justification to operate per se "in measuring the responsibility of states for injury to foreign investors' property".[131] Furthermore, it is claimed that the extent of the minimum standard does not go beyond identifying the superiority of international law in determining the international minimum standard of treatment which foreign investors should receive from the host state.[132]

However, as Choudhury argues rightly, according to the measures set by the Tribunal in the *Neer* case, only "egregious conduct" may be regarded as a violation of an international minimum standard by the host state. Accordingly, a violation of the international minimum standard would not arise if the action of the government "fell short of being outrageous".[133]

1.3.3 The Protection for Foreign Investment under other Fundamental Principles of International Customary Law

The principle of fair and equitable treatment is considered to be a fundamental principle in international customary law and the most important principle in protecting foreign investors' rights. It provides a primary level of protection for foreign investors, since it is based on fairness and equity. However, although this principle has been interpreted in various ways, the most common claim before international investment tribunals is the violation of the fair and equitable treatment principle by the host country.[134] In addition, arbitral tribunals are concerned with the unity of international investment law and the need for consistency. Therefore, investment tribunals "are very restricted to principles cited by

129 Westcott (n 125) 411.

130 *Elettronica Sicula S.p.A (ELSI) (United States of America v Italy)* (Judgment) ICJ Reports 1989, 15, para 128.

131 Alireza Falsafi, 'The International minimum standard of treatment of foreign investors' property: A Contingent Standard' (2007) 30 Suffolk Transnatl L Rev 317, 362.

132 Ibid 362.

133 Choudhury (n 127) 298.

134 Subedi (n 7) 86.

previous tribunals over the meaning of 'fair and equitable treatment'".[135] This can be seen clearly in the view of the British Court of Columbia that the interpretation of the fair and equitable treatment standard should not go beyond the pre-existing rules of customary international law.[136]

Notwithstanding the view that a fair and equitable standard of treatment is a higher standard than the international minimum standard is not accepted by developed countries, it led to controversy. However, it has been clearly demonstrated by the North American Free Trade Agreement (NAFTA) Commission that whenever the standard of "fair and equitable" was used by NAFTA it was not considered to be a higher standard than the international minimum standard defined in international customary law.[137] Regardless of the debate regarding whether the principle of fair and equitable treatment offers better protection than the international minimum standard of treatment for aliens and their investment under customary international law, tribunals have generally taken the position that the right to a stable and predictable business environment is consistent with the standard under customary international law.[138] The relation between the two principles (international minimum standard and a fair and equitable standard of treatment) will be discussed further in Chapter Three.

Although there is no agreed definition of the principle of full protection and security, it is found in many international foreign investment agreements.[139] In *Noble Ventures v Romania*, it was claimed that Romania was supposed to grant Noble Ventures "full protection and security" by enforcing its laws and providing police protection to the foreign investors situated on its territory.[140] It has been observed that this principle was developed by the United States to provide a firmer basis in customary international law and it has been admitted in many arbitral awards, such as the Iran-US claims, that the failure to provide full protection and security for foreign investment creates liability in the host country.[141]

135 Mishra and Mishra (n 128) 114.

136 Ibid.

137 Sornarajah (n 8) 128.

138 Matthew C Porterfield, 'State Practice and the (Purported) Obligation under Customary International Law to Provide Compensation for Regulatory Expropriations' (2011–2012) 37, NCJ Intl L & Com Reg 159, 167-168.

139 Subedi (n 7) 90.

140 *Noble Ventures v Romania*, ICSID Case No ARB/01/11 Award (12 October 2005), para 111.

141 Sornarajah (n 8) 128.

However, it is worth noting that the initial norms of customary international law relating to FDI were restricted to general principles, including the legal doctrine of state responsibility and the principle of state sovereignty and exclusive territorial jurisdiction.[142] Traditional international law addresses FDI issues in the light of central principles of customary international law, such as the principle of territorial sovereignty, which grants the State the right to admit aliens or to exclude them from its territory, and to "take the property of private persons in pursuit of public purposes".[143] The principle of nationality determines the interest of states in appropriate treatment for their nationals and their property abroad.

In addition, relying on the customary practice on compensation, some raise the point that new principles have emerged that could qualify as being generally accepted as a part of customary law, owing to new developments in the international treatment of investments.[144] Compensation is one of these emerging principles; it is now generally recognised that a foreign investor has the right to compensation in the case of expropriation by the host country, although the conditions for payment of compensation are still a controversial issue. As a result, the absence of established customary principles led countries to conclude thousands of BITs in the 1990s.[145]

1.3.4 Current Level of Protection of Foreign Investment under Customary International Law

One challenge facing foreign investors in relation to the protection provided by customary international law is that the enforcement of its norms relies mostly on diplomatic and military action by the home state of the investor, the result and institution of which is extremely unclear.[146] Therefore, there is an on-going debate about the actual extent of legal protection provided under customary international law[147] and it is argued that it provides insufficient instruments for the protection of foreign investment.[148] Some countries questioned whether customary international law applies as an international minimum standard given that, as mentioned above, many developing countries, especially those in

142 Wouters, de Man and Chanet (n 21) 265.
143 Leal-Arcas (n 24) 74.
144 Ibid 75.
145 Dumberry (n 20) 676.
146 Wouters, de Man and Chanet (n 21) 265.
147 Dumberry (n 20) 676.
148 Vandevelde (n 32) 159.

Latin America, followed the Calvo Doctrine under which foreign investors are not entitled to better treatment than local investors. In addition, the content of some principles in customary law is vague, including that of the international minimum standard.[149]

Lester observed that some principles of international customary law such as "fair and equitable treatment" received much criticism and countries' fears on its scope have led states to attempt to set boundaries on it. Even the latest efforts by the European Union and Canada to establish Comprehensive Economic and Trade Agreement (CETA) leave issues such as direct expropriation, indirect expropriation, and "fair and equitable treatment" quite broad and undefined. [150]

However, others believe that customary international law currently has an important role to play in the foreign investment arena for a number of reasons. According to Gazzini, BITs only make up 13% of the bilateral investment relationships between countries, and significantly, there are no BITs covering relationships between developed states. Moreover, he notes that some key players in foreign investment, such as Japan and Brazil, have only concluded a handful of BITs. Unlike BITs, international customary law is integrated with bilateral and multilateral rules.[151] Relying on the *Chorzów Factory* case,[152] the Court reached the conclusion that the question of liability and compensation is governed by customary international law. The Permanent Court of International Justice (PCIJ) announced that:

> [A]ccording to customary international law, if a state has committed a wrong it is liable to pay reparations. The amount of such reparations must be sufficient to eliminate the consequences of the illegal act and to place the wronged party in the situation it would have been had the illegal act not taken place.[153]

149 Vandevelde (n 32) 159.

150 Simon Lester, 'Reforming the International Investment Law System' (2015) 30 Md J Intl L 70, 78.

151 Gazzini, (n 85) 691.

152 *Factory At Chorzów, Germany v Poland* (Judgment) No 13, 1928 PCIJ (ser A) No 17 paras 27–28.

153 Salacuse (n 74) 446.

Another point supporting the significance of international customary law is that there is a close link between the general principles of public international law and the agreements that directly regulate international investment, as well as there being a "high degree of interpenetration and supplementation between international law and domestic law".[154] For example, the actions in dispute must be attributable to the host state, no matter whether or not the actual performer was part of its government, in order to find that a host state has violated its obligations under an international investment agreement.[155] The issue of attribution to the host state was examined deeply by the tribunal in the case of *Al-Tamimi*. This will be discussed later in Chapter Three.

A further significant advantage of customary international law in international investment issues is that it can be used to help determine whether or not a specific act should be considered a State act, while BITs rarely provide for this matter.[156] In the absence of sufficient widespread and convincing practice, the tribunal should announce that no customary norm has yet emerged.[157] This happened in *Marvin Feldman v Mexico* regarding the customary norm that supposedly "requires a state to permit cigarette exports by unauthorised resellers".[158] However, in the absence of any established norm forbidding a certain conduct, international tribunals can exercise a degree of discretion.[159] Thus, in the case of *Compañía del Desarrollo de Santa Elena, S.A. v Costa Rica*, the Tribunal stated:

> No uniform rule of law has emerged from the practice in international arbitration as regards the determination of whether compound or simple interest is appropriate in any given case. Rather, the determination of interest is a product of the exercise of judgement, taking into account all of the circumstances of the case at hand and especially considerations of fairness which must form part of the law to be applied by this Tribunal.[160]

---

154 Guiguo Wang (n 66) 21.

155 Ibid.

156 Ibid.

157 Gazzini (n 85) 695.

158 *Marvin Roy Feldman Karpa v United States of Mexico* (Award) (ICSID Case No ARB(AF)/99/1) para 115.

159 Gazzini (n 85) 695.

160 *Compañía del Desarrollo de Santa Elena S.A. v Costa Rica*, ICSID Case No ARB/96/1 Award (17 February 2000), para 103.

Nevertheless, it is believed that the customary rules which should be respected and followed are settled rules that have been practised by nations for a long time. The District Court of Columbia criticised the decision in McKesson Corp. v Iran. Pointing out that "international courts have over a period of decades followed the custom of granting only simple interests", the court stated:

> [I]n enforcing customary international law, the Court is constrained to follow the custom, not the rare exceptions, even if there are strong policy reasons to believe that the exception should be the rule.[161]

It could be argued that customary rules in the field of international investment law presently have a number of strengths compared to treaties. First, customary rules may be applied to amend the relevant treaty provisions in some cases, if a long time has elapsed after the treaty was originally concluded. Gazzini argues that if a customary rule would lead to more favourable treatment of the investor, this may modify treaty provisions, pointing to the fact that international customary law provides more protection for international foreign investment.[162] Moreover, it may be inclined to give priority to the customary rule if the conflict between treaty provision and the rules of customary law cannot be resolved through interpretation under Article 31(3) (c) of the Vienna Convention on the Law of Treaties 1969. Therefore, Subedi argues that foreign investors are now eligible for the protection of international customary law principles even in the absence of a BIT between the home and host states. This is because most principles of international investment law are recognised in customary international law.[163]

Although in practice there are difficulties with the content of international law, which restrict the host state's treatment of foreign investors, the content of customary law continues to be significant, incorporated as it is into modern investment agreements through treatment standards, such as the international minimum standard and the fair and equitable standard of treatment.[164]

161 *McKesson Corp. v Iran,* 116 F-Supp 2d 13, 41 (DDC 2000), excerpts in 95 AJIL (2001) para 633.
162 Gazzini (n 85) 714.
163 Subedi (n 7) 105-106.
164 Sornarajah (n 8) 119-120.

1.4 The Protection of Foreign Investment under BITs

Notwithstanding that the content of BIT concluded between one state and another may differ from those concluded between other states, the provisions and the basic feature for all BITs are almost the same. Generally, provisions of BITs deal with the following essential areas: (i) definition of investment and investor; (ii) admission of foreign investors; (iii) fair and equitable treatment of investors; (iv) expropriation and compensation; and (v) dispute settlement.[165]

In order to complete the investigation concerning the protection provided under international law, it is necessary to examine the protection under BITs. As the following section will show, BITs now play an important role in the development of international investment law and international law generally, impacting particularly noticeably on the second of these areas. This section examines this issue from three perspectives: the impact of BITs on the development of customary international law in the area of international investment law, the role of BITs in protecting foreign investment and finally the role of BITs in attracting foreign investment.

1.4.1 BITs: A New Form of Customary International Law in International Investment Law?

In general, developing countries no longer oppose the application of customary international law norms and instead, have granted foreign investors more protection by using BITs to attract foreign investment.[166] As signatories to BITs, over 170 states have agreed to treat foreign investors in accordance with international law standards and, in practice, they have agreed to resolve their disputes through international arbitration.[167] Nevertheless, the emergence of BITs has prompted debate amongst arbitrators and academics concerning the extent to which these agreements now represent a new form of customary international law in international investment law.[168] Opinions on this issue are divided.

Some scholars[169] believe that these BITs are indeed the new customary international law since the principles of customary international law have

165 Subedi (n 7) 108-109.
166 Dumberry (n 20) 680.
167 Ryan (n 53) 725-726.
168 Dumberry (n 20) 680.
169 Aditya Kutty and Sindhura Chakravarty, 'A Multilateral Investment Agreement: Poison or Antidote?' (2010) 22(1) Sri Lanka JiL 89, 94-95.

effectively been incorporated into these modern investment protection agreements.[170] In other words, these treaties constitute evidence of customary international law because of the strong similarities which can be found in the language of BITs, the common structure, the processes they contain, and the huge number of states participating in the negotiation of international investment agreements.[171] According to Ryan, contemporary international investment law takes its legitimacy and authority from about 3,000 BITs and a number of multilateral investment treaties, regardless of the fact it originated as a form of customary international law.[172] In addition, some argue that the functional value of treaty regimes is that they reflect many legal principles and interpret them into commonly perceived goals, attitudes and values in the international investment law field. This functional value of treaties may eventually lead to the development of the status of customary international law.[173]

Some scholars, such as Kutty and Chakravarty, support this view as well, believing that BITs have an influence on customary international law, as reflected in their contribution to the consolidation of existing customary norms and to the crystallisation of new norms of customary international law.[174] Article 31 (3) of the VCLT provides that when interpreting a treaty, "there shall be taken into account, [...] (C) together with the context: any relevant rules of international law applicable in the relations between the parties". The rules of international law here include customary international law, in addition to written international treaties.[175] It can be argued that Western countries aim to preserve some customary international law rules through BITs, because they have encountered a high level of resistance to these on the part of developing countries.[176]

However, other scholars reject the notion that BITs represent the new customary international law, for a number of reasons, the most important being that these agreements lack two crucial elements of customary international law. First, the condition of consistent state practice is not met by these BITs. Second, they also lack any *opinio juris*.[177] In addition, BITs effectively create a *lex specialis* between the parties and their provisions,

170 Kohona (n 57) 153.
171 Salacuse (n 74) 430.
172 Ryan (n 53) 725-726.
173 Schlemmer (n 73)545-546.
174 Kutty and Chakravarty (n 169) 94-95.
175 Guiguo Wang (n 66) 22.
176 Sornarajah (n 8) 173.
177 Ibid 233.

no matter how uniform they may be[178] serving simply to define specific rules regulating investments between the signatories.[179] As Mosoti notes, "the popularity of BITs should not be taken as evidence in support of customary international law".[180] In supporting this view, Sornarajah argues that it may be difficult for even the definite rules in BITs to establish themselves as principles of customary law,[181] and cites the example of the rule of prompt, adequate and effective compensation in the case of expropriation by the host state.[182] Consequently, both in terms of theory and practice BITs do not seem to be capable of creating customary law.[183]

Nevertheless, whether or not BITs are a new form of international customary law in the area of international investment law, what is important is how effective they are in protecting foreign investment.

1.4.2 The Role of BITs in Protecting Foreign Investment

One of the main objectives of BITs is to increase the legal protection of foreign investors.[184] This is because countries "could bilaterally decide on what rules of protection would apply".[185] In addition, it has been observed that the reason for establishing these treaties is to provide *lex specialis*, due to the lack of clarity in the rules of investment protection.[186]

It can be argued that BITs provide significant protection for foreign investment which can be seen in number of instruments. First, the majority of these treaties contain provisions determining the procedures that allow foreign investors to take action to defend their rights directly if these are violated by the host state.[187] In addition, BITs typically offer two features protecting foreign investors against discriminatory treatment of their investment: the first is a guarantee of national treatment and

178 Victor Mosoti, 'Bilateral Investment treaties and the Possibility of a Multilateral Framework on Investment at the WTO: Are Poor Economies Caught in Between?' (2005-2006) 26 Nw J Intl L & Bus 95, 132.
179 Salacuse (n 74) 430.
180 Mosoti (n 178) 132.
181 Sornarajah (n 8) 233.
182 Although the USA consistently supports this rule, not all BITs adopt this formula. See Sornarajah (n 8) 233.
183 Sornarajah (n 8) 232 .
184 Zakia Afrin, 'Foreign Direct Investments and Sustainable Development in The Least-Developed Countries' (2004) 10 Ann Surv Intl & Comp L 215, 226.
185 Sornarajah (n 8) 232.
186 Mosoti (n 178) 132; Sornarajah (n 8) 232-233.
187 Schlemmer (n 73) 544-545.

the second, a guarantee of most-favoured-nation treatment.[188] Further protection is offered by provisions in a typical BIT that guarantee that foreign investments covered will receive fair and equitable protection, full protection and security against the most dangerous sources of political risk, and that the host state will exercise reasonable care to protect foreign investment from specific kinds of harm.[189] With specific reference to expropriation, the host state cannot expropriate any investments covered under the terms of the BIT unless certain conditions are met, including the payment of compensation. Most BITs also guarantee investors' rights to transfer payments related to an investment into a freely exchangeable currency. Some BITs also oblige the host state to provide compensation for foreign investors in the case of war or civil disturbance.[190] All these guarantees will be discussed in further depth in Chapter Three of this book.

However, it is possible to identify a number of concerns regarding BITs as an instrument of protection. First of all, investment treaties BITs may be vague or ambiguous and consequently restrict the sovereignty of states. At the same time, they do not offer international tribunals and courts any guidance on the scope of the obligations and rights of the respective parties under these treaties. According to Schill, these shortcomings have led to a growing number of contradictory and inconsistent interpretations of investment protection norms by international courts and arbitral tribunals, not only in reference to different BITs but to the provisions within a treaty.[191]

It is said that BITs attempt to offer protection for foreign investment by establishing rules covering the host state's treatment of foreign investors and specifying how those rules are to be enforced.[192] In other words, the rules and norms contained in BITs aim to control and regularise the behaviour of a host government toward investment by the other regime member.[193] In cases of dispute, the enforcement process provides for international mechanisms outside the jurisdiction of the host state to enforce the rules.[194] Although some BITs control the action of the host

188 Kenneth J Vandevelde, 'The Political Economy of a Bilateral Investment Treaty' (1998) 92 *Am J Intl L* 621, 630.
189 Kenneth J Vandevelde, *Bilateral Investment Treaties: History, policy, and Interpretation* (OUP 2010) 108, 109.
190 Ibid.
191 Schill (n 23) 66-67.
192 Kutty and Chakravarty (n 169) 95.
193 Salacuse (n 74) 431-432.
194 Kutty and Chakravarty (n 169) 96.

state more than others, almost all of these treaties serve the function of creating an agreed legal framework for the protection of foreign investment and contain the same topics.[195] While some of these treaties include more general principles and fewer specific rules, presupposing the need for good will, because of the requirement to balance the competing interests of both state parties, in general, BITs usually contain specific provisions as mentioned above.[196] Given these similarities among BITs with respect to their content and scope, it is likely that arbitrators will refer to previous arbitral awards.[197]

While Judge Schwebel believes that BITs are a tool to constrain the freedom of the State,[198] the key question for host governments which are BIT signatories is the degree to which they are able to maintain control over foreign investment. As Sornarajah has observed, the erosion of the host nation's regulatory environment is significant in some BITs, with those treaties signed with the US typically containing provisions related to rights of entry and national treatment.[199]

1.4.3 Evaluating the Role of BITs in Attracting Foreign Investment

In general, most countries seek to attract foreign investments by using a variety of instruments.[200] Typically, developing countries believe that they need investment treaties and developed countries are willing to begin the process of providing such agreements.[201] In recent years, BITs have become a universal way of protecting foreign investment. According to the United Nations Conference on Trade and Development (UNCTAD), by the end of 2012, the international investment agreements (IIA) regime consisted of 3,196 agreements, which included 2,857 BITs and 339 "other

195 According to Kutty and Chakravarty (n 169) 95-96 almost all BITs contain the following elements: (A) Scope of Application (B) Conditions for the Entry of Foreign Investment (C) General Standards of Treatment of Foreign Investments (D) Monetary Transfers (E) Operational Conditions of the Investment (F) Protection Against Expropriation and Dispossession (G) Compensation for Losses (H) Investment Dispute Settlement.

196 Kohona (n 57) 152-153.

197 Salacuse (n 74) 431-432.

198 Subedi (n 7) 108.

199 Sornarajah (n 8) 231-232.

200 Deborah L Swenson, 'Why Do Developing Countries Sign BITs?' (2006) 12 UC Davis J Intl L & Policy 131,132.

201 Jason Webb Yackee, 'Do We Really Need BITs? Toward A Return to Contract in International Investment Law' (2008) 3 Asian J WTO & Intl Health L & Policy 121, 121.

IIAs", such as integration or cooperation agreements with an investment dimension.[202]

However, the role of BITs in attracting foreign investment has been extensively debated among scholars. Some hold that these treaties help developing countries to attract investment and improve their investment environment by providing overseas investors with enforceable rights to protect their assets. Others claim that the dispute settlement provisions of BITs and the significant increase in treaty litigation against host countries and the legal protection of BITs have a detrimental effect on the regulation of public and environmental welfare and on the pace of development. [203]

Studies examining the effect of BITs in enhancing the flow of foreign investment to signatory countries have reached conflicting conclusions. Some studies claim to have found a positive impact of BIT on foreign investment flow. Neumayer and Spess, who investigated data from 119 countries for the period 1970 to 2002, reached the conclusion that once a host state started to negotiate additional BITs there was an increase in its share of foreign direct investment.[204] Salacuse and Sullivan obtained similar results in a study of foreign investment flows between 1998 and 2000 for more than 100 developing states and the foreign investment flows of the US to 31 countries over a ten-year period. They found that BITs concluded by the US played a significant role in enhancing investment flows for both signatories.[205]

However, UNCTAD in 1998, reported only a small positive link between BITs and an increase in foreign investment. UNCTAD noted that:

> Following the signing of a BIT, it is more likely than not that the host country will marginally increase its share in the outward FDI of the home country [...] The effect, however, is usually small. [206]

202 United Nations Conference on Trade and Development (UNCTAD), *World Investment Report 2013; Global Value Chains: Investment and Trade for development* <http://unctad.org/en/PublicationsLibrary/wir2013_en.pdf> accessed 3 May 16.

203 See Yackee (n 201) 121; Kevin P Gallagher and Elen Shrestha, 'Investment Treaty Arbitration and Developing Countries: A Re-Appraisal' (2011) Global Development and Environment Institute Working Paper 11/01, 1 <http://ase tufts edu/gdae> accessed 3 May 2016.

204 Cited in Vandevelde (n 32) 185.

205 Ibid.

206 Ibid.

UNCTAD concluded that BITs play a "minor and secondary role in attracting foreign direct investment".[207] The same conclusion was reached by Tobin and Rose-Ackerman, who examined the FDI flows for 62 countries from 1980 to 2000.[208] Although large numbers of BITs were signed during the 1990s, no clear evidence was found to support claims that they encouraged foreign investment.[209]

As a result, over time these conflicting views and results have led to confusion on whether BITs are vehicles for attracting investment flows.[210] It is argued that there no strong evidence of either the benefits of BITs or their disadvantages.[211] Thus, it cannot be said with certainty that treaties act as an instrument for attracting foreign investment.[212] The high level of enthusiasm among countries, especially developing countries, to conclude BITs may be misplaced, given the absence of compelling evidence of their benefits. In contrast, they appear to carry a serious risk because, as previously noted, the number of cases brought by foreign investors against host states increased dramatically in the late 1990s, following an earlier surge in the numbers of BITs which had been concluded.[213]

Overall, it seems that the attraction of foreign investment involves a number of factors and BITs alone are not sufficient for this purpose. Yackee has argued rightly that it is inappropriate to expect BITs to provide "a quick and easy cure" [214] for those developing countries which have been less successful in attracting foreign investment and if they wish to increase their flows of foreign investment, they should do more than simply signing and ratifying these treaties.[215]

207 UNCTAD, *World Investment Report 2004: The Shift Towards Services*, (2004) para 302 <www.unctad.org/en/docs/wir2004.en.pdf> accessed 4 May 2016.
208 Cited in Vandevelde (n 32) 185.
209 Kutty and Chakravarty (n 169) 100.
210 Vandevelde (n 32) 185.
211 Kutty and Chakravarty (n 169) 100.
212 Swenson (n 200) 131; Kutty and Chakravarty (n 169) 100.
213 Kutty and Chakravarty (n 169) 100.
214 Jason Webb Yackee, 'Do Bilateral Investment Treaties Promote Foreign Direct Investment? Some Hints from Alternative Evidence', (2010) 51 Va J Intl L 397, 438, 439.
215 Ibid 439.

1.5 Effects of the Absence of Global Comprehensive Treaties on Protecting Foreign Investment

According to Subedi, the absence of multilateral international treaties at a global level has compounded the existing confusion, since international courts and tribunals offer different interpretations of rules relating to foreign investment. Furthermore, every state incorporates its own interpretations of customary international law in BITs or other legal tools in order to favour its own national interests.[216]

Efforts to create a comprehensive international investment treaty that would protect foreign investment started in the 1920s, lost momentum and then resumed in the early 1960s. To be specific, in 1929 and 1930, two conferences were held with the aim of establishing international minimum standards of treatment to protect the person or property of foreigners. However, both initiatives failed due to resistance from Latin American, East European and ex-colonial states.[217] Since then, despite intermittent attempts to do so, countries have failed to create a multilateral international agreement on the promotion and protection of foreign investments on a global level.[218]

Nevertheless, since the first WTO Ministerial Meeting in Singapore in 1996, the argument concerning the need for an international investment treaty has continued. The WTO Ministerial Meetings in 1996, 2001 and 2004 encouraged member countries to integrate different investment agreements into a comprehensive and global treaty.[219] The purpose of the 1990s negotiations between OECD members on a Multilateral Agreement on Investment (MAI) was to liberalise investment regimes and provide higher standards of investment protection.[220]

Some of the reasons behind the failure to conclude a comprehensive multilateral international agreement have already been pointed out. Conflicting ideological approaches are adopted by developed and developing countries regarding the protection of foreign investment. Drafts of multilateral agreements aimed at providing more protection for foreign investment have been resisted by the capital-importing states.[221]

---

216 Subedi (n 7) 122.
217 Peter T Muchlinski, *Multinational Enterprises & the Law* (2nd edn, OUP 2007) 654.
218 Loibl and Evans (n 25) 745.
219 Mosoti (n 178) 102-103.
220 Loibl and Evans (n 25) 745.
221 Sornarajah (n 8) 236.

Within the OECD, the tendency of developed countries to discuss and negotiate multilateral agreements among themselves and then expect them be signed by developing countries has led to a failure to ratify a comprehensive international investment treaty. In negotiation and discussion of a multilateral investment framework under the umbrella of the WTO, developing countries assert the right to participate fully in shaping its outcome.[222]

Two arguments can be raised on the effects of the absence of global comprehensive treaties on protecting foreign investment. It may be argued that even if an international multilateral investment treaty was concluded at a global level, it is not certain that countries and international courts and tribunals would stop relying on international customary law. As this discussion has shown, currently, despite the huge number of BITs and multilateral investment agreements in existence, customary international law still influences many aspects of international foreign investment.[223] Therefore, Matsushita, Schoenbaum and Mavroidis question the necessity for a comprehensive international treaty on foreign investment, arguing that the absence thus far of such a treaty has not stopped the progress of the liberalisation of foreign investment.[224] Sauvé also maintains that a comprehensive international treaty on investment is unlikely to enhance FDI in every signatory country because it is not expected that all countries would act identically with regard to investment policies such as liberalisation, privatisation, competition, macroeconomic, tax, the fight against corruption and the elimination of excessive administrative red tape in FDI policy.[225]

Conversely, Leal Arcas argues that a comprehensive international investment treaty would have several advantages for improving protection of foreign investment in international investment law. First, it would serve as a guide for a new generation of bilateral and regional investment agreements, enhancing the coherence of the international legal framework of foreign investment. Second, there would be a reduction in the transaction costs and an increase in the benefits of foreign investment, due to greater coordination among countries. Finally, if a comprehensive

222 Leal-Arcas (n 24) 129-132.

223 Subedi (n 7) 122.

224 Mitsuo Matsushita, Thomas J Schoenbaum and Petros C Mavroidis, *The World Trade Organization Law, Practice, and Policy* (2nd edn, OUP 2006), 849.

225 Pierre Sauvé, 'Multilateral rules on investment: is forward movement possible?' (2006) 9 JI Econ L 325, 349-350.

agreement was issued under the aegis of WTO, it would help to clarify the relationship between the GATS, the TRIMs Agreement and BITs.[226]

Overall, it can be argued that the existence of a global comprehensive treaty of foreign investment would enhance the protection of foreign investment, because at least countries will find one set of international rules upon which to judge their investment.

1.6 Conclusion

This chapter examined the protection mechanisms for foreign investment currently provided under international law. It began by tracing the historical evolution of international investment law and then discussed the protection of foreign investment provided under customary international law. The protection of foreign investment under BITs was analysed. Finally, the possible effects of the absence of comprehensive global treaties covering foreign investment on protection for foreign investors were investigated.

It is argued that the Calvo Doctrine has reflected the position of developing countries, especially those of Latin America and the Hull Formula has reflected the American and Western approach; both became an ideology for each side. In other words, the issue of protection of foreign investment under international law has been affected significantly by the international relations between developed and developing countries and their respective approaches toward this topic. Despite major disagreements concerning the ability of customary international law to provide the necessary degree of protection for foreign investors, since most principles of international investment law are recognised in customary international law, this continues to play an important role in this context, even in the absence of BITs between a home and host state.

It is argued that for reasons of both theory and practice, BITs are unlikely to create customary law, notwithstanding the similarities among them, and they should not be expected to provide the solution to developing countries' lack of success in attracting foreign investment. Nevertheless, despite their limitations, BITs are likely to reduce risks for foreign investors more than other instruments by controlling unfair action by the host state. However, it can be argued that the existence of a comprehensive

226 Leal-Arcas (n 24) 134-135.

global treaty covering foreign investment would represent a number of advantages with regard to promoting protection of foreign investment. While this chapter examined the protection of foreign investment under international law, the evolution of the law and policy of foreign investment in Oman will be analysed in the next chapter.

Chapter 2: Overview on Foreign Investment Related Laws and Policy in Oman

2.1 Introduction

The 1990s economic development plans of the Sultanate of Oman showed a strong understanding among policymakers of the strong relationship between Oman's future social, economic and political development and its ability to attract more foreign direct investment.[227] International organisations such as the IMF in 2013 warned the Omani Government that it needed to increase its non-oil revenues as a part of a fiscal adjustment strategy intended to tackle recent increases in public spending. This spending, funded by higher oil revenues, was intended to expand public sector employment, provide higher wages and benefits, create unemployment benefits for Omanis, and find new infrastructure and social investment projects.[228]

The aim of this chapter is to discuss the evolution of foreign investment law and policy in Oman. To set the discussion in context, a preliminary overview about the Sultanate of Oman will be provided, highlighting its geographical importance, rich history and the new era of economic development that began in 1970. Following this, the background to the Omani legal system and the role of its Basic Law will be analysed in order to facilitate understanding of the general legal environment in Oman. It will show how Omani foreign investment law has evolved with the aim of providing better protection for foreign investment, and will begin by outlining the previous foreign investment regime, especially the 1974 Foreign Business Investment law (FBIL) and its subsequent amendments. Finally, the new features of the 1994 FCIL will be analysed.

227 Kamal Mellahi and Cherif Guermat, 'What Motivates Foreign Direct Investment? The Case of Oman' (2002) 3 Exeter Business School (Working Paper 02/01) <http://business-school.exeter.ac.uk/documents/papers/management/2002/0201> accessed 28 April 2016.

228 International Monetary Fund, *Oman-2013 Article IV Consultation Concluding Statement of the IMF Mission* (14 May 2013) <www.imf.org/external/np/ms/2013/051413.htm> accessed 28 April 2016.

2.2 Overview of Oman

The Sultanate of Oman is situated in the south-east of the Arabian Peninsula and covers some 309,000 square kilometres.[229] It has a population of 4,438,554[230] and the gross national per capita income is 24,765 US$.[231] Historically, Omanis have played an important role in trade with different parts of the world since the third millennium BC.[232] During the 16th-18th centuries, Oman benefitted from its location to become a trading power and major maritime centre, forming part of a trading network covering the area from Zanzibar in East Africa to India.[233]

Although Great Britain was closely involved and influenced the Omani policy from the mid-nineteenth century, unlike its neighbours Oman never entered into a governing agreement. Therefore, the British government was under no obligation to defend Oman,[234] and the Sultanate sustained full international responsibility as an independent and sovereign state throughout the nineteenth and twentieth centuries.[235] Before the discovery of oil in the 1960s followed by its commercial scale production and export in 1967, Oman's budget was wholly funded by religious taxes (*zakat*) and customs duties,[236] and the Omani people mainly depended on subsistence agriculture and fishing for their livelihood.[237] During the reign of Sultan Said Bin Taimur (1932-1970), the country was closed to foreign investment for three reasons: first, the civil war in the country between the Sultan and Imamate in the internal region,[238] second, the Sultan adopted a "policy

229 World Bank and International Finance Corporation, *Doing Business 2014, Economy Profile: Oman* 5 <www.doingbusiness.org/data/exploreeconomies/oman/~/media/giawb/doing%20business/documents/profiles/country/OMN.pdf> accessed 2 August 2014.

230 National Centre for Statistics and Information <https://www.ncsi.gov.om/Pages/NCSI.aspx> accessed 5 June 2016.

231 World Bank and the International Finance Corporation (n 229) 5.

232 John Duke Anthony, 'Oman, the Gulf and the United States', in B R Pridham (ed), *Oman: Economic, Social and Strategic Developments* (Croom Helm 1987) 177.

233 Oxford Business Group, *The Report: Oman 2012* (Oxford Business Group 2012) 231.

234 Federal Research Division, *Oman, a country study* (Kessinger 2004) 16.

235 Alastair Hirst, 'Contemporary Mercantile Jurisdiction in Oman' (1992) 7 Arab LQ 3, 3.

236 Federal Research Division (n 234) 60.

237 Bridget McKinney, 'Privatisation: Oman and Egypt' (1997) 25 Intl Bus Lawyer 126, 131.

238 Khaldoun Hassan Al-Naqeeb, *Society and State in the Gulf and Arab Peninsula: A Different Perspective* (1st Routledge 2012) 95.

of isolation";[239] and third, before 1970, the Sultan's financial position was fundamentally synonymous with the Sultanate's public finances,[240]

Following the accession of Sultan Qaboos in 1970, the Sultanate's economic strategies and development changed radically.[241] Oman's main need as a developing country was to reform its national and international financial structure, as well as initiating a programme of economic and political development.[242] Therefore, Sultan Qaboos took the necessary steps to modernize his country, including stabilising the political situation, providing education for the whole population and establishing a legal framework that would help Oman achieve economic development.[243] Consequently, in 1971, the Omani government announced the first government budget and initiated its first Five-Year Development Plan (1976-80). This focused on investment in infrastructure and was to be achieved by direct contracts between the government and the private sector.[244]

The development of the Omani economy has been somewhat uneven. It witnessed rapid growth from 1970 to 1986, and then as a result of the 1985-86 collapse in oil prices, the period from 1986 to 1989 was one of economic retrenchment. From 1990 onwards, Oman has further developed in economic terms.[245] However, some researchers believe that the Sultanate faces some economic difficulties, such as providing suitable housing and services, especially water; increasing food production through stimulating agriculture and decreasing urban migration.[246] Addressing these difficulties needs combination of solutions, including foreign investment in these areas.

It is rightly said that nowadays Oman occupies the most strategic location among the GCC states[247] being situated at the north-western

239 J H A McHugo, 'The Practice of Law by Foreign Lawyers in the Sultanate of Oman' (1985) *7 Mich YBI Legal Stud 89*, 90.

240 Federal Research Division (n 234) 96.

241 McKinney (n 237) 131.

242 Loukas A Mistelis, 'Regulatory Aspects: Globalization, Harmonization, Legal Transplants, and Law Reform-Some Fundamental Observations' (2000) 34 Intl L 1055, 1055.

243 Ellen Kerrigan Dry, 'Corporate Governance in the Sultanate of Oman' (2003) 3 Rich J Global L & Bus 45, 47.

244 See McKinney (n 237) 69.

245 Helen Chapin Metz, 'Oman', in Helen Chapin Metz (ed), *Persian Gulf States: Country Studies* (Library of Congress 1993) 251, 268.

246 Federal Research Division (n 234) 27.

247 Oxford Business Group (n 233) 231.

corner of the Indian Ocean[248] and the entry point to the Strait of Hormuz,[249] which is the most important maritime gateway in the world, connecting the Arabian Gulf and Arabian Sea.[250] It is estimated that 60% of the world's existing oil and natural gas resources come from the Arabian Gulf[251] and about 40% of world's oil passes through the Strait of Hormuz.[252] By taking advantage of its 2092 km-long coastline and its modern ports, Oman has the chance to become the major Indian Ocean shipping lane linking Europe and East Asia.[253] With its secure location on the Arabian Peninsula and its relative distance from unstable areas such as Iraq and Iran, Oman has proved a reliable and consistent supplier of oil and gas to the Far East, without the burden of heavily increased insurance imposed on other regional suppliers. It is a safe and useful transit point for other Gulf States.[254]

With all these advantages, Oman potentially has much to offer foreign investors. However, its ability to capitalise on this attractive position will depend to a great extent on whether its legal and institutional environment is conducive to expanding "its foreign investment potential".[255] The key question is: does Oman benefit from its strategic location to attract and protect foreign investment? Before answering this question, it is necessary to provide some general background on the legal system and the evolution of the foreign investment law in the Sultanate.

2.3 The Evolution of the Omani Legal System

Although there was no written law in Oman before 1970, the general law applied in the country was Islamic Law or *shari'a*.[256] The modern Omani legal system started in 1970, with the accession of Sultan Qaboos. There

248 Anthony (n 232) 178.
249 Chapin Metz (n 245) 314.
250 Geoffrey F Gresh, 'Traversing the Persian Gauntlet: U S Naval Projection and the Strait of Hormuz' (2010) 34 Fletcher F World Aff 41, 43.
251 Ibid 41.
252 Oxford Business Group (n 233) 231.
253 Ibid 12.
254 William F Pepper, 'Foreign Capital Investment in Member States of the Gulf Cooperation Council Coniderations, Issues and Concerns for Investors' (1991) 6 Arab LQ 331, 332.
255 Pepper (n 254) 332.
256 Hirst (n 235) 3.

was a great need at this time to create a legal system and issue laws to support two significant developments. First, the economic circumstances of the country began to change in the early 1970s, due to oil production and large-scale infrastructure projects.[257] Second, Oman began to establish strong relationships with Western institutions, with the aim of exploiting them to enhance its business activities.[258] A modern legal framework is a precondition to enable the flow of foreign capital to any state.[259] It should be noted that Oman's experience in the evolution of its legal system is unusual for two reasons: first, the relatively late start (1970s) of its struggle to begin modernising the country, and second, the fact that since Oman had never been colonised, it had not inherited any legal framework from a European nation that would serve as a foundation for a new Omani legal system.[260]

Currently, there are two kinds of legislation in the Sultanate. Royal decrees, promulgated by the Sultan, form the primary legislation, while Ministerial Decisions are the secondary source. These are usually issued under specific powers conformed by Royal Decree on the relevant executive or ministerial body.[261] Therefore, no regulations are considered binding unless issued by royal decree or ministerial decision: both of these are promulgated in the *Official Gazette of the Sultanate of Oman* (*OGSO*). Thus, the most remarkable characteristic of the Omani legal system is its simplicity and easy accessibility, due to the fact that since 1973 all royal decrees, including laws, have been numbered and published in *OGSO*, as well as in an annual compilation known as *Al-Mujallad* (literally, 'the Compendium').[262]

It is argued that in order to satisfy its need for rapid and logical development, Oman put itself in a position where it is able to choose from different legal systems.[263] Therefore, the Sultanate has applied a "pragmatic approach" of issuing legislation as it is needed to deal with problems instead of adopting a foreign legal system that might not fit with

---

257 Ibid.

258 Leon G R Spoliansky, 'Modern Business Law in the Sultanate of Oman' (1979) 13 Intl L 101, 102.

259 Mistelis (n 242) 1057.

260 McHugo (n 239) 90.

261 Khalil Mechantaf, 'The Legal System and Research in the Sultanate of Oman' (July 2010) <www.nyulawglobal.org/globalex/oman.htm> 12 accessed 28 April 2016.

262 McHugo (n 239) 91- 92.

263 Thomas W Hill, 'The Commercial Legal System of the Sultanate of Oman' (1983) 17 Intl L 507, 508.

the "country's needs".[264] However, it can be argued that the lack of strong legal institutions in Oman had two relatively negative outcomes. Firstly, this meant that the legal system was slow to develop. Secondly, and more significantly, there is a tendency to issue laws that are viewed as necessary in a piecemeal and ad hoc basis, without any clear long-term strategic vision for the country, whereas the laws should frame and contribute to the economic development of the country.

It is possible to distinguish two main stages in the Omani legal system since 1970. The first stage, spanning the 1970s and 1980s, witnessed the establishment of the modern Omani state, and the main focus was on issuing the laws necessary for organising, running, and securing the country and also for creating an environment that was conducive to economic development. Originally, the Omani government believed that establishing a modern legal system would be a lengthy process.[265] One characteristic of the Omani legal system during this era was the priority and importance that was given to commercial and business laws. This can be seen in the large number of such laws promulgated from the early 1970s in different areas of business law. Key examples include Royal Decree 3/1974 on the Commercial Register Law, the Commercial Companies Law Royal Decree 4/1974, Royal Decree 5/1974 on FBIL, Royal Decree 6/1974 on the Law for the Protection of Developing Industries, and Royal Decree 7/1974 on the Banking Law.

In the subsequent years, further sectoral business legislation was put in place, such as the Commercial Agencies Law promulgated by Royal Decree 26/1977, the Customs Management Law Royal Decree 35/1978, the Law for the Organisation and Encouragement of Industry by Royal Decree 1/79, and the Insurance Companies Law by Royal Decree 12/1979. In addition, a number of important laws in other areas were introduced at this stage, such as the Interpretation of Certain Terms and General Provisions by Royal Decree 3/1973, the Criminal Law by Royal Decree 7/1974, and the Law Regulating the Administrative Apparatus of the State by Royal Decree 26/1975 amended by Royal Decree 13/1976. These laws, addressing what were considered to be the most pressing issues of the day, preceded the introduction of constitutional and civil laws by many years, since these did not appear until the second stage.

264 McHugo (n 239) 90.
265 Ibid.

Clearly, Oman could not establish international trade without certain laws being applied in the country. Consequently, whether it was planned or not, this approach by the Omani government led to the creation of an "integrated and interrelated" business legal system.[266] It is believed that this "has closed most of the loopholes through which foreign interests avoided submission to Omani jurisdiction and control".[267] This situation encouraged foreigners who planned to operate in Oman to understand these laws and comply with them.[268] However, during the 1970s and the early 1980s commercial lawyers still faced difficulties in certain unregulated areas. Since laws in some important areas, such as contracts and tort, had not been promulgated at that stage, there was no alternative law to turn to. [269]

The second stage began in the 1990s, when developments in the Omani legal system reflected the greater maturity of the modern Omani state and its increasing integration with the international community. During this decade, the focus shifted to completing and modernising the legal structure of the country and the legal system started to respond to demands from international organisations for Oman to become a fully constitutional state. This progress in the Omani legal system was to be expected, as the Sultanate's greater integration with the world community generated more development and demand for new laws. This was reflected in the redrafting of a number of its older laws, such as FCIL in 1994, and later the Labour Law by Royal Decree 35/2003.

Change is also discernible in the nature of the new legislation issued during this era. Whereas the laws enacted in the 1970s addressed the pressing need to establish the basic requirements for trade, those enacted in the second stage addressed the needs arising from an increasingly complex and sophisticated national and international business environment. Examples include the Law of Arbitration in Civil and Commercial Disputes (Arbitration Law) by Royal Decree 47/1997; the Finance Law by Royal Decree 47/1998, the Law of Intellectual Property by Royal Decree 82/2000, the Banking Law by Royal Decree 114/2000, the Law of Money Laundering by Royal Decree 34/2002; the Law on the Protection of Consumers by Royal Decree 81/2002; and the Privatization Law by Royal Decree 77/2004.

266 Spoliansky (n 258) 102.
267 Ibid.
268 Ibid.
269 Nowadays, all commercial areas are regulated, due to the country's modernization and commercial development. See McHugo (n 239) 92.

These laws reflect the influence of Oman's attempts to attract foreign investors and its preparation in the late 1990s for accession to the WTO, finally achieved in 9 November 2000.[270]

The most significant development during this era was the issuing of the Basic Law.[271] On November 6, 1996, Sultan Qaboos issued the Basic Law of the Sultanate of Oman. Although Oman was the latest Arab country in issuing a constitution,[272] it is believed that Omani Basic Law has two features: first, it reflects both tribal and Islamic concepts to form a vision of a harmonized Omani state. Second, it adopted international standards, especially in the areas of criminal, commercial, company, banking, procedural, foreign investment and arbitration law.[273] It can be said that Oman is trying to strike a balance in its legal system between its national culture and international standards and demands. It applies predominantly international standards, especially in those areas covering interaction with the international community, while it applies Islamic *shari'a* in a small number of laws that deal mainly with personal matters within the local society.

2.4 The Role of the Basic Law

The role of the Omani Basic Law is controversial; Miller believes that the issuing of this Law represented a significant step toward state formation and democratization. However, Siegfried argues that the effect of this Basic Law on political life and legal development is not clear. Nevertheless, all the commentators agree that the issuing of the Omani Basic Law represented a significant step on the way to state formation.[274] In addition, it can be argued that the promulgation of the Basic Law played a crucial role in the development of the Omani legal system and of political life in Oman, since all the laws issued by the Sultan through Royal Decrees must be consistent with the Basic Law. Moreover, the Basic Law has been used to decide, determine, identify and clarify a number of important issues that

---

270 WTO, 'Oman-Member organisation' <www.wto.org/english/thewto_e/countries_e/oman_e.htm> accessed 29 April 2016.

271 The Omani Constitution.

272 Nikolaus A Siegfried, 'Legislation and Legitimation in Oman: the Basic Law' (2000) 7 Islamic L & Society 359, 359.

273 Ibid 360.

274 Ibid 359.

may help to shape future development with regard the implementation of the rule of law in the country.

While Article 2 of the Basic Law declares that *shari'a* forms the basis for Omani legislation, some argue that Oman actually relies on three fundamental "parallel interrelated" sources in its legislation. These are (1) Islamic law, which is in turn derived from four sources applied respectively (the Quran, the Sunna, *ijma* and *qiyas*); (2) a statutory system of law expressed in Royal Decrees and Ministerial Decisions, and (3) private international law, applied to commercial and financial transactions.[275] In fact, Royal Decrees and Ministerial Decisions, the only instruments by which legislation is issued, may be based on various sources. Nevertheless, these sources are interdependent. An effort has been made during recent decades to develop the legislation needed for the governmental system and the administration of justice.[276]

Although Oman's legal system, like those of all the Islamic nations in the region, is based on *shari'a*, Western countries have also influenced its system by means of commerce-related laws that developed in the twentieth century based upon the French pattern.[277] This is due to the fact that the Napoleonic Code has been widely applied in the Middle East and has been adopted in countries such as Egypt,[278] from which Oman has benefited via the skills of its consultants, administrators and professionals. This has led to Oman widely applying the Napoleonic Code in its legal system.[279] Although Oman does not completely apply the Napoleonic Code taking into account the differences in the content of the Omani Civil and Family laws, it can be argued that the application of the Islamic Law in Omani law is limited to specific parts of the Omani legal system.

For instance, in criminal, commercial and all business related laws, Oman does not apply *shari'a* rules.[280]

---

275 The Sunna refers to examples or precedents based on the Prophet Muhammad's words or acts as recorded in the Hadith or tradition; *Ijma* is scholarly consensus and *Qiyas* if the process of reasoning by analogy. *Shari'a* is the source of both Civil and Family Law in Oman. See Hill (n 263) 507.

276 Hill (n 263) 508.

277 Spoliansky (n 258) 101.

278 See Chibli Mallat, 'From Islamic to Middle Eastern Law a Restatement of the Field (Part II)' (2004) 52 Am J Comp L 209, 209.

279 Hill (n 263) 508.

280 For example, in criminal law, Oman does not apply *Huddod* and *Qisas*, which are forms of punishment in Islamic Law. In commercial law, it allows interest and the court applies this in normal banking loans which is against *shari'a* principles.

A second important feature of the Omani Basic Law is that it enshrines principles and the protection of basic human rights, thus establishing a basis for commitment to protection of human rights. These rights are emphasised in a number of provisions. Article 28 guarantees the freedom to practise religion. The freedom of opinion and expression is secured by Article 29. Article 31 guarantees the freedom of the press, printing and publication. Citizens' right of assembly within the limits of the Law is ensured by Article 32. In addition, Article 34 provides that citizens have the right to address the public authorities on personal matters or on matters related to public affairs, in the manner and under the conditions laid down by the Law. However, it can be argued that these declared rights might be weakened because most of these articles stipulate that these rights should be granted in accordance with the applicable laws, which may sometimes limit them. Moreover, there is much doubt concerning how effectively these provisions provide real and full protection of the basic human rights, because there is a need for enough experience and examination. Nevertheless, the existence of all these provisions is a good basis for full human basic rights.

The sovereignty of the Law and the independence of the judiciary from the executive authority are other important principles determined by the Basic Law. Article 59 states that the sovereignty of the Law is the basis of governance in the State. Rights and freedoms are guaranteed by the dignity of the judiciary and the probity and impartiality of the judges. Moreover, Article 60 declares that the judicial power is independent and vested in the Courts of Law. In addition, Article 61 states that "there is no power over the judges in their rulings except the law. [...] No party may interfere in a law suit or in matters of justice; such interference shall be a crime punishable by law".

However, the mentioned sovereignty of the Law and independence of the judiciary in Oman may be weakened due to the lack of full separation of the three powers. The Sultan is the head of all three powers: judicial, legislative and executive. According to Royal Decree 9/2012 he is the president of the Judiciary Council, and he is also the president of the Oman Council, which consists of two councils (the *Majlis Alshura* (Parliament) and the State Council). Moreover, he is also the Prime Minister according to Article 42 of the Basic Law. In addition, according to the same article and law, the Sultan promulgates and ratifies laws. Although members of the *Majlis Alshura* are fully elected by the people, they still do not have the power to issue laws, their current role regarding legal issues being limited to:

- Reviewing draft laws prepared by the Ministries and other government authorities before their promulgation.
- Submitting what is deemed as appropriate for promotion of the economic and social laws in force in the Sultanate.[281]

In addition, according to Royal Decree 14/94, the Ministry of Legal Affairs is the body responsible for preparing, reviewing and developing royal decrees, laws, regulations, ministerial decisions, draft treaties and international conventions that the government intends to sign or join. It also reviews any contracts that impose an obligation on the government exceeding half a million Omani Rials, and issues official legal opinions and interpretations of royal decrees and laws.[282]

2.5 The Evolution of Foreign Investment Law in Oman

2.5.1 The Establishment of the Foreign Investment Regime

Oman is an oil-producing country. Thus, the special needs of international investment in "natural resources and public utility" projects must be recognised by special legislation.[283] The provisions of the FBIL 1974, amended by Royal Decrees 2/1977 and 16/1978 formed the basis of the legal framework that guided foreign investors establishing business in Oman, especially during the 1970s and 1980s. The fact that the FBIL was issued in 1974, only four years after the accession of Sultan Qaboos and at a time whilst a war was still being fought in the south of the country, is a sign of the importance attached to regulating foreign investment from the early years of the Sultan's rule, especially in the context of the policy of expanding Omani companies with Omani equity participation.[284]

It has been rightly pointed out that there is a significant relationship between the legal framework and the likelihood of foreign investors

281 *Majlis Alshura* website <www.shura.om/en/preface.new.asp> accessed 29 April 2016.

282 Ministry of Legal Affairs website <www.mola.gov.om/eng/index.aspx> accessed 29 April 2016.

283 Bridget McKinney, 'Economic Reform Legislation in Oman' (1995) Intl Bus Lawyer, 131.

284 Spoliansky (n 258) 103.

investing in a country. Foreign investors largely target countries which have a good legal infrastructure, especially where freedom of contract, protection of property and property rights are guaranteed by a legal system and by proper rules "of secured transactions" and where the judicial system is perceived to be fast and efficient.[285]

It has been argued that the FBIL was intended to control foreign investment in the country's economy. This is because Oman was not free from the international approach regarding foreign investment during those decades. Like many developing countries, Oman was concerned about the implications of foreign investment at that time. In this respect it was similar to all the GCC States, whose laws all adopted a similar stance.[286] Therefore, the Omani Government was caught on the horns of a dilemma. On the one hand, the country needed foreign investment, especially in the oil sector, whilst on the other, it was wary of foreign investment and the need to defend the national interest.

As a result, during the 1970s and 1980s, Oman was not willing to provide absolute protection to foreign investors or to grant them any incentives.[287] Indeed, foreign investment was discouraged by laws that provided for a "high degree of screening or sectoral restrictions and barriers".[288] The provisions of this law were mainly designed to protect the interests of the Omanis. The use of the word "unlawful" in Article 1 of the FBIL reflects the strongly restrictive stance concerning foreign investors:

> It shall be unlawful for any non-Omani national, whether a natural or juristic person, to engage in trade or business in the Sultanate of Oman or to acquire an interest in the capital of an Omani company except as provided in this Law.

Therefore, the main effects of this law were to make it known that non-Omanis who wished to establish business and trade in Oman would not be granted a licence unless a number of conditions were met, and also to prohibit foreign investors from any business activity in Oman without the permission of MoCI, as stated by Article 2.[289]

---

285 Mistelis (n 242) 1056-1057.
286 Spoliansky (n 258) 103.
287 Mellahi and Guermat (n 227) 4.
288 Ibid.
289 Spoliansky (n 258) 103.

This restrictive approach can be seen in a number of provisions of the FBIL and in the foreign investment regime generally. First of all, there was the number of governmental bodies involved in issuing licences for foreign investors. Article 3 stated that:

> The license (authorization) required in accordance with Article (2) of this law shall not be granted unless [...] (b) the paid up capital referred to may be decreased to a minimum of thirty thousand Omani Rials in accordance with the recommendation of the Committee for Foreign Capital Investment and the reasonable economic reasons which are given by the Committee and are approved by the Minister of Commerce and Industry after the approval of the Development Council.

This extract shows the required authorization was threefold: the Committee for Foreign Capital Investment (CFCI), the Minister of Commerce and Industry, and the Development Council. Having this number of governmental bodies involved in the decision to granting a licence presented a significant obstacle.

Another feature of the restrictive approach of this law is that the Law and the subsequent amendments did not permit foreign ownership to exceed 65%. According to Article 3 (C):

> The proportion of Omani shareholding in the Capital and share of profits is not less than that determined by the Committee for Foreign Capital Investment and is under no circumstances less than 35%.

This requirement of 35% Omani participation in shareholding in the capital and share of profits was a challenge. Moreover, in practice, the Foreign Capital Investment Committee usually insisted on an Omani participation of 51% and, in certain circumstances, even greater.[290]

Moreover, foreign investment was only exempted from paying revenue and income taxes for a period of five years if the Minister of Commerce and Industry ruled that a project involving foreign capital was regarded as an Economic Development Project. According to Article 10:

290 McHugo (n 239) 132.

> The Minister of Commerce and Industry may, at his discretion, declare a project in which non-Omani capital is being invested to be an Economic Development Project. Each Economic Development Project shall be exempt from taxes imposed upon its revenue and income, but not other taxes generally applicable to Omani business, for a period of five years from a date to be fixed by the Minister of Commerce and Industry.

Those companies owned by foreign investors were subject to income tax of 20% if the profits of a company with 35-51% local participation exceeded OMR 20,000, whereas the majority of local-owned companies paid only 15%.[291]

Finally, the Law also prohibited foreign investors from involvement in a number of business and trade activities in Oman, representing a further obstacle to entry and foreign ownership. Article 5 (b) stated that:

> For the purposes of this Law, the following shall be deemed not to be engaged in trade or business in the Sultanate of Oman:
>
> i. Service as an official of the Government of the Sultanate and service or employment by persons engaged, hired or retained by the Government of the Sultanate;
>
> ii. individual employment in the Sultanate;
>
> iii. individual service in the Sultanate as an officer, director or manager of an Omani commercial company;
>
> iv. any non-Omani bank which has a representative office in the Sultanate but does not transact any banking business in Oman there from;
>
> v. any non-Omani business which has no permanent establishment in the Sultanate, does not have any

291 W M Ballantyne and A R Monico, 'Latest Trends in Corporation Law and Other Developments in Kuwait, Saudi Arabia, Bahrain, Qatar, the United Arab Emirates and Oman' (1978) 6 Intl Bus Law 666, 668.

officer, director, employee or agent in the Sultanate for more than 30 days in any calendar year and transacts no business in the Sultanate through any such officer, director, employee or agent when such personnel is in Oman.

vi. any non-Omani business which has no permanent establishment, assets or officers, directors, employees or agents in the Sultanate and has only occasional and isolated transactions in the Sultanate;

vii. any non-Omani press representatives, whether of newspapers, magazines, radio, television or motion pictures, provided that such representatives are in the Sultanate solely for the purpose of reporting events occurring therein; and

viii. any non-Omani company engaged in the business of providing international transportation by air or sea; provided that such company does not provide domestic service within the Sultanate.

This article lays out further restrictions on participation in trade or business for foreign investors. Therefore, as Mellahi and Guermat rightly observe, the 1974 law governing investment in Oman and the amendments that followed it clearly discriminated against foreign investors, giving priority to Omani investors.[292]

Failure to comply with the FBIL led directly to a strict position being adopted by the judicial authority, as was made clear in *Case 43/84*, heard on 31 March 1985. The case had been brought to the Authority for the Settlement of Commercial Disputes (ASCD)[293] by a foreigner of Bangladeshi origin who had an agreement with an Omani establishment to carry on a business in Oman, and on his own behalf, but under the name

292 Mellahi and Guermat (n 227) 4.

293 Historically, commercial disputes were settled by a judicial body established in May 1974 in the MoCI called the Committee for the Settlement of Commercial Disputes. In 1997 this was replaced by the Commercial Court by Royal Decree 13/97 See McHugo (n 239) 92.

of the Omani establishment to which he paid a commission of 10 per cent of the value of every contract he carried out.

The ASCD held that the agreement was void, stating that the provisions of FBIL were intended for the public/common good which overrode the interests of private individuals and the Law was linked with "public policy" or "public order". Thus, whether or not the illegality of the agreement had been raised by the defendant, the ASCD was disposed to strike down the agreement on its own initiative. Therefore, according to McHugo, this case served as a warning to all foreign companies to ensure they complied with FBIL provisions.[294]

However, amendments to the FBIL were intended to ease these restrictions somewhat. For example, the 1978 amendment to Article 3 was a step towards easing the conditions imposed on foreign investors aiming to invest in Oman, since it reduced the minimum amount of capital from OMR 150,000 to OMR 30,000 at the recommendation of the CFCI, based on a reasonable reason. Article 3 (b) provided that:

> The licence (authorization) required in accordance with Article 2 of this law shall not be granted unless all the following conditions are fulfilled: [...]
> that the paid up capital of the Omani Commercial Company shall not be less than that determined by the Committee for Foreign Capital Investment referred to in Article 9 hereof and is under no circumstances less than OR 150,000. However, the paid up capital referred to may be decreased to a minimum of thirty thousand Omani Rials [...].

The CFCI was responsible for approving any foreign interest in shares in an Omani company; this included the cases of shares with an Omani company when the foreign company obtained an interest that was less than absolute ownership.[295] In addition, in Article 6 there were specific exemptions to enable a foreign investor, whether a company, institution or individual, to establish business in Oman under its "own name and on its own account"[296] following approval from the MoCI. According to Article

294 John McHugo, 'Joint Ventures in the Sultanate of Oman' (1987) 2 Arab LQ 130, 133.

295 McHugo (n 294) 134.

296 Ibid 131.

6 (a-e), these exemptions could be applied in a number of instances. The Article states:

> The following shall be exempted from the provisions of Article 3 hereof:
>
> a. Companies, institutions and individuals which are engaged in activities in the Sultanate of Oman by virtue of agreements or special contracts concluded with the government of the Sultanate or its public institutions;
>
> b. Companies, institutions and individuals which are engaged in a project declared to be an Economic Development Project;
>
> c. Companies, institutions and individuals who are engaged in a profession which the Council of Ministers has declared to be a profession of critical need and shortage in the Sultanate of Oman;
>
> d. Companies and institutions which are licensed banking institutions in the jurisdiction of their organization; and
>
> e. Companies, institutions and individuals which are exempted by Decree of the Sultan.

However, invoking these exemptions might be not easy, as the approach applied during the implementation of the FBIL did not favour foreign investment. For example, in 1982 the MoCI conducted a review of the FBIL, and prohibited foreign investment in the trade and service sectors, on the basis that these sectors were sufficiently developed, using this as an incentive to benefit Omani interests.[297] This prohibition clearly shows the level of discrimination against foreign investors under the FBIL regime.

2.5.2 The New Foreign Investment Regime Post-1994

The new foreign investment era started on 16 October 1994 with the issue of FCIL which replaced the FBIL 1974. Article 4 of FCIL states clearly that:

297 Pepper (n 254) 337.

"The Foreign Business and Investment Law issued by the Royal Decree 4/74 referred to above shall be hereby abrogated". It is thought that the rapid changes in foreign investment-related legislation are indicative of the Omani government's desire to provide the guarantees needed to attract foreign investment to Oman.[298] This shift in attitude reflects the Omani government's new approach towad attracting foreign investment during the 1990s, which, according to Mellahi and Guermat, was motivated by two main reasons: the fall in the price of oil and pressure from the World Bank and International Monetary Fund (IMF) to seek foreign investment and further integrate its economy into the global economy.[299]

This new position toward reducing the obstacles to foreign investment was accompanied by a number of developments during this period, such as the conference held in 1995 (2020 Vision Oman). This event was intended to establish development targets in various national sectors to be achieved by 2020 and to provide guidance for the Omani government's development plans, including foreign investment.[300] In addition, the Omani Centre for Investment Promotion and Export Development (OCIPED) was established in 1997 to assist foreign investors in various respects. During the same period, Oman also made preparations to become a member of the WTO, ratified the agreement and acceded to membership on 9 November 2000.[301]

Although both the old and new laws provide that foreign investors cannot be involved in any foreign investment without a licence from the MoCI, this is couched in softer language in Article 1 of the FCIL:

> Non-Omanis – whether natural of juridical persons – shall not conduct any commercial, industrial or tourism businesses or otherwise participate in an Omani Company except with a licence from the Ministry of Commerce and Industry to be issued in accordance with the Provisions of this Law.

298 McKinney (n 283) 131.

299 Mellahi and Guermat (n 227) 5.

300 Howard L Stovall, Emad Tinawi, Yael Katz, and Harold Uliman, 'Middle East Commercial Law Developments', (1998) 32 Intl L 411, 417-418.

301 WTO, *Trade Policy Review: Report by the Secretariat: Oman WT/TPR/S/201* (2008) 65, <www.wto.org/english/tratop_e/tpr_e/s201-02_e.doc> accessed 6 January 2015.

This can be seen in the revoking of the word "unlawful" which was used in the corresponding Article of the original law.[302]

It can be argued that the significance of FCIL is that it removed a number of restrictions on both entry to local business enterprises and ownership in most sectors.[303] First, Article 2 (1) of FCIL increases the allowable percentage of foreign ownership over that stipulated in FBIL. The essential principle in Article 3 of FBIL and Article 2 of FCIL is that to operate a business in Oman, all foreign investors must have an Omani as a shareholder. While under FBIL in practice the permitted percentage of foreign ownership was not more than 49%,[304] FCIL set these levels of foreign participation in an Omani company, starting from 49%. This can be increased to 65% provided the capital invested is not less than OMR 150,000 (US$ 390,000) after a decision by the MoCI following a recommendation from the CFCI.

Moreover, with the approval of the Development Council, the percentage of foreign investment can be increased to 100% of the company's capital, subject to two further conditions: first, the capital sum invested must be at least OMR 500,000 (US$ 1.3 million) and second, the project must contribute to the development of the national economy. This change was made because Omani policymakers realised that for foreign investors the ability to maintain and to exercise financial and operational management over the company plays an important role in investment decisions.[305]

However, in practice there are two exceptions to Article 2 of FCIL. The first relates to multilateral treaties and permits up to 70% foreign participation in companies, in accordance with Oman's commitments and applicable regulations under the WTO.[306] The second concerns those countries that have an agreement with Oman and in this case the provisions of that treaty apply. Thus, for example, American companies

302 An English translation ot the Law has been produced by the Oman Chamber of Commerce and Industry <http://images.mofcom.gov.cn/om/table/wgtz.pdf> accessed 30 April 2016.

303 Mellahi and Guermat (n 227) 6.

304 McKinney (n 283) 131.

305 Ibid.

306 World Trade Organization, *Trade Policy Review* 61; Ernst & Young 'Doing business in Oman An executive's guide to doing business in Oman' (January 2011) 12 <http://vae.ahk.de/fileadmin/ahk_vae/Startseite_Oman/Doing_business_in_Oman__Final_.pdf> accessed 29 June 2014.

can own up to 100% of the capital under the FTA between Oman and the USA.[307]

It is believed that under FCIL, in the case of those companies with less than 50% of foreign ownership, separate Foreign Investment Clearance will no longer be required in order to enter on Oman's commercial registration and seek "authorisation to conduct business"[308] there. In contrast, under FBIL, the CFCI enjoyed a "significant measure of administrative discretion"[309] in how it defined the national economic sectors in which the presence of foreign business would be beneficial and this impacted on whether or not authorisation was granted to foreign investors.[310] Moreover, in the context of the FCIL's approach intended to encourage foreign investment, in 1997 the MoCI called on all Omani public joint-stock companies to allow at least 49% non-Omani ownership by issuing an internal directive requiring corporate articles.[311]

An additional significant step is that Article 7 of FCIL reduces the number of authorities involved in granting licences to foreign investors, compared with the previous law, as it declares clearly that with regard to obtaining a licence for establishment of a new company, approval need only be sought from the MoCI: "Licensing shall be granted to the projects subject to this Law without the need for obtaining prior approvals from any authorities outside the Ministry". The only exception to this is for companies that are 100% foreign-owned, where the approval of the Development Council is needed.

A further important development in FCIL concerns the exemption from income tax and customs duties on imports of equipment and raw materials required for production, offered to companies with foreign ownership. In association with the supportive approach of foreign investment applied in FCIL during the 1990s, the Omani government issued a number of commercial laws intended to create incentives for foreign investment. These involved relieving foreign-owned companies of the higher tax rate to which they were then subject, by establishing five-year tax exemptions

307 Deloitte, 'International Tax: Oman Highlights 2014' <www.deloitte.com/content/dam/Deloitte/global/Documents/Tax/dttl-tax-omanhighlights-2014.pdf> accessed 29 June 2014.

308 McKinney (n 283) 131.

309 Ibid.

310 Ibid.

311 See Royal Decrees 87/96, 89/96 and 90/96; Stovall, Tinawi, Katz, and Uliman (n 300) 418.

for companies engaging in an extensive variety of activities.[312] Article 8.1 of FCIL states:

> Companies licensed to be incorporated pursuant to this Law and carrying out its activity in one of the following areas shall be exempted from income tax:
> One) Industry and Mining.
> Two) Export of locally manufactured or processed products.
> Three) Tourism promotion including operation of hotels and tourist villages, but excluding management contracts.
> Four) Production and processing of farm products including poultry farming, processing or manufacturing animal products and agro-industries.
> Five) Fishing and fish processing.
> Six) Exploitation and provision of services such as public utility projects, but excluding management contracts and project execution contracting [...].

In addition, according to Article 9.1:

> Foreign Investment projects mentioned in this Law can be exempted from paying custom duties on plant and machinery imported by them for setting up the projects. They can also be exempted from paying custom duties on raw materials needed in the manufacturing process which are not available in the local markets, for a period not exceeding 5 years starting from the date of commencing production. This exemption can be renewed once.

However, the difference between the two exemptions granted should be noted, namely, that Article 8.1 states that companies "shall be exempted from income tax", whereas Article 9.1 announced that they "can be exempted from (paying) custom duties". In other words, it is mandatory to provide the exemption with regard to taxes, but with regard to customs duties, it is optional. The amendment in the Law on Income Tax that came into force in 2010 introduced full equality of treatment between completely Omani-owned companies and foreign companies, regardless

312 Stovall, Tinawi, Katz, and Uliman (n 300) 418.

of the percentage of foreign participation.[313] This equality in tax payment is an important development for foreign investors, to reduce their fear of discrimination. Moreover, another instrument to attract foreign investment was the launch of a 12% "flat rate corporate tax", applied as well from January 1, 2010. This flat-rate tax, one of the most favourable in the GCC, is expected to help Oman to secure more direct investment. In addition, Oman does not apply personal income tax or wealth tax.[314] However, all legal guarantees and weaknesses in FCIL will be examined in further depth in Chapter Four.

2.6 Conclusion

This chapter introduced foreign investment related laws and policies in Oman. After briefly tracing Oman's history as a trading nation, the focus shifted to an analysis of the evolution of the Omani legal system and the role of Omani Basic law, to provide a background for the environment of the developments in investment law in Oman since 1970. Two key pieces of legislation were discussed and compared: the FBIL and its more recent successor, the FCIL.

Oman has benefited greatly from its strategic location over the centuries and in more recent times, it has embarked on an ambitious development programme that involves attracting foreign investment. The key question to be addressed in the following chapters is whether Oman has been able to utilise this rich history and strategic position to attract and provide legal protection for foreign investment.

This chapter argues that the promulgation of the Basic Law was important for attracting foreign investment to Oman since the Law defines the Omani policy and attitude toward many issues concern foreign companies. The existence of the Law is important as a basis for the development and protection of these rights as the Law emphasises the sovereignty of the law, and the independence of the Judiciary and judges, and criminalises any interference in judges' work.

It is clear that the cautious stance of Omani regulations toward foreign investment during the 1970s and 1980s, which was seen under the FBIL was because the country was focusing mainly on providing the basic needs

313 Ithraa <www.ithraa.om> accessed 16 June 2015.

314 According to the Income Tax Law issued by Royal Decree 28/2009 Oxford Business Group (n 233) 295.

for Omani citizens and due to the weak realisation of the importance of FDI. This was obvious in many features, such as in the number of governmental bodies involved in issuing licences, rules regarding the permitted percentage of foreign ownership, income tax regulations covering foreign-owned enterprises, and restrictions on business and trade activities open to foreign investors in Oman.

The shift in developing countries' attitude toward provision of better protection for foreign investment during the 1990s, in addition to pressure from international and internal factors, was reflected in the promulgation of the Omani FCIL 1994. It is argued that the law took a more welcoming attitude towards foreign investors, offering them more protection than the previous law. Nevertheless, it seems the law was intended to balance attracting foreign investment with keeping national control in certain key areas.

This policy at national level is complemented by a development in Oman's commitments under international agreements. The legal guarantees and weaknesses under Oman's international and regional obligations will be examined in the next chapter.

Chapter 3:
Legal Guarantees and Weaknesses under Oman's International and Regional Obligations

3.1 Introduction

There is a widespread belief that investment treaties are important tools both for host countries wishing to attract foreign investment and for states wanting to protect the foreign investment of their citizens.[315] Therefore, Oman has signed many agreements -bilateral agreements such as Oman's BITs and FTAs, regional such as the GCC, and multilateral international such as the WTO (GATS, TRIPS, TRIMS) - to address mainly or partly the issue of protection of foreign investment. The extent to which these international and regional obligations on Oman provide adequate guarantees and protection can be evaluated.

Therefore, this chapter will examine the legal guarantees and weaknesses under Oman's international and regional obligations. It will provide an overview of Oman's international investment and investment-related agreements. This will include the analysis of Oman›s International investment related agreements such as those with the WTO Agreements, the GCC, Oman›s BITs, and its FTA with the USA. These are Oman›s main related international agreements. It important to mention that although this chapter generally follows the approach of examining Oman›s commitments under the WTO, GCC, BITs, and Oman›s FTAs, this will be changed in many areas according to the level of the strength of Oman›s commitments under these agreements.

The extent to which the obligations provided by international treatment standards included in these agreements form an important element of protection will be investigated. This will be by focusing on three kinds of treatment standards: national treatment provisions, MFN treatment provisions, and minimum standards treatment provisions. Then, the possible risk of expropriation in Oman's treaties will be evaluated by examining the strength of protection offered in these agreements and whether or not their provisions contain clear conditions for compensation.

315 Michael Ewing-Chow, 'Thesis, Antithesis and Synthesis: Investor Protection in BITs, WTO and FTAs' (2007), 30 UNSWLJ 548, 548.

The case of *Al-Tamimi* will be referred to throughout the chapter in order to derive the legal lessons behind it. Another aspect which merits discussion in this regard is how Oman's international treaties deal with taxes, custom duties and money transfer and what are Oman's obligations with regard to these three issues.

The effectiveness of dispute settlement provisions in those treaties dealing with foreign investment in Oman will also be investigated, by analysing the guarantees and challenges under the Dispute Settlement Body (DSB) of the WTO, the ICJ, Oman's BITs, the Oman-USA FTA dispute settlement provisions, and the ICSID.

Al-Tamimi will serve here as an illustrative example of an international foreign investment dispute against Oman and the impact of this case on the Sultanate's foreign investment law and policy will be analysed.

3.2 Oman's International Investment Agreements

3.2.1 Overview of Oman's International Investment Agreements

As part of the Sultanate's efforts to market itself as an investment-friendly country, Oman has signed most of the important multilateral treaties on trade and investment as well as a large number of BITs. Even though there is no conclusive evidence that entry into investment treaties is directly associated with an increase in foreign investment, as mentioned earlier,[316] it is clear that the Omani government is keen to ratify international trade and investment agreements as a means of integrating the Omani economy with international trade as part of its attempts to diversify its economy. According to Article 42 of the Omani Basic Law,[317] it is the responsibility of the Sultan or a person designated by him to conclude international treaties and agreements.

Despite Oman's long history as an independent nation, it only became a member of the United Nations in 1971.[318] It is also party to many international organisations, such as the WTO and GCC. As occurred

316 Ewing-Chow (n 315) 548.

317 Basic Law of State, art 42 states: "His Majesty the Sultan discharges the following functions: [...] Signing international conventions and treaties according to the provisions of the Law or authorising their signature and promulgating Decrees ratifying the same".

318 United Nations, 'Member States' <www.un.org/en/members/index.shtml> accessed 19 November 2014.

elsewhere in the world, Oman witnessed a boom in the number of BITs it signed from the 1990s onwards. Since 1991, the Sultanate has signed 34 BITs, the first BIT with Tunisia in 1991 and the latest with Bulgaria in 2014.[319] However, with regard to the protection of foreign investment, the most significant treaties involving Oman are its agreements with the GCC and the WTO and its FTA with the United States, because of the comprehensive guarantees provided under these agreements and their effect on Oman's foreign investment policy. For this reason, these agreements will be analysed here.

3.2.2 The WTO Agreements

Oman viewed accession to the WTO as a vital step towards attracting more FDI, obtaining access to other major regional and international markets through trade liberalisation and tariff reduction, and improving its financial and economic credibility. Therefore, the time-consuming efforts involved in the accession process, either at national level or later within the WTO, were considered worthwhile. Internally, the application went through a number of steps; in December 1994 the Council of Ministers decided that Oman should seek observer status and an application to participate on this basis was submitted in January 1995, with acceptance being received in October 1995.[320] Oman officially applied to join the WTO on 22 April 1996, under Article 12 of the WTO Agreement, finally becoming a member on 9 November 2000.[321] No known reservations were expressed to its application.[322]

Whether GATT was a suitable forum to discuss the issue of foreign investment policies was controversial. Many developing countries argued that allowing foreign investment and regulating this should be a purely internal matter, whereas others argued that international trade law should be involved in the case of applying policies and regulations restricting the ability of foreign companies to invest locally. However, ultimately, countries arguing for the involvement of international trade law won and

319 See Supreme Council for Planning, 'Agreements' <https://www.scp.gov.om/en/Agreements.aspx> accessed 7 June 2016 A full list of bilateral investment agreements concluded by Oman can be found in Appendix A.

320 Ministry of Commerce and Industry 'WTO Agreement' <www.mocioman.gov.om/Main-Menu/Agreements/wto/wto-agreement> accessed 13 October 2014

321 WTO, *Trade Policy Review Report by the Secretariat: Oman* (2014) 10 <www.wto.org/english/tratop_e/tpr_e/g295_e.pdf> accessed 24 September 2014.

322 WTO 'Oman and the WTO' <www.wto.org/english/thewto_e/countries_e/oman_e.htm> accessed 5 May 2016.

the TRIMs agreement was adopted.[323] During the WTO Uruguay round of multilateral trade negotiations, the notion emerged of regulating foreign investment as a part of international trade.[324]

Following Oman's accession to the WTO, Oman became subject to the obligations of the TRIMs. Hence, Omani investment and commercial laws should not contain any trade-restrictive investment measures. However, the effectiveness of the role of WTO agreements regarding the protection of foreign investment in Oman can be viewed from two sides. On the one hand, the limitations of the WTO agreements can be noticed in a number of areas. Mavroidis has argued that the implementation of protection provisions provided by the WTO agreements can vary among Member States. For example, members might or might not provide national treatment for services traders. In addition, members might use an exemption from applying MFN treatment relying on Article II of GATS on the basis of political reasons.[325] In addition, it is observed that although the WTO has addressed investment matters in specific provisions and practice, there has been a lack of a comprehensive and systematic way of dealing with those issues related to investment. For example, a very small number of governmental measures are covered in the TRIMs agreement for goods; the GATS agreement prevents countries and industries from applying important principles such as national treatment.[326] Therefore, Ewing-Chow has argued that foreign investment provisions in the TRIMS offer a "thin form" of protection.[327]

On the other hand, the WTO agreements can play a significant role in providing protection for foreign investment in Oman, as the country is under obligations to provide the protection needed in a number of areas. For example, the TRIPS Agreement requires it to provide protection for the intellectual property rights of Trans-national Corporations (TNCs).[328]

---

323 Subedi, (n 7) 55, 56.

324 Ibid 55.

325 Petros C Mavroidis, 'Regulation of Investment in the Trade Regime: From ITO to WTO' in Zdenek Drabek and Petros C Mavroidis (eds) *Regulation of Foreign Investment: Challenges to International Harmonization* (World Scientific Publishing 2013) 30, 31.

326 Thomas L Brewer and Stephen Young 'Investment Issues at the WTO: the Architecture of Rule and the Settlement of Disputes' (1998) 1 J Intl Econ L 457, 468.

327 Ewing-Chow (n 315) 549.

328 Subedi (n 7) 56.

In addition, although according to Article 1 the scope of the TRIMs Agreement is limited to dealing with "investment measures related to trade in goods only", Oman is under an obligation to eliminate all TRIMs that are "not in conformity with the provisions" of the TRIMs Agreement within five years of its date of entry into force.[329] In addition, Article 5.4 of TRIMs obliges Oman to not amend any laws under which the existing foreign investments were established. This provision can be regarded as a tool of protection for FDI from any unexpected changes in or amendments of laws or measures governing foreign investment in the Sultanate that may lead to less favourable treatment for the investment concerned.

Moreover, according to Article 6.2 of TRIMs, Oman as a member is under an obligation to "notify the Secretariat of the publications in which TRIMs may be found, including those applied by regional and local governments and authorities within" the country. Furthermore, Oman is obliged by Article III of the GATS agreement to provide transparency, not only by publicizing its laws and regulations but also "by disclosing investment-related information". However, it is ambiguous whether this article provides protection against misleading information or unclear procedures which may result in less favourable treatment being granted to foreign investors at any stage of FDI in Oman. In addition, although Article 5 of the Omani FCIL places responsibility for defining the investment areas on the CFCI, this article does not oblige the CFCI to publicize the investment fields that are available for foreign investors.[330] What is clear is that Oman will be in violation of its commitments under the WTO Agreement if it fails to ensure the transparency of all related trade and investment measures. It is pointed out that since Oman joined the WTO, there have been no claims that Oman maintains any measures that are not in compliance with the WTO TRIMs provisions.[331]

3.2.3 Oman's Agreements with the GCC

There has been slow progress in the economic achievements of the GCC since its establishment on 8 June 1981.[332] However, the desire of the GCC

329 Agreement on Trade-Related Investment Measures (TRIMs) 1995, art 5 (1,2).

330 Article 5 of the FCIL states: "The said Committee [...] shall make recommendations in respect of the following: 1 The identification of the investment fields".

331 Bureau of Economic and Business Affairs, *2015 Investment Climate Statement – Oman* (May 2015) <www.state.gov/e/eb/rls/othr/ics/2015/241691.htm> accessed 5 May 2016.

332 The GCC has six Member States: Bahrain, Kuwait, Oman, Qatar, Saudi Arabia, and the United Arab Emirates.

Member States to encourage investment among them, strengthening and integrating their economies, was one of the most important reasons for establishing this organisation. This approach is reflected in a number of agreements and provisions existing amongst the GCC countries. For example, Article 4 of the GCC Charter makes it clear that economic development and the formulation of similar regulations, especially in the business field and specifically "economic and financial affairs; commerce, and customs" has been the organisation's main focus since it was established.[333] In 1983 all six member states signed an agreement establishing a regional free trade area, which introduced freedom of movement for workers and free movement of goods among member states.[334] The Unified Economic Agreement between the Countries of the GCC (GCC Economic Agreement) [335] is arguably the most important and comprehensive agreement between the six countries.[336] Although it consists of some nine chapters and thirty-three articles, few of its provisions deal with foreign investment specifically. Oman must accord investors from GCC member States the same treatment as their Omani counterparts, with Article 3 of the Agreement stating:

> GCC natural and legal citizens shall be accorded, in any Member State, the same treatment accorded to its own citizens, without differentiation or discrimination, in all economic activities, especially the following: (1) Movement and residence (2) Work in private and government jobs (3) Pension and social security (4) Engagement in all professions and crafts (5) Engagement in all economic, investment and service activities (6) Real estate ownership (7) Capital

333 Charter of the Gulf Cooperation Council 1981, art 4 gives four objectives:
(1) Effect coordination, integration and interconnection between Member States in all fields in order to achieve unity between them
(2) Deepen and strengthen relations, links and scopes of cooperation now prevailing between their peoples in various fields
(3) Formulate similar regulations in various fields including the following: Economic and financial affairs; Commerce, Customs and Communications; [...]
(4) [...] and encourage cooperation by the private sector for good of their peoples.

334 Gonzalo Villalta Puig and Bader A1-Haddab, 'The Constitutionalisation of Free Trade in the Gulf Cooperation Council' (2011) 25 Arab LQ 311, 314.

335 Adopted by the GCC Supreme Council in the 22nd Session; 31 December 2001 in Muscat, Oman.

336 Amr Daoud Marar, 'The Cooperation Council for the Arab States of the Gulf' (2004) 10 Law & Bus Rev Am 475, 481.

movement (8) Tax treatment (9) Stock ownership and formation of corporations (10) Education, health and social services.

While this article seems to be an assertion of the provisions of the Preamble of the Agreement, it is clear that investors from GCC Member States are not subject to FCIL with regard to the issues included in the article. This is because the article obliges the GCC member states to accord nationals of other GCC states equal treatment to that given to their own citizens. The agreement stipulates that the treatment of members should be "without differentiation or discrimination". Therefore, all non-Omani GCC investors must receive the same treatment as Omani nationals in all economic activities, including the payment of taxes as well as ownership of real estate.

In addition, the Article 5 of the GCC Economic Agreement obliges the six countries to 'unify' all regulations related to investment and to grant national treatment to all investments owned by natural and legal citizens of GCC Member States.[337] Although Oman is committed in its regulations to treating GCC foreign investors equally to Omani nationals, there are no known efforts among the GCC states with regard to unifying their investment-related laws.[338]

In 2003 the GCC States established a customs union.[339] Later, in January 2008, the GCC signed an agreement to establish a common market for services.[340] Finally, 2008 witnessed the application of a common market, a big step for GCC members. Although the creation of the common

337 GCC Economic Agreement 2001, art 5 states:
"For the purpose of enhancing local, external, and intra-GCC investment levels, and provide an investment climate characterized by transparency and stability, Member States agree to take the following steps:
1 Unify all their investment-related laws and regulations.
2 Accord national treatment to all investments owned by GCC natural and legal citizens [...]".

338 For example, Oman is drafting its new foreign investment law in collaboration with the World Bank Group not other GCC States. See K Rejimon, '100% ownership for foreign investors in Oman?' *Times of Oman* (Muscat, 27 January 2016) <http://timesofoman.com/article/76347/Oman/Government> accessed 4 May 2016.

339 Benjamin Smith, *Market Orientalism: Cultural Economy and the Arab Gulf States* (Syracuse University Press 2015) 183.

340 WTO, *Trade Policy Review Report by the Secretariat: Oman WT/TPR/S/295* (2013), 23, <www.wto.org/english/tratop_e/tpr_e/s295_e.pdf> accessed 8 January 2015.

market may challenge the local agency system within these countries, its establishment made it much easier for investors from GCC states to operate in other GCC countries. In 2014 Oman and Bahrain were the only GCC countries which had succeeded in having two GCC countries, Saudi Arabia and the UAE, among their top-five foreign investor states. Nevertheless, some service-sector companies, particularly in property and retail, have succeeded in operating in other GCC countries.[341] An example is Majid AlFutaim, a UAE citizen who has invested in all GCC countries. It is anticipated that by 2020, the total investment of Majid Al Futtaim in Oman will be OMR 515 million ($1.3 billion).[342]

It may be argued that although such agreements may extend the market for investors within the member states (and in some cases for companies established outside the region), there is a concern that such regional organisations might introduce discriminatory policies against companies and investors from non-member states.[343] Nevertheless, whether a country has the right to grant preferential treatment to certain nationalities will be discussed later.

In addition, Article 31 of the GCC Economic Agreement raises a question about the limits that Oman has in its bilateral agreements or FTAs. This article states:

> No Member State may grant to a non-Member State any preferential treatment exceeding that granted herein to Member State [...] [or] conclude any agreement that violates provisions of this agreement.
>
> It is clear that this article imposes an obligation on each member states of the GCC. It obliges GCC members not to 'water down' this preferential treatment by granting it to nationals of states which are not members of the GCC.[344] Oman is not in violation of this article by ratifying the FTA with the USA, since the treatment granted to the USA citizens does not exceed what is granted to Member States of the GCC. However, it seems that the FTAs between Oman

341 Smith (n 339) 183.

342 Robert Anderson, 'Majid Al Futtaim plans $1.3bn investment in Oman malls', 2 May 2016 <www.gulfbusiness.com> accessed 4 May 2016.

343 Muchlinski (n 217) 262.

344 Hussain Agil and Bruno Zeller, 'Foreign Investments in Saudi Arabia' (2012) 15 Intl Trade & Bus L Rev 60, 68.

and the USA and Bahrain and the USA[345] have raised concern among other GCC Member States and that is why currently GCC States have started to negotiate FTAs with other parties as a bloc rather than as individual states. Thus, they have concluded FTAs with Singapore in 2013 and with European Free Trade Association (EFTA) States in 2014,[346] whereas the FTA with the EU is not ratified yet.[347]

3.2.4 The Oman-US FTA

The most significant treaty following the WTO Agreement was Oman's FTA with the USA. However, this was not the first trade agreement between these two nations, as the trade relationship between them has deep historical roots, dating back to 1833 when Oman signed a treaty of Amity and Commerce, becoming among the first Arab States to do so.[348] This was followed by a number of trade agreements with the USA: the Investment Protection Agreement in 1976, the Agreement on Economic and Technical Cooperation in 1980, the Memorandum of Understanding Regarding the Continuation of Limited Services in 1996 and the Trade and Investment Framework Agreement (TIFA) on 7 July 2004, which is regarded as a preliminary step toward the FTA.[349]

Generally, the FTA, which consists of twenty two chapters, grants US investors and investment the same treatment as those of Oman and the GCC.[350] Chapter Ten of the FTA deals comprehensively and clearly with the investment issues between the two parties, whereas, the WTO Agreements lacks this comprehensive investment protection clause. The Oman-USA FTA covers all aspects of investment, including enterprises,

345 The USA-Bahrain FTA entered into force on 11 January 2006. See Office of the US Trade Representative, 'Bahrain FTA' <https://ustr.gov/trade-agreements> accessed 5 May 2016.

346 EFTA States include Iceland, Liechtenstein, Norway and Switzerland. The FTA Agreement entered into force on 1 July 2014. See <www.efta.int/> accessed 5 May 2014.

347 Gulf Business <www.gulfbusiness.com/> accessed 5 May 2016.

348 MoCI, 'Highlights of the Free Trade Agreement (FTA) between the Sultanate of Oman and the United States of America', 6 <www.mocioman.gov.om/> accessed 16 September 2014.

349 Ibid.

350 Ibid.

debt, concessions, contracts and intellectual property.[351] Chapter Ten of the FTA guarantees six essential forms of protection for foreign investment: non-discriminatory treatment, the minimum standard of treatment of aliens, protection from expropriation, free transfer of funds, freedom from performance requirements and the right to hire executives regardless of their nationality.[352] All these rights are backed by a comprehensive dispute settlement system[353] described in Chapters Ten and Twenty.

However, in referring to investment, Chapter Ten, Article 10.2.1 of the FTA states: "In the event of any inconsistency between this Chapter and another Chapter, the other Chapter shall prevail to the extent of the inconsistency." It is unclear what the possible effects of this article on the protection of foreign investment and investors' rights may be, in a case of inconsistency between the provisions in Chapter Ten, which deals fully with the protection of foreign investment, and the aforementioned "other Chapter", since the latter will prevail. It can be said that, for better protection of foreign investment in both countries, this article may need to be amended to grant the foreign investment provisions superiority in the case of contradiction or inconsistency between them and other provisions in the agreement.

In the *Al-Tamimi* case, the "investor of a party" defined under Article 10.27 of the Oman-USA FTA raised a debate between Mr Al-Tamimi (the Claimant) and Oman (the Respondant). Oman raised two objections; first, that the Claimant was a US-UAE dual national and therefore should be excluded from claiming under the Oman-USA FTA according to Article 10.27 of the FTA. Second, the Claimant lacked a genuine connection to the US.[354] However, the tribunal rejected the Oman argument and stated that:

> In any event, as a matter of interpretation of Article 10.27, the Tribunal does not consider that the language of "dominant and effective nationality" is intended to prevent dual citizens of both the United States and a third-party State, such as the UAE, from invoking the US–Oman BIT – even where

351 USTR, 'Statement of Why the United States – Oman Free Trade Agreement is in the Interest of US Commerce' 7 <www.ustr.gov/webfm_send/2650> accessed 13 December 2014.

352 USTR, 'United States – Oman Free Trade Agreement Summary of the Agreement' 9 <www.ustr.gov/webfm_send/2648> accessed 3 January 2015.

353 USTR (n 351) 7.

354 *Al-Tamimi* (n 11) Procedural Order No 5 (15 March 2013).

> the nationality of the third-party State is predominant. Rather, the Tribunal considers that the provision is aimed at preventing claims by dual nationals of both State parties (i.e. the United States and Oman) from seeking to use the FTA to claim against their own State of dominant and effective nationality – thereby defeating the purpose of the FTA to apply investment protection only to "investors of the other Party".[355]

The "covered investment" and the entry into force of the Oman-USA FTA was another debated issue raised by the *Al-Tamimi* case. Oman challenged that the OMCO–Emrock and OMCO–SFOH Lease Agreements were not "covered investments" under the Oman-USA FTA, because OMCO terminated the OMCO–Emrock Lease Agreement under cover of a letter dated 20 July 2008.[356] This meant that the lease agreement was not in existence as of the date of entry into force of the FTA on 1 January 2009. The Claimant argued that OMCO sent a second termination on 17 February 2009, which proved that the earlier termination letter was ineffective.[357] The Tribunal rejected Oman's argument and founds that it possessed "jurisdiction *ratione temporis* over the OMCO–Emrock Lease Agreement, which remained in existence as of 1 January 2009"[358] and stated that:

> In light of this evidence, the Tribunal finds that the second termination notice of 17 February 2009 must be taken to have superseded the earlier notice of 20 July 2008, with the effect that the earlier notice was rendered ineffective. In other words, the specification of a 2009 termination date in the second termination notice ("we hereby terminate [...] with immediate effect") effectively waived the earlier purported termination date.[359]

---

355 Ibid para 274.
356 *Al-Tamimi* (n 11) paras 96, 100.
357 Ibid para 105.
358 Ibid para 293.
359 Ibid para 292.

3.3 The Guarantees Provided by Treatment Standards and the Challenges they Present

Although there is debate concerning the meaning and scope of the international minimum standards of treatment, most Regional Trade Agreements (RTAs), BITs, FTAs and other related investment treaties provide basic standards of treatment, including national treatment and MFN treatment, as protection instruments for foreign investors.[360] It is clear that the inclusion of these in Oman's BITs, in addition to the treatment standards accorded under the Oman-USA FTA, offer protection for the home state investments and investors who are investing in Oman.

The reason that the WTO includes the treatment standards in its agreements is that this organisation's essential mission is to liberalise international trade.[361] Therefore, WTO agreements include national treatment and MFN standards to protect foreign investment. The following discussion will examine the role of these standards of treatment in Oman's international agreements.

3.3.1 Protection under National Treatment Provisions

The aim of the principle of national treatment is to prevent discrimination on the grounds of the nationality of ownership of a foreign investment.[362] In order to evaluate accurately the application of this principle in the case of Oman, there are two simple criteria: (1) are foreign investors and Omani investors placed in a "comparable setting"? and (2) is the treatment granted to foreign investors at least as favourable as the treatment granted to Omani investors?[363]

It can be said that Oman's commitment with regard to the implementation of national treatment can be categorised into absolute national treatment guarantees and those which contain exceptions. National treatment protection is provided under the WTO agreements, the GCC Singapore FTA and Oman's BITs, contains exceptions, whereas the Oman-USA FTA contains absolute application of the principle of national treatment. This is clear as Article 10.3 of the Oman-USA FTA, which extends national treatment not only to the operation but also to the establishment, acquisition, expansion, management, conduct, and sale or other disposition

360 Subedi (n 7) 80.
361 Sornarajah (n 8) 269.
362 Subedi (n 7) 94.
363 See Dolzer and Schreuer (n 91) 179.

of investment/investors after they enter the host state, whether it is Oman or the USA. Paragraphs 1 and 2 of the mentioned article state that:

> 1. Each Party shall accord to investors of the other Party treatment no less favourable than that it accords, in like circumstances, to its own investors with respect to the establishment, acquisition, expansion, management, conduct, operation, and sale or other disposition of investments in its territory.
>
> 2. Each Party shall accord to covered investments treatment no less favourable than that it accords, in like circumstances, to investments in its territory of its own investors with respect to the establishment, acquisition, expansion, management, conduct, operation, and sale or other disposition of investments.

According to Dolzer and Schreuer, the use of the phrase "no less favourable", in paragraphs 1 and 2, seems to assume that national rules may provide less protection for foreign investors than those of the general obligations of international law. Therefore, it recognises that other rules might offer greater protection for foreign investments.[364] Consequently, Oman is obliged to provide higher protection for American investment and investors than for its own nationals, in those instances where the general rules of international law are more protective than Omani national regulations.

While the words "in like circumstances" stated in paragraphs 1, 2 of Article 10.3 of the FTA may raise a debate, as will be seen later in *Methanex Corporation v USA*, the Tribunal in the *Al-Tamimi* case took a narrow approach in to this provision, stating that:

> However, to provide a relevant comparison for a national treatment claim, any comparator investor must still be in materially the same circumstances as the Claimant. The Tribunal does not accept the Claimant's submission that "the Jebel Wasa Quarry should be understood as being in like circumstances with all limestone quarries in Oman". The

364 Ibid 178.

> Claimant must point to evidence that a domestic operator which possessed the same or substantially similar approvals as the Claimant, and carried out the same or substantially similar material conduct (including the Claimant's repeated violations of the terms of those approvals) was treated less harshly or according to a different standard[365]

Therefore, it is clear that if there is an absence in one respect of complete similarity between the foreign investor's case and treatment of a national investor, this will not establish a violation of the national treatment clause. This was apparent in both tribunals' interpretation of the words "in like circumstances" in *Methanex* and *Al-Tamimi*. In addition, "in like circumstances" should be applied in the key factors of the investment. For example, the Tribunal in *Al-Tamimi* investigated "like circumstances" with regard to the treatment of Mr. Al-Tamimi himself and the Jebel Wasa limestone quarry. Evidence was provided by the Respondent that the Claimant was not the only case in Oman to be investigated by the Omani authorities for quarrying violations since in a 2013 report, 193 cases had been referred to the public prosecutor's office, including cases where operators were investigated for "extending the areas that were allocated to them".[366] This convinced the Tribunal that the claimant had failed to prove "like circumstances". Consequently, the Tribunal in the *Al-Tamimi* case dismissed the Claimant's national treatment claim on the basis of Article 10.3 of the FTA that the Respondent had breached the national treatment.[367]

Importantly, the Tribunal in *Al-Tamimi* concluded that since Oman imposed fines in the first instance against OMCO, the Omani-owned company and Mr AlWaily, an Omani citizen who was prosecuted along with Mr Al-Tamimi, this constituted evidence that Mr Al-Tamimi had been not targeted because he was a foreigner and therefore, there was no breach of national treatment.[368] Thus, even though the host states' action against the foreign investor was wrong in its conclusion, since it treated the foreign investor and its own citizens equally, there was no violation of national treatment.

365 *Al-Tamimi* (n 11) para 463.
366 Ibid para 466.
367 Ibid para 467.
368 Ibid.

Although there are slight differences in its application, the principle of national treatment is found in three main areas under the WTO Agreements.[369] The first is trade in goods. Oman is obliged under the terms of Article III paragraph 1 of GATT not to apply to imported or national products any protection measures such as discriminatory internal taxes, other internal charges, laws, regulations and other relevant requirements.[370] Moreover, if Oman grants products imported to the Sultanate treatment less favourable than that granted to its own similar products in respect of all laws, regulations and requirements, Oman will be in a violation of GATT Agreement. Paragraph 4 of GATT Article III states that:

> The products of the territory of any contracting party imported into the territory of any other contracting party shall be accorded treatment no less favourable than that accorded to like products of national origin in respect of all laws, regulations and requirements affecting their internal sale, offering for sale, purchase, transportation, distribution or use.

According to Wang, this paragraph in GATT Article III is the most significant in creating the "background and terminology of national treatment of the GATS".[371] Again, the exceptions given to the WTO's Agreement member states may weaken the full implementation of national treatment to like products, as will be discussed later.

The second area is Oman's obligation to apply national treatment in trade in services for foreign investment of all WTO members, as stated in Article XVII of GATS:

---

369 WTO 'Principles of the trading system: trade without discrimination' <www.wto.org/english/ thewto_e/whatis_e/tif_e/fact2_e.htm#nondiscrimination> accessed 24 November 2014; Wei Wang, 'National Treatment in Financial Services in the Context of the GATS/WTO' (2003) 6 Stud Intl Fin Econ & Tech L 149, 150.

370 The General Agreement on Tariffs and Trade (GATT) 1948, art III para 1 states: *The contracting parties recognize that internal taxes and other internal charges, and laws, regulations and requirements affecting the internal sale, offering for sale, purchase, transportation, distribution or use of products, and internal quantitative regulations requiring the mixture, processing or use of products in specified amounts or proportions, should not be applied to imported or domestic products so as to afford protection to domestic production.*

371 Wei Wang (n 369) 152.

> 1. In the sectors inscribed in its Schedule, and subject to any conditions and qualifications set out therein, each Member shall accord to services and service suppliers of any other Member, in respect of all measures affecting the supply of services, treatment no less favourable than that it accords to its own like services and service suppliers.

Therefore, the only condition for national treatment is to apply treatment not less favourable. It is pointed out that the purpose of the national treatment clause is to oblige a host state to make no negative differentiation between foreign and national investors.[372] In addition, according to this article, the words "in the sectors inscribed in its schedule" means that Oman is not obliged to apply national treatment to service sectors not scheduled; therefore, the Sultanate would not be violating the national treatment rule under the GATS agreement if it took discriminatory measures against services and service suppliers of any other WTO Members in those sectors.[373]

The third area in which the national treatment principle is applied in trade relates to intellectual property rights. Oman would be in breach of its commitments under the TRIPs Agreement if it offered foreign investors treatment less favourable than it granted to its own citizens in protecting the intellectual property rights of foreign investment, as stated in Article 3.1 of the Agreement: "Each Member shall accord to the nationals of other Members treatment no less favourable than that it accords to its own nationals with regard to the protection of intellectual property".

However, it should be noticed that one weak aspect of the application of this principle in the area of goods, services, or item of intellectual property under the WTO agreements is that the national treatment rule only applies once products entered the market. Therefore, Oman has the right to charge customs duty at the import stage without being deemed to have violated the principle of national treatment, even if it does not apply an equivalent tax on its national products.[374] This can regarded as a challenge for foreign investors unless they are protected by a BIT, FTA or regional agreement with Oman. Therefore, although it is argued that the national treatment obligations under the GATS are binding on both pre-

372 Wenhua Shan, 'Genderal report' in Wenhua Shan (ed) *The Legal Protection of Foreign Investment A Comparative Study* (Hart Publishing 2012) 3, 22.

373 Wei Wang (n 369) 159.

374 WTO (n 369).

entry and post-entry measures, Wang argues that the non-generality of the application of the principle under the GATS weakens its value.[375] One difference between national treatment in the case of goods and of services is that in the former case it is unqualified, whereas in the latter certain sectors and sub-sectors are the subject of specific commitments recorded in the schedule of commitments of each Member.

Despite their previous reservations about the principle of national treatment, developed countries now tend to include the national treatment principle in their investment treaties, since most economic sectors in developing countries are now controlled by nationals. Consequently, in recent years there has been a tendency among developed countries to raise the issue of international responsibility "on the basis of discrimination" due to the host country's failure to provide treatment no less favourable than that it accords to its own nationals to foreign investors.[376]

The significance of the principle of national treatment as a tool to protect foreign investment can be seen in the significant number of cases arising from investment treaties in which it is claimed that this has been violated.[377] The Tribunal in the case of *Methanex Corporation v USA* illustrates the difficulty of applying the national treatment principle when dealing with WTO agreements due to the failure to use the terms used in the WTO or GATT agreements.[378] The Tribunal found that the term "like products" as it appears in GATT Article III is different from the term "like circumstances", which was used as a key element in granting non-discriminatory treatment to foreign investment.[379] The Tribunal made clear that the words "in like circumstances" mean that the Tribunal should compare the foreign investor to those most closely comparable among domestic investors.[380] In this case, Methanex as a manufacturer of methanol should be compared to other US-based methanol manufacturers in similar circumstances. The Tribunal did not accept that Methanex

375 Wei Wang (n 369) 183.

376 Sornarajah (n 8) 202.

377 Ibid.

378 *Methanex Corporation v USA* (Final Award on Jurisdiction and Merits) 3 August 2005 NAFTA, ICSID, pt IV c B s 10.

379 Ibid B ss 29, 30.

380 Ibid B ss 28, 29. See Howard Mann, 'The Final Decision in *Methanex v United States:* Some New Wine in Some New Bottles' (2005), 1 <www.iisd.org/pdf/2005/commentary_methanex.pdf> accessed 7 May 2016.

should be compared with manufacturers of all gasoline additives.[381] Therefore, the GATT term "like products" could not be applied in this case.

All Oman's BITs call on the contracting parties to apply the national treatment standard. For example, Article 3.1 of the Oman-UK BIT, Article 4.1 of the Oman-India BIT, Article 3.1,2 of the Oman-Korea BIT, and Article 3.2 of the Oman-Germany BIT all oblige Oman to accord the investment and investors of those countries treatment not less favourable than is accorded to Omani investors. In addition, some BITs define what would be regarded as less favourable treatment, in an attempt to provide helpful clarification in case of future dispute. For example, Article 3.3 of the Oman-Germany BIT specifies the situations which should be considered as less favourable treatment:

> [U]nequal treatment in the case of restrictions on purchase of raw or auxiliary materials, of energy or fuel or of means of productions or operations of any kind, unequal treatment in the case of impeding the marketing of products inside or outside the country.

However, each BIT includes its own exceptional situations in which national treatment of the other contracting party does not apply. These exceptions relate mostly to customs and tax matters such as Article 3.3 of the Oman-Korea BIT and Article 4.3 of the Oman-India BIT. In addition, Article 3.3. of the Oman-Germany BIT grants each contracting state the right not to apply the principle of national treatment on three grounds: "public security, public health or morality". This article raises two issues: first, these exceptions potentially permit less favourable treatment on the specified grounds of public security, public health or morality. Therefore, this might weaken the article by granting both parties the latitude to not apply the national treatment standard on these grounds. A question also arises as to the situation if Oman took a less favourable measure against German investment or investors in Oman, but it was not included under one of the less favourable treatment articles mentioned above.

It is worth noting that Article 2.3 on national treatment of the FTA between the GCC and Singapore applied national treatment in accordance with Article III of the GATT 1994.[382] In addition, it took a similar approach

381 *Methanex Corporation v USA* B ss 28, 29.
382 GCC-Singapore FTA 2008, art 2.3 (1, 2).

of applying exceptions to national treatment as it states clearly in Article 6.4.3:

> The provisions of paragraphs 1 and 2 of this Article shall not apply to customs duties and charges of any kind imposed on or in connection with importation, the method of levying such duties and charges, other import regulations and formalities, and measures affecting trade in services other than laws, regulations, procedures and practices regarding government procurement covered by this Chapter.

3.3.2 Protection Offered under MFN Provisions

The role of the MFN standard is to ensure that the contracting parties treat members' investments and investors in a way at least as favourable as they treat third parties.[383] Thus, the standard ensures equally favourable treatment by the host state for all foreign investors of different nationalities.[384] Oman is normally obliged by the WTO agreements not to discriminate among WTO members by granting one or some of its trading partners favourable treatment, such as applying lower customs duties.[385]

However, the application of MFN in Oman's international agreements can be divided mainly into two kinds: a full MFN guarantee and agreements that include exceptions.[386] Under the first group, Oman is bound by Article 31 of the GCC Economic Agreement which prohibits Member States from granting MFN treatment exceeding that granted in the Agreement to Member States. Therefore, Oman is not allowed to offer in its BITs or FTAs any better treatment to any country than that which is granted to GCC Member States. Thus, although the agreements established between the GCC Member States should work within the WTO framework, these effectively grant the GCC Member States preferential treatment compared to that accorded by the WTO agreements.

In addition, Article 10.4 (1, 2) of the Oman-USA FTA obliges both parties to grant the investor and investment of each party treatment not less favourable than that which it accords in like circumstances, to investors of any non-party. This means that Oman can be found to have breached its obligations under the FTA investment chapter if it grants investors

383 Dolzer and Schreuer (n 91) 186.
384 Muchlinski (n 217) 628.
385 WTO (n 369).
386 GCC-Singapore FTA 2008 does not include MFN treatment.

from GCC Member States more favourable treatment with regard to the establishment, acquisition, expansion, management, conduct, operation, and sale or other disposition of investments.

However, the significant example of the exceptions applied to Oman's commitment in providing MFN is under the WTO agreement and Oman's BITs. The application of the MFN principle can be found in all three main areas under the WTO agreement. First, Article I of the GATT obliges Oman to accord MFN treatment in the trade of goods to like products of other WTO Members. Second, Article II of the GATS obliges Oman to afford treatment that is no less favourable than that which is granted to nationals regarding the trade in services, as defined by the first article of this agreement. Third, Article 4 of the TRIPS obliges Oman to extend any benefits accorded to one state with regard to the protection of intellectual property rights to all WTO members.[387]

Nevertheless, the exceptions included in the WTO agreements can be considered as weaknesses in applying MFN under these agreements. For example, if an FTA is established, countries can enjoy favourable treatment in the trade between them, allowing them to exclude products from outside. This exception would cover Oman's FTA with the United States and the GCC FTA with Singapore. Moreover, Oman can grant developing countries special access to its market.[388] Oman can also increase barriers against products that are regarded to be unfairly handed by particular countries.[389] Finally, all WTO members are allowed to declare exemptions from the MFN standard lasting up to 10 years according to Article II Paragraph 6 of GATS,[390] which obviously weakens this obligation. As a result, Oman can rely on these exceptions to exclude itself from applying MFN under the WTO.

In addition, bilateral negotiations tend to pose a challenge to the application of MFN, since they do not extend the MFN to other countries in the WTO which are not parties in the negotiation. This is because of the lack of transparency and the fact that the negotiation reflects the interest

387 WTO (n 369).

388 Ibid.

389 Ibid.

390 General Agreement on Trade in Services (GATS) 1995 paras 5, 6 state:
"5 The exemption of a Member from its obligations under paragraph 1 of Article II of the Agreement with respect to a particular measure terminates on the date provided for in the exemption.
6 In principle, such exemptions should not exceed a period of 10 years. In any event, they shall be subject to negotiation in subsequent trade liberalizing rounds".

of the two countries.[391] Therefore, Voon argues that regional or free trade agreements have negatively affected MFN treatment and the non-discrimination principle, to the extent that MFN has become the exception rather than the rule.[392] This is because almost all WTO members accord MFN treatment to specific members through such agreements.[393] It can be argued conversely that BITs and FTAs enhance the application of the MFN between the contracting states. Shill maintains that the MFN principle plays an important role in elevating the foreign investment protection in BITs to a multilateral level.[394]

All Oman's BITs contain MFN provisions. For example, Article 3.1 of the Oman-UK BIT, Article 3.2 of the Oman-Germany BIT, Article 2.3 of the Oman-Netherlands BIT, Article 2.4 of Oman-Austria BIT, and Oman's other BITs oblige Oman to accord the investment and investors from those countries treatment not less favourable than that which is accorded to any third party investment or investors. These articles in Oman's BITs with other countries would enable foreign investors from those countries to benefit from any favourable treatment granted to a third party. However, the exceptions set out in specific clauses within each BIT weaken the full application of MFN to these countries. A clear example of this is the Oman-Netherlands BIT which states in Article 2.4 that:

> If a Contracting Party has accorded special advantages to nationals or persons of any third State by virtue of agreements establishing customs unions, economic unions or similar institutions, or on the basis of interim agreements leading to such unions or institutions, that Contracting Party shall not be obliged to accord such advantages to nationals or persons of the other Contracting Party.

---

391 Ministry of Economy, Trade and Industry, 'Most-Favoured-Nation Treatment Principle', <www.meti.go.jp/english/report/data/gCT9901e.html> accessed 14 January 2015.

392 Tania Voon, 'Eliminating Trade Remedies from the WTO: Lessons from Regional Trade Agreements' (2010) 59 Intl & Comp LQ 625, 628.

393 Ibid.

394 Stephan W Schill, 'Investment Treaties: Instruments of Bilateralism or Elements of an Evolving Multilateral System' (4th Global Administrative Law Seminar, Viterbo, June 2008) 12 <www.iilj.org/gal/documents/schill.pdf> accessed 16 January 2015.

Thus, in such cases, Oman is relieved of the obligation to provide MFN treatment; the same is true of the exceptions mentioned in each BIT. As a result, according to interviews with an Omani policymaker and a foreign investor, it seems that MFN treatment is accorded fully in practice only to foreign investors from the GCC Member States and the USA.[395]

However, to what extent are the effects of an MFN clause included in other treaties? There are two arguments in this regard. Dolzer and Schreuer note that, in practice, no tribunal has allowed the invocation of the principle in a way that has led to a regime change to the basic treaty, including the MFN clause. They argue that the MFN clause will apply only to the extent that "the provision in the other treaty is compatible in principle with the scheme negotiated by the parties in the basic treaty".[396]

This means there is a need to understand the circumstances which make both treaties "compatible in principle".[397]

Others argue, however, that the MFN clause should operate in all areas of other treaties to which the state is a signatory, "regardless of any comparison or judgement on compatibility".[398] So, to what extent might foreign investors benefit from the MFN clause? Although Subedi notes that the latest trend is in favour of extending the MFN rules to cover the areas of jurisdiction and administration of justice, the different views given by international investment tribunals kept the door open. For example, the International Institute of Sustainable Development's (IISD) Model International Agreement on Investment for Sustainable Development adopts the approach that the MFN clause should be applied to substantive but not procedural provisions.[399] Therefore, it is believed that whether MFN treatment would cover dispute settlement provisions is a very controversial issue. Hence, it is suggested that exclusion of dispute settlement from the application of MFN to should be clearly stated.[400]

In *Emilio Agustin Maffezini v Kingdom of Spain (Maffezini)*[401] the case involved a dispute concerning the interpretation of an MFN clause in an Argentina-Spain BIT. The wording of the MFN article in the treaty adopted

395 Interview with policymaker 3 (Muscat, Oman, 20 August 2014); interview with foreign investor 4 (Muscat, Oman, 5 September 2014).
396 Dolzer and Schreuer (n 91) 191.
397 Ibid.
398 Ibid.
399 Subedi (n 7) 214- 215.
400 Shan (n 372) 21- 22.
401 *Emilio Agustin Maffezini v Kingdom of Spain (Maffezini)* (Decision on Jurisdiction) 25 January 2000 (ICSID Case No ARB/97/7).

the broad approach,[402] as is the case for most of Oman's BITs, and the ICSID Tribunal rejected the respondent's claim of a narrow interpretation of the principle. The ICSID Tribunal decided that, by virtue of the MFN clause of the 1991 Argentina-Spain BIT, the claimant had the right to import the more favourable jurisdictional provisions of the 1991 Chile-Spain Agreement and concluded that:

> [I]f a third-party treaty contains provisions for the settlement of disputes that are more favourable to the protection of the investor's rights and interests than those in the basic treaty, such provisions may be extended to the beneficiary of the most favoured nation clause as they are fully compatible with the *ejusdem generis* principle.[403]

Therefore, the practice of international tribunals in this case decided that this broader interpretation of the MFN was applicable. Consequently, this ruling should provide more protection for all state parties that are signatories to BITs with Oman containing MFN treatment provisions. It is observed that even before the *Maffezini* case, the MFN treatment provisions were understood to extend the benefits granted by one state to all states which have concluded BITs, including the MFN standard "applicable to that benefit".[404]

3.3.3 Protection Offered under the International Minimum Standards Treatment Provisions

In order to evaluate clearly the role of international minimum standards as an obligatory principle of foreign investment legislation applying to the Sultanate it is necessary to first identify the various interpretations that exist of the concept of international minimum standards. Sornarajah notes that the idea that specific international minimum standards of foreign investment exist in customary law, the violation of which incurs state liability, remains highly contentious.[405] This is due to the fact that

---

402 Argentina-Spain BIT 1991 art IV, para 2 states:
"In all matters subject to this Agreement, this treatment shall be no less favourable than that extended by each Party to the investments made in its territory by investors of a third country".

403 *Maffezini* (n 401) paras 21, 56.

404 Vandevelde (n 189) 359.

405 Sornarajah (n 8) 345.

some argue it is difficult to identify the content of international minimum standards.[406]

Although the WTO agreements do not use the words "international minimum standards" specifically in their provisions, it is argued that the doctrine of state responsibility is used to apply not only to minimum but also maximum standards of treatment in international treaties such as the WTO agreements.[407] Therefore, it is clear that the WTO agreements themselves represent minimum standards of protection to be provided by the signatory states. A significant example of this is the TRIPS agreement that establishes these standards by requiring member countries to comply with the substantive obligations of the WIPO agreements, together with the Paris and the Berne Conventions.[408]

Therefore, Ewing-Chow takes a broader view, arguing that the violation of international agreements, such as those within the WTO framework, is covered under investment treaties and breaching these would be regarded as a violation of international minimum standards of treatment and therefore, a breach of international law. Consequently, if a host state breaches the terms of a WTO agreement the foreign investor can take action against it on the basis of a violation of international minimum standards by using investment treaty arbitration, without the need pressurise the home state to take action under the WTO Dispute Settlement Body (DSB).[409]

However, there is considerable debate as to whether the international minimum standards is the origin of the principle of fair and equitable treatment or not. Some believe that fair and equitable treatment is merely the international minimum standards and others say fair and equitable treatment is an independent standard.[410] This chapter takes the approach that the principle of international minimum standards is the origin of fair and equitable treatment because currently it is widely included under international minimum standards. This can be seen in the interpretation applied by the NAFTA, Singapore-USA FTA,[411] and declared clearly under Article 10.5 of the Oman-USA FTA as mentioned above. The wording under

406 Sornarajah (n 8) 128.

407 Subedi (n 7) 173.

408 See WTO 'Overview: The TRIPS agreement' <www.wto.org/english/tratop_e/trips_e/intel2_e.htm> accessed 26 November 2014.

409 Ewing-Chow (n 315) 570.

410 Dolzer and Schreuer (n 91) 124.

411 Sornarajah (n 8) 204.

the Oman-USA FTA is similar to that of Article 1105 of the NAFTA.[412] Muchlinski observes that this paragraph is a response to the suggestion made by NAFTA's arbitral decisions that the international minimum standard is additive to the international law standard.[413] In addition, Saleem argues that the broad interpretation of minimum international standards by international tribunals led countries like the USA and Canada to restrict the interpretation of the principle by referring in their agreements to the interpretation of the principle applied in international customary law.[414]

However, it seems that the use of the principle of "fair and equitable treatment" in Oman's BITs instead of the principle of international minimum standards is merely the converse of this. Oman's BITs do not use the term "international minimum standard"; instead, some of them call for a treatment in accordance with "fair and equitable treatment" and declare the investment shall enjoy "full protection and security". This wording can be found in the BITs relating to Oman-UK (Article 2.2), Oman-Germany (Article 2.2) and Oman-Netherlands (Articles 2.2 and 2.3). Other BITs request parties to provide "fair and equitable treatment", for example the Oman-Sweden BIT (Article 2.3), the Oman-Brunei BIT (Article 2.3) and the Oman-India BIT (Article 3.2). Therefore, Vandevelde observes that it is rare for a dispute to be raised in BIT arbitration relying on the breach of international minimum standards.[415]

Nevertheless, according to Article 10.5 paragraph 1 of Oman-USA FTA, Oman is obliged to accord American investment and investors treatment in accordance with customary international law, including two kinds of standards: fair and equitable treatment, and full protection and security. Therefore, paragraph 1 makes it obvious that both of these principles are understood to form part of international minimum standards. Although it has been argued that this paragraph applies international minimum

412 Regarding the Minimum Standard of Treatment, North American Free Tarde Agreement (NAFTA) 1994, art 1105 para 1 of the NFTA states: "1 Each Party shall accord to investments of investors of another Party treatment in accordance with international law, including fair and equitable treatment and full protection and security".

413 Muchlinski (n 217) 683.

414 Hadi Saleem, 'Comments of Professor Hadi Saleem', J Arab Arbitration (2016) 29, 819.

415 Vandevelde (n 189) 395.

standards as a part of the fair and equitable standard,[416] the aforementioned Oman-USA FTA paragraph declares the opposite.

It can be argued that the Oman-USA FTA adopts a narrow definition of the concept of international minimum standards, as it states clearly in Article 10.5.3 of the FTA that:

> A determination that there has been a breach of another provision of this Agreement, or of a separate international agreement, does not establish that there has been a breach of this Article.

This article clearly seeks to prevent the possibility of a dispute occurring on the basis of a breach of international minimum standards if either contracting party breaches another provision of the FTA, or a separate international agreement. Therefore, it would be helpful for the states that are party to an investment treaty to clarify the scope of the minimum standards.[417]

It seems that this narrow interpretation of this principle arose because the US lawyers who submitted the first draft[418] of this agreement benefited from the past experience of controversial interpretation of this article, when the Tribunal in *SD Myer, Inc. v Government of Canada* ruled that a violation of the national treatment standard meant a violation of the minimum standard.[419] The main point in the criticism made by the USA's lawyers on the ruling was that the international minimum standard is merely international customary law.[420] Therefore, for greater certainty, paragraph 1 prescribes the customary international law minimum standard of treatment of aliens as the minimum standard of treatment to be afforded to covered investments. Article 10.5 Paragraph 2 of the

416 Muchlinski (n 217) 683.

417 Ewing-Chow (n 315) 570.

418 The US submitted the first draft for the basis of the Oman-US FTA in negotiations. See MoCI (n 348).

419 *SD Myer, Inc. v Government of Canada* (Partial Award) 13 November 2000 NAFTA Arbitration 40 ILM 1408 para 266. The Tribunal states: "Although modern commentators might consider Dr Mann's statement to be an overgeneralisation, and the Tribunal does not rule out the possibility that there could be circumstances in which a denial of the national treatment provisions of the NAFTA would not necessarily offend the minimum standard provisions, a majority of the Tribunal determines that on the facts of this particular case the breach of Article 1102 essentially establishes a breach of Article 1105 as well".

420 Ewing-Chow (n 315) 569.

Oman-USA FTA emphasises that the meaning of the minimum standard of treatment in Paragraph 1 is the customary international law minimum standard of treatment of aliens,[421] in order to avoid such an interpretation by international tribunals. In addition, the concepts of "fair and equitable treatment" and "full protection and security" do not require treatment in addition to or beyond that which is required by that standard, and do not create additional substantive rights.

Subedi maintains that it is difficult to assume that such an agreement between the US and other parties regarding the interpretation and scope of the minimum standards of treatment is an accurate application of international customary law.[422] For Sornarajah, applying the principle of international minimum standard is problematic when it comes to investment protection because of the lack of clarity of the contents.[423] This view is supported by tribunals' opinion that the international minimum standards are capable of being developed in the modern context; they are not static.[424]

Consequently, one purpose of FTAs is to provide guidance on how to interpret some of the key principles of foreign investment in the case of disputes between parties.[425] Hence, it seems that the US FTA's approach is to define the scope and the nature of the principle of international minimum standards, in order to avoid any disappointing interpretation by the international tribunal.[426] One of these controversial areas is the balance between providing the international minimum standard of treatment including "fair and equitable treatment" and "full protection and security" and the host country's right to apply its national laws. In the *Al-Tamimi* case, the Tribunal made this differentiation clear by stating that:

421 Oman-USA Free Trade Agreement (FTA) 2009 art 10.5 states that:
"1 Each Party shall accord to covered investments treatment in accordance with customary international law, including fair and equitable treatment and full protection and security
2 For greater certainty, paragraph 1 prescribes the customary international law minimum standard of treatment of aliens as the minimum standard of treatment to be afforded to covered investments".

422 Subedi (n 7) 247.

423 Sornarajah (n 8) 346.

424 See *ADF v United States*, ICSID Case No ARB (AF)/00/1 (NAFTA) Award (9 January 2003), para 180, citing *Mondev International Ltd v United States* ICSID Case No ARB (AF)/99/2 Award (11 October 2002) with approval.

425 Subedi (n 7) 246.

426 This is also the case for US FTAs with countries such as Chile and Singapore See Subedi (n 7) 246-247.

> A State must be permitted to take a legal position in relation to the alleged or perceived violation of its existing laws, even if that position turns out ultimately to be wrong, provided it does so in good faith and with appropriate due process. To impose international liability in such a context would significantly undermine States' long-recognised right to reasonably exercise their police powers to enforce existing laws.[427]

More clearly, the Tribunal stated that:

> The Tribunal agrees with the Respondent's submission that the number of environmental citations previously issued against the Claimant make plain that both his arrest and prosecution were undertaken by the State authorities for a legitimate purpose, rather than the furtherance of a covert political agenda.[428]

The important question raised in *Al-Tamimi* by the Tribunal, referring to Article 10.5 of the Oman-USA FTA is which party has the burden of establishing the content of an applicable rule of customary international law?[429] The United States argues that the minimum standard of treatment incorporated in Article 10.5 reflects a standard that develops from State practice and *opinio juris*, as expressly stated in Annex 10-A, rather than an autonomous, treaty-based standard.[430] According to Article 10.5 of the FTA the burden is on a claimant to prove that this custom has become binding on the other party, since the claimant is the party who relies on a custom.[431] The Tribunals applying Article 1105 of NAFTA Chapter 11 in many cases such as in *Cargill Inc. v. Mexico*, *ADF v. United States*, *Glamis Gold v. United States*, and *Methanex v. United States*, confirm that a party who intends to rely on a rule of international customary law must prove its existence.[432] Moreover, a tribunal must look to the elements set forth in Annex 10-A; specifically, the "general and consistent practice of States that they follow

427 *Al-Tamimi* (n 11) paras 163-164.
428 Ibid para 164.
429 Ibid Procedural No 11 (26 May 2014).
430 Ibid.
431 Ibid.
432 Ibid.

out of a sense of legal obligation," taking into consideration as well the criteria recognized by the ICJ.[433] Then, the claimant must show that the respondent has engaged in conduct that breached the established rule.[434]

However, it is worth commenting that the burden of proof of the content of customary international law remains an outstanding issue. For example, Judge de Castro's dictum in the *Fisheries Jurisdiction (United Kingdom of Great Britain and Northern Ireland v Iceland)* case states that:

> International customary law does not need to be proved; it is of a general nature and is based on a general conviction of its validity [...] Only regional customs or practices, as well as special customs, have to be proved.[435]

The ICJ states that:

> [T]he burden of establishing and proving rules of international law cannot be imposed upon any of the parties, for the law lies within the judicial knowledge of the Court.[436]

On the other hand, some argue that the more widespread the practice of international customary rule, the less proof is needed, and the less widespread the practice, the more proof is needed. In addition, where the practice is not at all widespread, the onus is upon the party seeking to rely on it to prove it.[437]

The Tribunal in *Al-Tamimi* found Oman did not breach the minimum standard of treatment, and it was not in violation of Article 10.5 of the Oman-USA FTA. The Tribunal's reasoning in its decision was as follows:

> There has, in short, been no credible evidence presented to the Tribunal that the Respondent was responsible for any loss or damage to any property at the Claimant's quarry site, or otherwise failed to act reasonably to protect the Claimant's

433 Ibid.

434 Ibid.

435 *Fisheries Jurisdiction (United Kingdom of Great Britain and Northern Ireland v Iceland)* ICJ Reports 1974, 79.

436 Ibid 9, para 17;181, para 18.

437 Olufemi Elias, 'The Relationship Between General and Particular Customary International Law' (1996) 8 Afr J Intl & Comp L 67, 83.

property. There is no evidence that Oman encouraged or fostered any looting or vandalism at the quarry site. To the extent that the Claimant was willing to abandon his property, he cannot equally assert that the Respondent failed to take steps to preserve it.[438]

It is clear that this conclusion of the Tribunal shows that the Tribunal investigated whether Oman failed to provide "fair and equitable treatment" and "full protection and security", even though it did not state it clearly. Therefore, it can be argued that because the wording of the international minimum standards provision under the FTA contains specific details, the Oman-USA FTA would provide more clarity in a case of arbitration, compared with the international minimum standard under other Oman's international agreements. For example, this is clear as 10.5.2 (a) of the FTA, which provides what "fair and equitable treatment" includes or 10,5,2 (b) on what "full protection and security" requires are ultimately intended to provide clarity and enable consistent interpretation, and are expected to help achieve better foreign investment protection. This is clear in Article 10.5.4, 5 and 6 by organising the treatment of foreign investment and investors during armed conflict or civil strife, in order to limit the possibility of ambiguity and minimise the likelihood of incorrect interpretation by international tribunals.

3.4 The Threat of Expropriation

3.4.1 Evaluating the Strength of Protection from Expropriation in the Agreements

The large number of BITs signed by Oman is assumed to provide greater protection for foreign investment from unfair expropriation and all of these have provisions covering protection from unfair expropriation.[439] In addition, Article 10.6 of the Oman-USA FTA provides protection from expropriation in accordance with international customary law as a basic protection for foreign investment. It can be noticed that these BITs signed by Oman with other countries follow a similar pattern in expropriation

438 *Al-Tamimi* (n 11) para 166.

439 See for example Oman-UK BIT 1995, art 5; Oman-Germany BIT 2007 art 4, Oman-Sweden BIT 1995 art 4 Oman-Netherlands BIT 2009 art 5; Oman-Brunei BIT 1998 art 4.

provisions,[440] by admitting the host country's right to expropriation on the basis of its sovereignty over its own territory, and provide almost the same conditions, namely, that the expropriation should be "for a public purpose in accordance with law on a non-discriminatory basis and against prompt, fair and equitable compensation", with more detail given in the Oman-USA FTA. However, there is no clause on expropriation in the Oman-Pakistan BIT. Therefore, the protection of foreign investment in the issue of expropriation is less under the Oman-Pakistan BIT, compared with Oman's other BITs. In addition, although the GCC-Singapore FTA does not contain an expropriation clause, it cannot be claimed that it offers less protection, because it contains a substantive chapter of dispute settlement.

The treaties set out conditions defining the cases in which the host state can apply expropriation. Importantly, under Article 10.6 (1), the Oman-USA FTA adds a fourth condition that is: "in accordance with due process of law and Article 10.5.1 through 10.5.3." Those four conditions in Oman's BITs and under Article 10.6.1 of the FTA are crucial in eliminating the chances of expropriation and nationalization by Oman, which the host state should consider before taking any such action. More important, in the *Al-Tamimi* case, the Tribunal made clear that these four conditions are "conjunctive rather than disjunctive" and should be "satisfied before an expropriation may be considered lawful".[441] This clarification by the Tribunal reduces the chance of expropriation by the host state and therefore, provides more protection for foreign investors.

With regard to the condition, "in accordance with due process of law" under Oman-USA FTA, the difficulty is that what can be regarded as a due process in a one country may not in another, as every state has different procedures to determine what is justice, and those procedures may produce different final judgments.[442] In *Bank Melli Iran v Pahlavi*, a US court stated, "A foreign judgment cannot be enforced if it was obtained in a manner that did not accord with the basics of due process."[443] Therefore, it can be agued that the condition of due process is a two-edged sword. On the one hand, it contains a protection of foreign investors' rights. On the

440 Stephen Olynyk 'A Balanced Approach to Distinguishing Between Legitimate Regulation and Indirect Expropriation in Investor-State Arbitration' (2012) 15 Intl Trade & Bus L Rev 254, 259.

441 *Al-Tamimi* (n 11) para 121.

442 Charles T. Kotuby, 'General Principles of Law, International Due Process, and the Modern Role of Private International Law' (2013) 23 Duke J Comp & Intl L 411, 424.

443 *Bank Melli Iran v Pahlavi*, 58 F.3d 1406, 1410, 1412 (9th Cir. 1995).

other hand, it may become a weapon that can be used by foreign investors, especially during a difficult time between the host state and the home state, as the investor may seek the help of his home country using its judiciary institution. A foreign investor may bring an arbitration case against the host state under the relevant BIT or FTA because of "fundamental breaches of due process."[444]

However, to solve the mentioned difficulty it is stated that international due process consists of "certain minimum standards in the administration of justice" with regard to the "elementary fairness and general application in the legal systems".[445] In *Society of Lloyd's v Ashenden* the court referred to "a concept of fair procedure simple and basic enough to describe the judicial processes of civilized nations".[446] In addition, Kotuby believes that currently it has become more common among national courts to apply the international concept of due process.[447]

A more fundamental question concerns what constitutes expropriation. This has been defined and argued widely in international tribunals and among scholars, as referring to not only the direct taking of foreign investors' property, but also any means used to neutralize the use or the benefit of the property of foreign investors, including "constructive taking", "regulatory taking" or "creeping expropriation", also known as indirect expropriation.[448]

Therefore, Article 10.6.1 of the Oman-USA FTA includes the words "either directly or indirectly through measures equivalent to expropriation". This constitutes a strong and comprehensive statement that if Oman takes any measures considered equivalent to expropriation of American investment and investors, this will be regarded as a breach of the FTA. Therefore, there is no need to rely on customary international law or the international tribunal to define whether an action is regarded as expropriation or not. In the *Al-Tamimi* case, the Tribunal stated that:

> Any claim for indirect expropriation based on the Respondent's actions after 17 February 2009 would also have to confront the express stipulation in Annex 10-B.4 (b) of the US- Oman FTA that non-discriminatory regulatory actions

444 Kotuby (n 442) 425 cites *Salem (U.S.) v Egypt*, 2 RIAA 1161, 1202 (1932).
445 Kotuby (n 442) 425.
446 *Society of Lloyd's v Ashenden*, 233 F.3d 473, 477 (7th Cir. 2000).
447 Kotuby (n 442) 430.
448 See Subedi (n 7) 152-155; Muchlinski (n 217) 587.

> by a State designed and applied to protect legitimate public welfare objectives, including protection of the environment – and, the Tribunal infers, the enforcement of Omani private property laws – do not constitute indirect expropriations.[449]

Therefore, action by Oman as a host country will not constitute an indirect expropriation in this case, provided two conditions are met, that the Omani government action is non-discriminatory, and the protection of public welfare objective is legitimate. However, if one of these conditions is not met, Oman will be committing indirect expropriation, even if the other condition is met. For example, if the action of Oman against a foreign investor was on the basis of a legitimise protection of public welfare objective, such as the protection of environment, but the action was on a discriminatory basis, the Omani government would be accountable. As another example, if the action by Oman against a foreign company was a non-discriminatory regulatory action but without serving legitimate protection of public welfare objectives, Oman as a party would be responsible for indirect expropriation. Nevertheless, it can be argued that all the host state's actions must be assumed non-discriminatory and legitimate unless it is proved otherwise by a foreign investor or claimant.

The *Al-Tamimi* case raised a debatable issue of whether an action by a governmental company can be attributed to the government of Oman. The Tribunal rejected the Claimant's claim that unlawful expropriation of his investment took place through a series of measures carried out by Oman. The Tribunal found that:

> [T]he conduct of OMCO, including its commercial decision to terminate the OMCO–Emrock Lease Agreement on 17 February 2009, cannot be attributed to the Respondent. OMCO did not exercise the necessary regulatory, administrative or governmental authority for its actions to be considered those of the Omani State.[450]

There are two arguments on the conclusion of the Tribunal. Saleem argued that the conclusion of the Tribunal in *Al-Tamimi* could be challenged on the basis that governmental companies play an important role in investment

449 *Al-Tamimi* (n 11) para 128.
450 Ibid para 122.

issues and they tend to establish contracts with foreign investors; a similar argument was raised in the *Maffezini* case.[451] In addition, Articles 5 and 8 of the Draft articles on Responsibility of States for Internationally Wrongful Acts govern such acts, as the Draft reflects international customary law.[452] Article 5 the Draft Articles on Responsibility of States for Internationally Wrongful Acts states that:

> The conduct of a person or entity which is not an organ of the State under article 4 but which is empowered by the law of that State to exercise elements of the governmental authority shall be considered an act of the State under international law, provided the person or entity is acting in that capacity in the particular instance.

Article 8 of the Draft states that:

> The conduct of a person or group of persons shall be considered an act of a State under international law if the person or group of persons is in fact acting on the instructions of, or under the direction or control of that State in carrying out the conduct.

It can be argued in counter that this dispute was governed by the Oman-USA FTA. In addition, the Draft article on Responsibility of States for Internationally Wrongful Acts is not binding, whereas the Oman-USA FTA is an international agreement binding on both parties. Furthermore, the Tribunal in *Al-Tamimi* investigated this issue and rightly decided that the case was ruled by Article 10.1.2 of the Oman-USA FTA, which states:

> A Party's obligations under this Section shall apply to a state enterprise or other person when it exercises any regulatory, administrative, or other governmental authority delegated to it by that Party.

It is clear that this article intends to apply narrow approach to exclude governmental companies from having a party's obligations. In addition,

451 Saleem (n 414) 813.
452 Ibid.

the FTA is a private agreement that has precedence over the general rules of international law. The Tribunal stated:

> [I]t is clear that the central element of the expropriation claim is the termination of the OMCO–SFOH and OMCO–Emrock Lease Agreements.[453]

> [I]n the language of Annex 10-B.2, there can be no expropriation because there has been no relevant action or series of actions by Oman which interfered with a tangible or intangible property right at Jebel Wasa.[454]

> [T]he legality of OMCO's termination of the OMCO–Emrock Lease Agreement must be resolved as a matter of private contractual law, not public international law.[455]

It is argued that home states aim to control the sovereignty of the host state by insisting that international law governs the international agreement and by applying the stabilization clause. [456] However, there is a need to strike a balance between two issues; first, Oman is a sovereign state, a member of the United Nations and entitled to apply its national laws in its territory. Second, foreign investors who possess and spend considerable amounts of money deserve, in return, compensation of an amount considered appropriate, in compliance with the regulations of the UN Charter of Economic Rights and Duties of States 1974. In addition, it is pointed out that there is a distinction between the host state's temporary interference with property rights as a legitimate exercise of regulatory powers over its own territory and the case of the permanent deprivation of the foreign investor's property rights.[457]

According to Sattoriva, the non-expropriatory standard of treatment incorporated in international investment agreements has played an important role in the considerable change in the protection of foreign

453 *Al-Tamimi* (n 11) para 122.

454 Ibid para 123.

455 *Al-Tamimi* (n 11) paras 122-123.

456 Muchlinski (n 217) 579.

457 Ibid 589.

investment in the last few decades.[458] Therefore, BITs and FTAs offer greater protection of foreign investment. As Subedi argues, the law on foreign investment has been internationally understood as the law included in BITs and regional investment treaties, not as that incorporated in international soft law instruments.[459]

3.4.2 The Issue of Compensation

Most of Oman's BITs and the Oman-USA FTA apply the same conditions for compensation, which must be "prompt, adequate, and effective". This is because most BITs concluded after 1960 apply the Hull Formula with regard to the standard of compensation for expropriation favoured by investors' home countries. Although Oman's BITs and its FTA with the USA are its main strong obligatory international agreements with regard to compensation, the challenge is that there is a lack of an international formation of a definite principle on the issue of compensation for expropriation of property, due to the absence of a multinational treaty or a uniform customary practice or sufficiently strong sources of international law such as treaty and custom.[460]

One of the reasons that led to the failure to formulate a multinational treaty on investment protection was disagreement on the standards of compensation to be offered for expropriated property.[461] While some scholars, such as Brownlie, tried to establish standards for compensation according to international law, others believe that there are no clear guidelines on the standards of compensations.[462] This deficiency may weaken the effectiveness of compensation as a tool for protection of foreign investment. In *Metalclad Corp. v United Mexican States*, on the basis of Chapter 11 Article 1110 of NAFTA the arbitral tribunal awarded the foreign investor (Metalclad) compensation on the basis that the denial of Metalclad's permit by the Mexican government was a violation of the principle of fair treatment provided under Article 1105 of NAFTA, having established expropriation under Article 1110 of NAFTA.[463] This ruling was

458 Mavluda Sattorova, 'Investment Treaty Breach as Internationally Proscribed Conduct: Shifting Scope, Evolving Objectives, Recalibrated Remedies?' (2012) 4 Trade L & Dev 315, 352.

459 Subedi (n 7) 118-119.

460 Sornarajah (n 8) 415-418.

461 Ibid 415-416.

462 Subedi (n 7) 191-193.

463 *Metalclad Corp v United Mexican States* (Award) 30 August 2000 (ICSID Case No ARB(AF)/97/1).

criticised on the basis that the tribunal interpreted Article 1110 harshly and considered a lawful regulatory act as an expropriation, which would render states unable to protect their national environment and public health.[464]

The Organisation for Economic Co-operation and Development (OECD) has issued two draft conventions on the limitations of expropriation and the rule of prompt, adequate and effective compensation.[465] However, Oman is not a member of the OECD. In addition, Oman's BITs and the FTA contain different criteria governing the compensation. Most of Oman's BITs contain an obligation on contracting parties to provide prompt and effective compensation, without defining the rules to guide the parties and tribunals in this regard, leaving scope for disagreement between the parties or for different interpretations among tribunals.

Nevertheless, it can be said that the Oman's BITs with Germany and Netherlands and Oman-USA FTA are good examples of attempts to define and delimit the issue of compensation. Article 4.2 of the Oman-Germany BIT and Article 4 (c) of the Oman- Netherlands BIT. Both of these include the condition that in case of expropriation, the host state should provide compensation equivalent to the expropriated investment before the actual expropriation or the threat of it becomes publicly known. This is good because it refers to a specific period and so minimizes the chances for the host state to delay paying compensation. Thus, if, for example, Oman decides to expropriate German or Dutch investors and this becomes known to the public before compensation is made, it will be regarded as a violation of the BIT terms. This condition is not contained in other Omani BITs.

Other examples of good protection for foreign investors are the conditions on compensation contained in the Oman-USA FTA, which require that compensation "should be paid without delay"[466], "must be equivalent to the fair market value of the expropriated investment, immediately before the expropriation took place (the date of expropriation)"[467], "must not reflect any change in value occurring because the intended expropriation

464 Joshua Elcombe, 'Regulatory Powers VS. Investment Protection Under NAFTA'S Chapter 1110: *Metalclad, Methanex*, and *Glamis Gold*' (2010) 68 U Toronto Fac L Rev 71, 74.

465 Sornarajah (n 8) 416.

466 Oman-USA FTA 2009, art 10 6 2 (a).

467 Ibid art 10 6 2 (b).

had become known earlier"[468], and "must be fully realizable and freely transferable".[469] It is asserted that "the fair market value must be no less than the fair market value on the date of expropriation, plus interest at a commercially reasonable rate for that currency, accrued from the date of expropriation until the date of payment".[470]

In addition, if the fair market value is denominated in a currency that is not freely usable the value applicable will be the fair market value on the date of expropriation, converted into a freely usable currency at the market rate of exchange prevailing on that date, plus interest, at a commercially reasonable rate for that freely usable currency, accrued from the date of expropriation until the date of payment".[471] These conditions included in Article 10.6 (2,3 and 4) of the Oman-USA FTA set up all the measures needed to provide fair compensation, and to protect foreign investors' rights by providing the necessary degree of clarification. The more clearly the terms of the investment agreement define the basis and conditions of the compensation, the more likely this is to reduce disagreement between parties and prevent a disappointing interpretation by the international tribunal, as demonstrated by the Oman-USA FTA and Oman's BITs with Germany and the Netherlands.

In the *Al-Tamimi* case the Claimant argued that the Omani Government's actions destroyed his multi-million dollar investment in the site, in violation of its obligations under the U.S.-Oman FTA, and caused losses and damages of approximately $560 million.[472] However, the Tribunal rejected his claim, stating that:

> For all of the foregoing reasons, and rejecting all claims and submissions to the contrary, [...] The Tribunal rejects all of the Claimant's requests for declaratory and compensatory relief.[473]

Although it cannot be claimed that this award is evidence that Oman guarantees compensation, to some extent this ruling is an investigation of Omani government practice in cases where compensation was claimed.

---

468 Oman-USA FTA 2009 art 10 6 2 (c).
469 Ibid art 10 6 2 (d).
470 Ibid art 10 6 3.
471 Ibid art 10 6 4 (a), (b).
472 *Al-Tamimi* (n 11) Request for Arbitration (5 December 2011), para 8.
473 Ibid Award, para 175.

3.5 Issues relating to Taxes, Custom Duties and Money Transfer

3.5.1 Taxes

The Omani government has adopted measures to increase the efficiency of its tax system and to improve the state's competitiveness, assumed to be an important incentive for foreign investment. This is clearly reflected in the fact that globally Oman is ranked tenth from a total of 189 countries, on the ease of paying taxes.[474] While Oman adopted in 2010 a tax regime to be implemented equally in all companies working in Oman, this section examines how Oman's international agreements address it.

Oman's international investment related agreements have three approaches in dealing with taxation issues. While Article 3.8 of the GCC Economic Agreement grants the advantage for foreign investors from GCC Member States to be treated like Omani nationals with regard to taxes,[475] some of Oman's BITs include an exception to the MFN and national treatment provisions in relation to tax matters. For example, Article 3.3 of the Oman-Finland BIT states: "The treatment mentioned above shall not apply to any advantage accorded to investors of a third state by either Contracting Party [...] or any international agreement or arrangement relating wholly or mainly to taxation". The GCC-Singapore FTA also excludes the provisions of the Agreement from applying to any taxation measures.[476] The main reason behind excluding tax issues from national treatment is that both parties have their binding regional agreements. For example, this is the case of Oman with the GCC and the case of Finland with the EU.

The third approach by some other BITs is to direct the contracting parties on how taxation issues are to be dealt with. For example, Article 3.5 of the Oman-Germany BIT specifies that income and capital taxes should be dealt with in accordance with the provisions of the Agreement for Avoidance of Double Taxation between the contracting states. If there is no such

---

474 World Bank and International Finance Corporation, *Doing Business 2015 Economy Profile: Oman* (World Bank Group 2014) 56 <www. doingbusiness.org//~/media/giawb/doing%20business/documents/ profiles/country/OMN.pdf> accessed 29 December 2015.

475 GCC Economic Agreement 2001, art 3.8 states that: "GCC natural and legal citizens shall be accorded, in any Member State, the same treatment accorded to its own citizens, without differentiation or discrimination, in all economic activities, especially the following: [...] 8 Tax treatment'.

476 GCC-Singapore FTA 2008, art 1.4.

agreement, the host state should apply the national tax law. Nevertheless, Oman has signed Agreements for Avoidance of Double Taxation with 32 countries.[477] Generally, the common pattern in investment and taxation agreements is to call on the contracting parties to solve claims of unfair taxation by consultation between the parties.[478]

It has been argued that excessive taxation may be regarded as indirect expropriation by the host state. However, others maintain that a uniform increase in taxation should not be regarded as a case of expropriation, but only those cases where a foreign investment is subjected to a unique and heavy taxation.[479] Therefore, the scope of the taxation exception has been addressed by only a few tribunals.[480] Nevertheless, no known taxation case has been brought against Oman.

3.5.2 Customs Duties

Since 1st January 2003, Oman has been obliged to provide "free movement of goods among the GCC States without customs or non-customs restrictions"[481] under the Implementation Procedures for the GCC Customs Union[482] effectively implementing the GCC customs union. In addition, it is obliged to apply "A Common External Customs Tariff for products imported from outside of the GCC customs union".[483] This tariff consists of "5% on all foreign goods imported from outside of the Customs union".[484] In response to its commitments as a member of the WTO and GCC, Oman issued the Royal Decree 67/2003 in order to implement the WTO Custom Valuation Agreement (CVA) on the basis of the GCC Common Custom Law and its Rules of Implementation and Explanatory Notes.[485] The transaction value is the first basis on which the customs value

---

477 These are Algeria, Belarus, Belgium, Brunei, Canada, China, Croatia, Egypt, France, India, Iran, Italy, Korea, Lebanon, Malaysia, Mauritius, Moldova Republic, Netherlands, Pakistan, Russia, Seychelles, Singapore, South Africa, Sudan, Syria, Thailand, Tunisia, Turkey, United Kingdom, Uzbekistan, Vietnam, and Yemen. PKF, *Oman Tax Guide 2013* (May 2013) 12 <www.pkf.com/media/1958939/oman%20pkf%20tax%20guide%202013.pdf> 12 accessed 7 January 2015.

478 Sornarajah (n 8) 405.

479 Ibid.

480 Vandevelde (n 189) 187.

481 Implementation Procedures for the GCC Customs Union, para II 2.

482 Signed in Qatar, 21-22 December 2002.

483 Implementation Procedures for the GCC Customs Union, para II 2.

484 Ibid para IV.

485 WTO (n 340).

is defined.[486] If this value cannot be determined, it is calculated using the methods established by the CVA.[487] This Agreement plays an important role in providing protection for investors from GCC Member States in Oman, and with investors from outside GCC. It is reported that between 80% and 90% of the 269 customs disputes between Oman and other states during the period from January 2008 to June 2013 were decided in favour of the importer.[488]

Some of Oman's BITs leave more leeway for the contracting states, by setting out exceptions from the granting of MFN treatment to investments and investors from each contracting state, if one of them grants any advantage to any investor from a third-party state on the basis of a "customs union, common market, free trade zone, regional economic agreement, multilateral international agreement or an agreement on avoidance of double taxation or facilitation of frontier trade". This is stated in the BITs that Oman has signed with Sweden (Article 3.3), the UK (Article 3.3 a,b), Germany (Article 3.4) and Brunei (Article 3.3). Therefore, it may be difficult to say that the excluding of custom duties from MFN treatment will weaken the protection accorded to foreign investment and investors of states parties in the Sultanate, as this is based on the will of all states parties and serves their national economic interest.

In comparison with these BITs, the Oman-USA FTA provides a number of protective measures for foreign investment and investors, improving the level of protection. For example, this FTA obliges Oman to publish in advance any regulations governing customs matters.[489] This will ensure the transparency of the Omani regulations for US foreign investment and investors. In addition, it obliges Oman to apply procedures providing for the release of goods within a period no greater than that required to ensure compliance with its customs laws and, to the extent possible, within 48 hours of arrival.[490] Moreover, it does not allow Oman to "increase any existing customs duty, or adopt any new customs duty, on an originating good".[491] Oman is also obliged to reduce its "customs duties on originating goods, in accordance with its Schedule to Annex 2-B."[492]. Consideration

486 Ibid.
487 Ibid.
488 Ibid.
489 Oman-USA FTA 2009, art 5 1 3.
490 Oman-USA FTA 2009, art 5 2 (a).
491 Ibid art 3 2 1.
492 Oman-USA FTA 2009 art 3 2 2.

is to be given to accelerating the elimination of custom duties upon the request of either party.[493]

All these articles guarantee that Oman will reduce its customs duties in accordance with the agreed schedule and, at the same time, will not increase its customs duties. However, the Oman-USA FTA contains vey specific exceptions, meaning that Oman is still bound to honour its commitments to reducing and not increasing customs duties under the Agreement. For example, the FTA specifies exceptional situations under which both parties can increase customs duty to the level established in its schedule, or stop reductions of tariffs, according to Article 2.3.4 (a) and (b) of the FTA. This can cover two cases: first, to raise customs duty back to the level established in its Schedule to Annex 2-B following a unilateral reduction; or to maintain or increase a customs duty as authorized by the DSB of the WTO. In addition, both parties may increase the rate of customs duty on a good on condition of not exceeding the lesser of:

> (i) the most-favoured-nation (MFN) applied rate of duty on the good in effect at the time the action is taken, and
>
> (ii) the MFN applied rate of duty on the good in effect on the day immediately preceding the date of entry into force of this Agreement.[494]

Therefore, it is clear that the customs duties provisions under the Oman-USA FTA provide better protection for American investment and investors compared to Oman's BITs.

3.5.3 Money Transfer

Whilst the issue of money transfer is important as a guarantee for foreign investment, the national interest of Oman should be taken into consideration. Therefore, on the one hand, Oman has obligations embodied in Article VIII sections 2 and 3 of the Articles of Agreement of the International Monetary Fund (IMF). The Agreement states in Article VIII Section 2 that: "no member shall without the approval of the Fund, impose restrictions on the making of payments and transfers for current international transactions." Thus, as a member state, Oman is not allowed

493 Oman-USA FTA 2009 art 3 2 3.
494 Ibid art 8.1 (b).

to impose any restrictions on so-called "current transactions"[495]. In addition, section 3 of the same article states that: "No member shall engage in, or permit any of its fiscal agencies referred to in Article V, Section 1 to engage in, any discriminatory currency arrangements or multiple currency practices". Hence, Oman is not allowed to impose any restrictions on payments and transfers relating to current international transactions, and or to engage in any discriminatory arrangements. As a result, due to the full guarantee of money transfer in the country, it is reported that the amount of money transferred from Oman by expatriates in 2013 was $9.1 billion, and increased in 2014 it to $10.29 billion.[496] Although a great part of this may be related to foreign workers in Oman, it shows the ease of money transfer policy in the country.

With regard to money transfer, Oman is obliged to treat foreign investors from the GCC Member States in the same way as its own citizens according to Article 3.7 of the GCC Economic Agreement.[497] Its BITs with Korea (Article 6.1), the UK (Article 6), Germany (Article 6.1,2), India (Article 7.1), and the Netherlands (Article 3), GCC-Singapore FTA (Article 5.12) and the conditions of the Oman-USA FTA (Article 10.7.1, 2) oblige Oman to enable money to be transferred freely and without delay in accordance with the applicable market rate of exchange on the day of transfer. The Oman-Germany BIT contains a back-up procedure to be applied in the absence of a foreign exchange market, in which case the parties should apply the rates applied by the IMF on the date of payment.[498]

Generally, international treaties adopt three basic approaches to money transfer.[499] The first approach allows foreign investors to transfer capital one year after the money has entered the host state. The second approach is to apply restrictions only during exceptional financial circumstances that affect the monetary stability of the host state. The third approach is not far from the second one; it is to reserve the right of both the host and the home country to preserve "the safety, soundness, integrity or financial responsibility of financial institutions". None of Oman BITs adopt the first

495 Dolzer and Schreuer (n 91) 192.

496 Haider Al Lawati, 'GCC countries need to address expat remittances', *Oman Daily Observer* (Muscat, 14 July 2015) <http://omanobserver.om/> accessed 11 May 2016.

497 GCC Economic Agreement 2001, art 3.7 states that: 'GCC natural and legal citizens shall be accorded, in any Member State, the same treatment accorded to its own citizens, without differentiation or discrimination, in all economic activities, especially the following: [...] (7) Capital movement".

498 Oman-Germany BIT 2007, art 6 3.

499 Dolzer and Schreuer (n 91) 193, 194.

approach. However, both foreign investors and the host state are greatly concerned about the condition of transfer of investors' funds into and out of the host country.[500]

On the other hand, one very important issue that needs to be considered is the right of Oman, as the host state, to protect the stability of its national financial market from the negative effect of large currency transfers into or out of the state, or sudden short-term capital inflows.[501] Therefore, it is believed that no treaty grants foreign investors an absolute right to transfer.[502] Thus, it is observed that in current BIT practice, the exceptions to money transfer have become more sophisticated.[503] Hence, the Oman-USA FTA contains very detailed exceptions to the application of free transfer without delay, and other guarantees provided under paragraphs 1 to 3 of Article 10.7. These exceptions are:

> (a) bankruptcy, insolvency, or the protection of the rights of creditors; (b) issuing, trading, or dealing in securities, futures, options, or derivatives; (c) criminal or penal offenses; (d) financial reporting or record keeping of transfers when necessary to assist law enforcement or financial regulatory authorities; or (e) ensuring compliance with orders or judgments in judicial or administrative proceedings.[504]

Whilst this article set some conditions for prevention of money transfer in the above cases, it stipulates that the application of its laws should be equitable, non-discriminatory, and in good faith. The challenge is how to ensure that these conditions are applied fairly. Overall, it can be stated that these exceptions should balance between providing the host state with the sovereign right to protect its national interest and at the same time not threatening the guarantee provided under this article if state parties apply it other than in the manner intended.

500 Dolzer and Schreuer (n 91) 1 191.
501 Ibid.
502 Ibid 193.
503 Shan (n 372) 56.
504 Oman-USA FTA 2009, art 10 7 4.

3.6 The Effectiveness of Dispute Settlement Provisions under Oman's International Agreements

Wang has argued that modern international investment law should be examined by investigating the dispute settlement mechanisms relating to international investment.[505] The effectiveness of dispute resolution by the national courts in the host state is always doubted, especially in developing countries.[506]

3.6.1 The Guarantees and Weaknesses under the DSB of the WTO

Although Oman has been a member of the WTO since 2000, reports show that to date, it has not been a party to any dispute in the WTO, with another WTO member either as a complainant or defendant.[507] In order to evaluate the guarantees provided by the DSB in the protection of foreign investment in Oman, it is important to examine two issues. Firstly, it is necessary to consider whether the objectives of the dispute settlement system cover the needs of foreign investment protection; secondly, and possibly more importantly, to consider whether in practice the system achieves these objectives.

The objectives are contained in Articles 3.2, 3.3 and 3.7 of the Dispute Settlement Understanding (DSU), and are intended to ensure that the international trading regime is secure and predictable, to guarantee the rights and obligations of the WTO members under the agreements covered, to make the provisions of the agreements clear and interpreted in accordance with customary international law,[508] to guarantee prompt

505 Guiguo Wang (n 66) 19-20.

506 Vandevelde (n 189) 427.

507 For example, see WTO (n 340) 10.

508 Understanding on rules and procedures governing the settlement of disputes (DSU), art 3.2 states that:
"The dispute settlement system of the WTO is a central element [...] to clarify the existing provisions of those agreements in accordance with customary rules of interpretation of public international Law Recommendations and rulings of the DSB cannot add to or diminish the rights and obligations provided in the covered agreements".

settlement of disputes between members,[509] and to ensure the withdrawal of WTO-inconsistent measures.[510] By putting these objectives in the context of Oman's commitments under the WTO agreements, the objectives of the dispute settlement system may serve relatively the needs of foreign investment protection; this will be analysed further later.

Whether in practice the guarantees of the WTO dispute settlement system can provide protection to foreign investment in Oman may raise two points of view. It can be argued that the WTO dispute settlement system provides foreign investors and investment in Oman with a number of guarantees, which are found in its agreements. At the outset, it can be argued that Oman's membership of the WTO was an important step forward in protecting foreign investment in the Sultanate. Under the WTO agreements Oman is obliged to resort to the WTO's dispute procedures in investment disputes involving Oman and other member states. In addition, Oman can also be brought before the DSB for breaching WTO regulations with respect to FDI.

The WTO dispute settlement system has the advantage of combining vrious mechanisms and appeal. Specifically, the DSU grants parties to a dispute the right to choose how to resolve this from four options: the first three, good offices, conciliation, and mediation can begin and be terminated at any time as stated clearly in Article 5. 3 of the DSU: "Good offices, conciliation or mediation may be requested at any time by any party to a dispute". The fourth option is arbitration. It is stated in Article 25.2 of the DSU that "resort to arbitration shall be subject to mutual agreement of the parties which shall agree on the procedures to be followed."

In comparison, the dispute settlement provisions under most BITs, FTAs and IIAs are less flexible and do not provide these instruments.[511] The DSB and DSU contain three instruments of protection; first, if there

509 Understanding on rules and procedures governing the settlement of disputes (DSU), art 3.3 states that:
"The prompt settlement of situations in which a Member considers that any benefits accruing to it directly or indirectly under the covered agreements are being impaired by measures taken by another Member is essential to the effective functioning of the WTO".

510 Ibid art 3.7 states that: "In the absence of a mutually agreed solution, the first objective of the dispute settlement mechanism is usually to secure the withdrawal of the measures concerned if these are found to be inconsistent with the provisions of any of the covered agreements".

511 Subedi (n 7) 256.

is any ruling or recommendation against Oman the DSB would monitor the implementation of such rulings and recommendations, according to Article 21.6.[512] Second, the DSB has the power to authorise retaliation if Oman does not comply with a ruling, as stated in Article 22.2 of the DSU.[513] BITs and FTAs lack both these protective mechanisms. Third, the complaining party may resort to the compensation provisions under Article 22.2 of the DSU.[514]

Foreign investment disputes, however, can benefit from the well-established dispute settlement body with its clear sets of responsibilities and authorities under the dispute settlement system of the WTO. States must exhaust all possible ways to solve the dispute with the state supposedly in breach in an amicable manner in order to invoke the DSU.[515]

Then according to Article 2.1 of the DSU,[516] the DSB has the authority to: "establish panels", and prepare Appellate Body reports', "maintain surveillance on implementation of rulings and recommendations", and "authorize suspension of concessions and other obligations under the WTO agreements". For example, under Article 27.2 of the DSU, any developing country Member has the right to request additional legal advice and assistance in respect of dispute settlement from the Secretariat. Therefore, if any developing country member initiates an investment dispute

512 DSU, art 21.6 states that: "the DSB shall keep under surveillance the implementation of adopted recommendations or rulings".

513 DSU, art 22 2 states that:
"If the Member concerned fails to bring the measure found to be inconsistent with a covered agreement into compliance [...] any party having invoked the dispute settlement procedures may request authorization from the DSB to suspend the application to the Member concerned of concessions or other obligations under the covered agreements".

514 Ibid art 22.2 states that:
"Such Member shall, if so requested, and no later than the expiry of the reasonable period of time, enter into negotiations with any party having invoked the dispute settlement procedures, with a view to developing mutually acceptable compensation".

515 Christopher Bovis, *EC Public Procurement: Case Law and Regulation* 1st, OUP 2006) 93.

516 DSU, art 2.1 states that:
"The Dispute Settlement Body is hereby established to administer these rules and procedures [...] Accordingly, the DSB shall have the authority to establish panels, adopt panel and Appellate Body reports, maintain surveillance of implementation of rulings and recommendations, and authorize suspension of concessions and other obligations under the covered agreements".

against Oman in the DSB, that country is entitled to qualified legal expert assistance from the Secretariat of the WTO.

Despite this limitation, the clear, flexible and relatively quick process of the DSU contributes to foreign investment protection. Article 4.3 of the DSU defines the time schedule from the beginning of the process of consultations.[517] Therefore, for example, if a member submits a request for consultations on a dispute with Oman, the latter is obliged to reply within 10 days and enter into consultations within a period of no more than 30 days from the date of receiving the request. Thus, according to this article, the requesting member will not have to wait until the end of the 60-day period set for consultations. The period it will have to wait before requesting panel establishment, will not exceed 30 days. This speed and flexibility are to the benefit of the foreign investor state.

However, the WTO dispute settlement mechanism has also been criticised for not providing suitable protection of parties' rights, thereby casting doubt on its ability to provide real protection for foreign investment. The DSU mechanism is to resolve state-state disputes, as the only possible approach under the WTO dispute resolution mechanism is inter-state remedies.[518] Hence, unilateral remedies to foreign investors are not possible under the WTO dispute settlement mechanism.[519] As a result, private performers in international trade may claim that the existing WTO system does not provide justice for them.[520] Nevertheless, it is believed that the right for the private sector to access the DSB might become real in future.[521] At that stage, the WTO DSB would serve as a more protective mechanism for foreign investment.

---

517 DSU, art 4.3 states that:
"If a request for consultations is made pursuant to a covered agreement, the Member to which the request is made shall, unless otherwise mutually agreed, reply to the request within 10 days after the date of its receipt and shall enter into consultations in good faith within a period of no more than 30 days after the date of receipt of the request, with a view to reaching a mutually satisfactory solution. If the Member does not respond within 10 days after the date of receipt of the request, or does not enter into consultations within a period of no more than 30 days, or a period otherwise mutually agreed, after the date of receipt of the request, then the Member that requested the holding of consultations may proceed directly to request the establishment of a panel".

518 See Bovis (n 515) 93; Sornarajah (n 8) 272.

519 See Bovis (n 515) 93.

520 Subedi (n 7) 257, 258.

521 Ibid 257.

McRae has argued that the WTO dispute settlement system has "limited effectiveness", for two reasons;[522] first, the only remedy that it might provide for the complaining party is to make the particular member remove an inconsistent measure. Second, the effectiveness of the types of sanction provided, namely, compensation and retaliation, is weak. There is much scepticism about whether practical remedies such as compensation and retaliation will make the violating country implement the WTO agreements. It is believed that compensation under the WTO system does not cover the losses caused by the offending measure and it is not "retroactive". Therefore, according to McRae, compensation and retaliation are merely sanctions with a "limited objective".[523] As a result, due to the lack of the compensation as a practical option under the WTO DSU, it is never used. Although there is limited use of retaliation, it is an incoherent tool, especially in view of the difficulties for a country with a small market initiating retaliation against a country with massive markets.[524] Therefore, Hsueh concludes that compensation and retaliation are not effective alternatives for the correction of WTO-inconsistent measures. They work only as temporary measures to persuade the respondent member to fulfil its commitments under the WTO agreements.[525]

Therefore, it is believed that the mission of the DSU is merely to stop the illegal act.[526] In addition, one scholar argues that the role of the WTO's DSB with regard to foreign investment cases is limited because its scope is restricted to the interpretation of the provisions of the TRIMs Agreement. As a result, so far the DSB has dealt with only a small number of foreign investment cases.[527] However, some argue that the lack of practicality and the informal nature of the WTO dispute settlement process contribute to the ineffectiveness of the WTO dispute settlement system. These limitations can be found in a number of features in the system, such as the "use of email for the exchange of pleadings, the use of conference rooms as courtrooms and the relative informality of panel and even Appellate Body

522 Donald McRae 'Measuring the Effectiveness of the WTO Dispute Settlement System' (2008) 3 Asian J WTO & Intl Health L & Policy 1, 8.

523 Ibid.

524 Ibid 13.

525 Ching-wen Hsueh, 'Direct Effect, WTO Compliance Mechanism and the Protection for Individuals: Lessons Learned from the EC' (2009) 4 Asian J WTO & Intl Health L & Pol'y 521, 528.

526 Ibid.

527 Subedi (n 7) 37.

hearings".[528] As a result, the whole process has become no more than a routine way to conduct relations between states, compared with the formal and pragmatic process of the ICJ.[529]

Overall, it can be argued that the DSB under the DSU generally provides soft protection for foreign investment, which can be seen through the mentioned doubts as to effectiveness and at the same time its advantages as a dispute settlement mechanism. For example, it was noted in *United States-Import Prohibition of Certain Shrimp and Shrimp Products*[530] that "the duty to negotiate a settlement cannot be converted into a duty to agree".[531] Therefore, it can be said that the WTO dispute settlement mechanism does not directly and strongly addressing foreign investment cases. As a result, it is not the ideal tool to do so.

3.6.2 The Guarantees and Weaknesses of the ICJ

As a member of the United Nations, Oman is *ipso facto* a party to the ICJ Statute, as noted in Article 93 (1) of the United Nations Charter.[532] It is therefore bound by the ICJ's decisions, as is stated clearly in Article 94 (1) of the Charter: "Each Member of the United Nations undertakes to comply with the decision of the ICJ in any case to which it is a party." According to Articles 7 and 92 of the United Nations Charter as the "principal judicial organ" of the United Nations, the ICJ is entitled also to deal with investment disputes. Furthermore, to avoid serious consequences in the case of non-compliance, Article 94 (2) of the Charter declares that:

> If any party to a case fails to perform the obligations incumbent upon it under a judgment rendered by the Court, the other party may have recourse to the Security Council, which may, if it deems it necessary, make recommendations

528 McRae (n 522) 13.

529 Ibid.

530 In *United States-Import Prohibition of Certain Shrimp and Shrimp Products* the Appellate Body emphasized the point that: "[N]o two negotiations can ever be identical, or lead to identical results" Appellate Body Report, *United States-Import Prohibition of Certain Shrimp and Shrimp Products*, T 122, WT/DS58/AB/RW (22 October 2001).

531 Chios Carmody, 'The Duty to Settle in WTO Dispute Settlement' (2011) 6 Asian J. WTO & Intl Health L & Policy 169, 193.

532 Oman was admitted on 7 October 1971.

or decide upon measures to be taken to give effect to the judgment.

This article shows the strong teeth of the ICJ in a case of enforcement. Enforcement is an important role which the ICJ would be able to play in the field of international law and it decisions in foreign investment cases. Vannieuwenhuyse argues that the enforcement power of the ICJ extends even to the ICSID award; by enforcing ICISD awards in the case of non-compliance in the execution of an ICSID award, the ICJ could play significant role.[533] In other words, although the foreign investor's consent to arbitration under the ICSID Convention will suspend the right to diplomatic protection according to Article 27.1 of the Convention, non-compliance with an ICSID award would be a reason to exercise diplomatic protection. For example, if Oman did not implement an ICSID dispute award, the foreign investor's home state could use the channel of diplomatic protection to bring Oman before the ICJ according to Part II.[534] It is worth mentioning that the *Anglo-American Oil Company*[535] case showed clearly the strength of the ICJ with regard to the protection of foreign investment, since Judge Carneiro argued that there must be full compensation granted for expropriated property.[536]

However, Muchlinski has pointed out two shortcomings of ICJ involvement in investment-related cases. Firstly, similarly to the difficulty under the WTO system, an individual foreign investor has no right to bring a claim against a sovereign state before the ICJ since Article 34 (1) of the ICJ Statute says: "only States may be parties to contentious cases before the Court". It seems that this is due to the classical notion of public international law that "only states have the right to bring international claims as they are the only subjects of that law".[537] The theory is that under international law the private individual lacks a legal personality enabling him to take action.[538] However, Muchlinski argues that a foreign corporation signing a contract with a state is subject to international law

533 Gauthier Vannieuwenhuyse, 'Bringing a Dispute Concerning ICSID Cases and the ICSID Convention Before the International Court of Justice' (2009) 8 Law & Prac Intl Cts & Tribunals 115, 118.

534 Ibid.

535 *Anglo-American Oil Company Case* (1952) ICJ Reports 93, para 151.

536 See Sornrajah (n 8) 428.

537 Muchlinski (n 217) 704.

538 Ibid.

and entitled to an international legal personality as a foreign corporation.[539] Nevertheless, no change has been made to the ICJ Statute. Therefore, the only recourse for a foreign investor is to convince his home state to take action before the ICJ on his behalf. The second criticism, raised by Dean Acheson, the former U.S. Secretary of State, concerns the questionable justiciability of the ICJ because of its lack of clear criteria; in his view, the ICJ should not interfere in specific politico-legal situations which are of essential interest to states.[540]

3.6.3 Protection Offered under Oman's BITs Provisions

It can be argued that the dispute settlement mechanism provided under Oman's BITs can be regarded as one of the strongest tools of foreign investors' protection in Oman. The fact that BITs allow individual foreign investors to take action in an international tribunal against states can be seen as a major development in international foreign investment law,[541] since they no longer need to persuade their home state to take action on their behalf against the host state.[542] The evidence of this is the hundreds of foreign investment cases before international tribunals relying on BITs.

All of Oman's BITs contain fairly similar provisions dealing with dispute settlement because these are derived from a very small number of common sources. These deal with two kinds of disputes: those between the contracting states themselves and those between the host state and foreign investors. In addition, all Oman's BITs contain arbitration clauses to be applied to resolve disputes' arising between the contracting states.[543] These BITs establish different rules and procedures for disputes between the contracting states themselves, and for disputes between contracting states and an investor from the other contracting state, another common approach in most international BITs.[544] For example, Article 7 of the Oman-UK BIT, Article 8 of the Oman-Sweden BIT, Article 9 of the Oman-India BIT, and Article 8.2 of the Oman-Netherlands BIT set rules in the case of a dispute between a state party and an investor from the other party. In

539 Muchlinski (n 217) 704.

540 Anna Spain, 'Examining the International Judicial Function: International Courts as Dispute Resolvers' (2011) 34 Loy LA Intl & Comp L Rev 5, 16-17.

541 Subedi (n 7) 94.

542 Ibid 95.

543 See Tiffany Ting Sun, 'Investor-State Dispute Settlement Provision in the Cross-Strait BIT: Possible Enhancement in its Operation' (2014) 7 Contemp Asia Arb J 195, 197- 198.

544 Ibid.

addition, Article 8 of the Oman-UK BIT, Article 7 of the Oman-Sweden BIT, Article 10 of the Oman-India BIT and Article 8.1 of the Oman-Netherlands BIT deal with disputes between the contracting states.

All of those BITs, bar one, also mention referring the dispute to the ICJ if a specific arbitral tribunal has been not been constituted within a period of four months. Only the Oman-Netherlands BIT (Article 8.3) does not specify a period of time within which the parties should reach an amicable resolution before starting the process of appointing an arbitrator from each party, using instead the vague phrase, "a reasonable lapse of time". Failure to specify this period of time may cause problems regarding when to begin appointing arbitrators.

Although some BITs refer to the United Nations Commission on International Trade Law (UNCITRAL), for example Oman-UK (Article 7), most of Oman's BITs specify ICSID for resolving investment disputes involving one of the contracting states and a foreign investor from the other contracting state, to be ruled by the ICSID Convention. Examples can be found in Oman's BITs with Sweden (Article 8.2) and India (Article 9.3 (a)). Although the period allowed for amicable settlement under the Oman-Germany BIT is shorter compared with some other BITs such as the Oman-UK BIT, it offers more options for settling disputes between investors and the contracting state, including the domestic court of the host state, ICSID, UNCITRAL, the ICC or any form of dispute settlement agreed upon by the parties.[545] Article 10 of the Oman-Austria BIT offers similar dispute settlement mechanisms to the Oman-Germany BIT, for example, the 60-day period for amicable settlement, and the jurisdiction over disputes between parties. The fact that the UK is the main investor in Oman may explain why the Oman-UK BIT is more detailed concerning procedures in the event of disputes between the contracting states. In contrast, the Oman-Sweden BIT gives more details in the case of dispute between an investor and the contracting party. It seems the more detailed the dispute settlement process is, the more foreign investment and investors' rights are protected, as there will be less vagueness in a detailed BIT.

545 Oman-Germany BIT 2007, art 10 gives three months from the date of receipt of request for settlement.

3.6.4 Dispute Settlement Mechanisms in the Oman-USA FTA

The FTA between the Sultanate and the USA contains the most detailed and comprehensive dispute settlement mechanism of all Oman's investment and trade agreements. Although Chapter 20 of the FTA deals with dispute settlement rules, Chapter 10, which focuses on investment, contains its own dispute settlement rules. However, the dispute settlement process set out under Section B, Articles 10.15 to 10.26 is different from that in Article 20. This merits further discussion. Why does Chapter 10 on investment contain only investor- state disputes and not deal with disputes between contracting states? What is the effect on the coherence and unity of the dispute settlement system in the agreement, when there are two separate different dispute settlement procedures in different chapters? The dispute settlement mechanism under Article 10 covers investor-state disputes whilst Article 20 focuses on states parties, Article 20.2 noting that: "this Chapter shall apply with respect to the prevention or settlement of all disputes between the Parties". It is worth noting that while the *Al-Tamimi* case, filed on 5 December 2011, was the first international dispute on the basis of Oman-USA FTA, the dispute lasted for more than four years (2011-2015) before ICSID raised any issue related to the lack of coherence and unity of the dispute settlement system in the agreement by the parties or the Tribunal.

Article 10 contains a detailed and organized definition and account of the dispute settlement process and the applicable law. It clearly describes the whole dispute settlement process, starting with negotiations and consultations (Article 10.14), then the arbitration process (Article 10.15), and finally the tribunal's decision. Oman consents to arbitration under Article 10.16. Therefore, if it violates investment rules under Section A of Chapter 10 on investment, the foreign investor from the USA has the right to submit a claim in accordance with Chapter II of the ICSID Convention, ICSID Additional Facility Rules and Article II of the New York Convention.[546]

546 Oman-USA FTA 2009 art 10.16 states that:
1 Each Party consents to the submission of a claim to arbitration under this Section in accordance with this Agreement
2 The consent under paragraph 1 and the submission of a claim to arbitration under this Section shall satisfy the requirements of:
(a) Chapter II of the ICSID Convention (Jurisdiction of the Centre) and the ICSID Additional Facility Rules for written consent of the parties to the dispute; and
(b) Art II of the New York Convention for an "agreement in writing".

The applicable law is clearly defined under Article 10.21 (1), (2) and (3). The process to be followed in case of a dispute is similarly detailed under Article 20, starting with consultations (Article 20.5), referral to the joint committee (Article 20.6), establishing a panel (Article 20.7), its report (Article 20.9) and implementation of its findings (Article 20.10), and then compliance review (Article 20.13).

The dispute settlement process under the FTA provides significant guarantees. In order to address the weakness under Oman's BITs which do not provide parties to the dispute with the right to appeal against the panel's report or the tribunal's award, the Oman-USA FTA states under Annex 10-D that the contracting states should consider within three years after the date of entry into force of the Agreement establishing a bilateral appellate body or similar mechanism to review awards rendered under Article 10.25. Therefore, the FTA acknowledges the weakness in the BIT dispute settlement system, and the FTA may provide in future better protection for foreign investment compared with other BITs by giving the chance for the contracting states to decide on the formation of the appellate body.

Another guarantee provided by Article 20.2 of the agreement is the broad scope of its application and its flexibility, since state parties are granted the right to establish a dispute settlement process in a number of circumstances: concerning the interpretation or application of this Agreement, or only on the occurrence of one of the following cases: if "A measure of the other Party is inconsistent with its obligations", if "the other Party has otherwise failed to carry out its obligations" or "A benefit the Party could reasonably have expected to accrue to it [...] is being nullified or impaired as a result of a measure, whether or not the measure conflicts with the provisions of this Agreement". Therefore, the USA can initiate the dispute process against the Sultanate if it believes that one of the mentioned cases has occurred.

In *Al-Tamimi*, although the USA was the home state of the claimant, surprisingly it made a written submission to address the issue of treaty interpretation, not serve the claimant's claim.[547] Article 10.19.2 of the U.S.-Oman FTA allows the non-disputing Party to make oral and written submissions to a tribunal. The claimant challenged the USA submission on two grounds that: "(a) it was untimely;[...] (b) it exceeded the United

547 *Al-Tamimi* (n 11), para 32.

States' permitted scope of participation under the FTA".[548] On 14 October 2014, the Tribunal issued Procedural Order No 12 admitting the United States' submission into the record, concluding that the submission was filed within a reasonable time, and the tribunal directed the parties to exchange memoranda with respect to the issue of the scope of the USA submission.[549]

In addition, the agreement does not specify a particular model or forum to be followed in order to a settle a dispute. Therefore, discretion rests with the complaining party to choose the forum in which to settle the dispute if any matter arises under this Agreement, or the WTO Agreement, or any other agreement to which both Parties are signatories, as stated in Article 20.4.1.[550] Paragraph 2 of this article states that: "The complaining Party shall notify the other Party in writing of its intention to bring a dispute to a particular forum before doing so." Therefore, for example, if the USA or its investor is the complaining party, it has the advantage of choosing the forum, and its only commitment is to notify the Omani party in writing of its intention to bring a dispute to a particular forum, without a need to secure the consent of the Omani party. Thus, the complaining party (the USA or its investor in this case) has the advantage of choosing its legal battleground.

Finally, the annual monetary assessment introduced by Article 20.11.5 works as a protective measure as this must be paid by the party complained against as a penalty. This measure under the FTA is not available under Oman's BITs or the DSU.[551] Overall, it can be seen from the above discussion that the Oman-USA FTA contains stronger guarantees in its dispute settlement provisions, compared with other Omani international agreements. Although the tribunal in *Al-Tamimi* rejected all of the Claimant's requests for declaratory and compensatory relief,[552] this case

548 *Al-Tamimi* (n 11), para 32

549 Ibid para 33.

550 Oman-USA FTA 2009 art 20 4 1 states that:
"1 Where a dispute regarding any matter arises under this Agreement and under the WTO Agreement, or any other agreement to which both Parties are party, the complaining Party may select the forum in which to settle the dispute".

551 Oman-USA FTA 2009, art 20 11 5 states that:
"The complaining Party may not suspend benefits if, within 30 days after it provides written notice of intent to suspend benefits or, if the panel is reconvened under paragraph 3, within 20 days after the panel provides its determination, the Party complained against provides written notice to the other Party that it will pay an annual monetary assessment".

552 *Al-Tamimi* (n 11).

raised by the claimant against Oman shows that on the basis of the dispute settlement mechanism provided under the FTA, US foreign investors' rights in Oman are protected by international tribunals.

However, the FTA raises a number of shortcomings, Article 20.5.1 of the Agreement, concerning the time limit within which the other party has to respond to the consultation request, is unclear, since the word "promptly" in Articles 20.5.1 and 20.5.3 does not specify the exact time allowed for replying to the request and seeking other views, which may lead to disagreement between the USA and Oman. Article 20.5.3 of the FTA states: "Promptly after requesting or receiving a request for consultations pursuant to this Article, each Party shall seek the views of interested parties [...] in order to draw on a broad range of perspectives." Although this article allows "interested parties" to submit their views,[553] it does not specify who these might be: other foreign investors, or non-governmental organisations? Moreover, it is unclear if a party such as Oman would breach this clause of the FTA if it failed to seek such views.

The second shortcoming concerns the transparency of the arbitral proceedings, which is another protection instrument. Article 10.20.1 requires both parties to the dispute to make all documents available to the public and Article 10.20.2 requires the tribunal hearing to be open to the public. However, the latter article cites some exceptions related to legally protected and confidential information.[554] It seems that it is left to the party concerned to define whether a document is confidential or not. These exceptions may weaken the transparency of the arbitral proceedings, as any party to the dispute may claim that the document submitted is protected or confidential information, while these documents may be vital in the case or the tribunal award.

Another shortcoming concerns the Joint Committee in the Agreement, which works as a protective instrument. This committee acts as a supervisory body for part of the dispute settlement process. According to

553 USTR (351) 7.

554 Oman-USA FTA 2009, art 10.20. 3 states that:
"The tribunal shall conduct hearings open to the public and shall determine, in consultation with the disputing parties, the appropriate logistical arrangements. However, any disputing party that intends to use information designated as protected information in a hearing shall so advise the tribunal The tribunal shall make appropriate arrangements to protect the information from disclosure
3 Nothing in this Section requires a respondent to disclose protected information or to furnish or allow access to information that it may withhold in accordance with Article 21 2 (Essential Security) or Article 21 4 (Disclosure of Information).

Article 10.21.3, the Joint Committee's interpretation of the FTA provisions is binding on a tribunal and provides that all decisions and awards of a tribunal should be consistent with that interpretation. In addition, Article 20.6 states that:

> If the consultations fail to resolve a matter within 60 days of the delivery of a Party's request for consultations under Article 20.5, 20 days where the matter concerns perishable goods, or such other period as the Parties may agree, either Party may refer the matter to the Joint Committee by delivering written notification to the other Party. The Joint Committee shall endeavour to resolve the matter.

Both Articles 20.5 and 20.6 made the right of a party to seek consultation and a joint committee optional by using respectively the words "Either Party may request consultation" and "either Party may refer the matter to the Joint Committee".[555] However, Joint Committee supervision is not applicable throughout the whole process of the dispute settlement process. According to Article 10.25 of the agreement, a tribunal may make an award against a respondent, not only for monetary damages, any applicable interest, or restitution of property, but may also award costs and attorneys' fees. This is important to ensure that foreign investors will be compensated for the cost of the award and the fees of the attorney.

3.6.5 Protection Offered under the ICSID

Since signing the ICSID Convention on 23 August 1995,[556] the Sultanate of Oman is under an obligation to resort to ICSID in disputes between Oman and nationals of other member states that adhere to ICSID. This means Oman is bound by any arbitral award or recommendation made by conciliators.[557]

According to Article 25.1 of the ICSID Convention, two conditions are necessary for entitlement to submit to the ICSID; first, both countries

555 Oman-USA FTA 2009, art 20 5 1 states that: 'Either Party may request consultations with the other Party with respect to any matter'.

556 ICSID, 'Member States' <http://web worldbank.org/apps/ICSIDWEB/about/pages/Member-States.aspx> accessed 4 December 2014. Some 150 states are members of ICSID.

557 The Preamble of the Convention on the Settlement of Investment Disputes Between States and Nationals of Other States 1966.

must be signatories of the ICSID convention. Second, both parties to the dispute, whether they are a state or foreign investor, must agree in writing to submit their dispute to the ICSID. Hence, if the parties to a dispute with Oman do not agree beforehand, in writing, to refer their dispute to the Centre, the Centre has no jurisdiction over the dispute.

Most of Oman's BITs make reference to the ICSID to resolve disputes between foreign investor and a contracting state.[558] Such provisions, for example, can be found in Oman's BITs with Germany (Article 10.2 (b)), Sweden (Article 8.2), Lebanon (Article 9.2.(C)) and India (Article 9.3 (a)). Indeed, in most BITs between states, the ICSID is the "sole or optional" dispute settlement method.[559] In addition, Oman has consented to the submission to arbitration, under the ICSID Convention and the ICSID Rules of Procedure under Article (10.16 (1,2)) of Oman-USA FTA. Therefore, in *Al-Tamimi*, Oman did not challenge the jurisdiction of the ICSID Tribunal.

Oman's membership of ICSID as a specialized and workable system of investor-state disputes offers a further strong form of protection for foreign investors in the Sultanate, for a number of reasons: first, ICSID proceedings and awards are fully independent of any kind of influence, compulsion, or review. Second, the unwillingness of a party to cooperate will not weaken or stop the proceedings of ICSID.[560] In this case the arbitrator will be appointed by the Centre according to Article 38 of the Convention, the tribunal will decide jurisdiction matters (Article 41) and the proceedings of the tribunal will not be stalled by non-appearance at hearings or non-submission of memorials by a party (Article 45). Thirdly, the tribunal's award will be final, binding and enforceable, even if one party fails to cooperate.[561] Finally, all member countries are obliged to enforce ICSID awards as they would final judgments by their own courts, as provided by Article 54 (1) of the ICSID Convention.

Foreign investors in Oman will prefer to seek the ICSID, as a reliable dispute settlement body, compared with the national courts. It is likely that the Omani national courts would be avoided for two reasons; first,

558 Some BITs do not refer to ICSID, for example, the Oman-UK BIT 1995 chooses the rules of the United Nations Commissions on International Trade Law (art 7), and the Oman-Brunei BIT 1998 chooses the International Court of Arbitration of the International Chamber of Commerce in Paris (art 9 2).

559 Muchlinski (n 217) 703.

560 Dolzer and Schreuer (n 91) 223.

561 Ibid 224.

they are the host country's courts. Second, it is a common approach among foreign investors and those involved in trade disputes generally to choose arbitration over the court system. Nevertheless, although ICSID currently is the most suitable mechanism of dispute settlement for investor-state disputes, it does not mean that the forum is in favour of the foreign investor.[562]

While one specific situation in which ICSID awards can be challenged is through the annulment of the award, Article 52 limits the grounds on which parties can request annulment and makes the rules in this regard precise, because of the potentially serious results in the event of the invalidation of an arbitral award.[563] In addition, there are specific conditions under which ICSID awards are subject to interpretation and revision by the parties under Articles 50 and 51 of the convention. Although state practice shows the enforcement of the arbitral award may be rejected on a particular basis, Oman is a signatory of the New York Convention,[564] and is therefore obliged to recognize and enforce the arbitral award according to Article 1.1 of this Convention.[565]

Criticisms have been raised regarding the ICSID dispute settlement system. Some, such as Carlos Garcia, [566] argue that the lack of an effective review and appeals process in investor-state disputes under ICSID,

---

562 Diana Marie Wick, ‚The Counter-Productivity of ICSID Denunciation and Proposals for Change' (2012) 11 J Intl Bus & L 239, 274.

563 Convention on the Settlement of Investment Disputes Between States and Nationals of Other States 1966, art 52 (1)
"Either party may request annulment of the award under the following grounds:
(a) that the Tribunal was not properly constituted;
(b) that the Tribunal has manifestly exceeded its powers;
(c) that there was corruption on the part of a member of the Tribunal;
(d) that there has been a serious departure from a fundamental rule of procedure; or
(e) that the award has failed to state the reasons on which it is based".

564 Oman signed the New York Arbitration Convention on the Recognition and Enforcement of Foreign Arbitral Awards 1958 (New York Convention) on 25 February 1999. New York Arbitration Convention, 'Contracting States' <www.newyorkconvention.org/contracting-states/list-of-contracting-states> accessed 25 January 2015.

565 New York Convention 1958, art 1.1 states that: "This Convention shall apply to the recognition and enforcement of arbitral awards made in the territory of a State other than the State where the recognition and enforcement of 8uch awards are sought".

566 The Mexican government's representative in investor-state arbitration in ICSID cited in Wick (n 562) 271.

combined with uncertainty in interpreting treaty rights, is a real weakness in the ICSID system. However, others argue that is not practical to create an effective review system with certainty in interpreting treaty rights when there are thousands of treaties containing different rights.[567] It is worth clarifying that when the applicable law is defined in the contract between Oman and the foreign investor, this would be applied by the ICSID tribunal. However, the outcome would be less clear if the applicable law lacked clarity or, more likely, if the arbitration were to proceed on the basis of consent stated in advance in a BIT where no choice of law is stated.[568] Nevertheless, the WTO has the advantage over ICSID regarding the issue of applicable law, because the former has a binding and comprehensive set of agreements.[569]

One final controversial area is the cost of ICSID proceedings. Some maintain that ICSID arbitration is expensive and time consuming, whilst others claim it is cheaper compared with ad hoc arbitration.[570] For example, in *Al-Tamimi* the tribunal stated that: "Under the US–Oman FTA and the ICSID Convention, therefore, the Tribunal has a broad discretion to determine "how and by whom" the expenses of this arbitration, including attorney's fees, should be paid"[571]

Then the Tribunal ordered that:

> the Claimant shall pay to the Respondent forthwith the sum of US$5,667,410.24, which comprises the Respondent's reasonable costs and expenses incurred in connection with this arbitration, including the cost of their legal representation, expert witness and consultants' fees, disbursements associated with this proceeding, and the Respondent's share of the ICSID arbitration costs and lodging fees paid.[572]

It can be argued that, taking into consideration the time and the effort that was made in this case, the cost is reasonable. In addition, a reasonable

567 Wick (n 562) 271.

568 See Dan Sarooshi, 'Investment Treaty Arbitration and the World Trade Organization: What Role for Systemic Values in the Resolution of International Economic Disputes?' (2014) 49 Tex Intl L J 445, 455.

569 Ibid 458.

570 Wick (n 562) 271.

571 *Al-Tamimi* (n 11) para 473.

572 Ibid.

cost is needed to ensure the seriousness of the claimant in raising disputes against the host states, because if the proceedings are very cheap, this will make it easy to bring parties before ICSID, regardless whether there is a serious reason to take action or not.

3.7 The Impact of the *Al-Tamimi* Case on Oman's Foreign Investment Law and Policy

3.7.1 The Facts of the Case

The *Al-Tamimi* dispute was brought before the ICSID by the Claimant Mr Adel A Hamadi Al-Tamimi, is a USA citizen born in the UAE, against the Respondent Sultanate of Oman.[573] While the main arguments of both parties have been furnished throughout the book, the Claimant submitted his notice of arbitration as mentioned earlier, on 5th of December 2011 declaring that the Omani Government's actions destroyed his multi-million dollar investment in the site, in violation of its obligations under the U.S.-Oman FTA and caused losses and damages of approximately $560 million,[574]

The Claimant argued that Oman's actions constituted a breach of Article 10.6 of the Oman-USA FTA.[575] The Claimant as well submited that Oman had breached its obligation under Article 10.5 of the Oman-USA FTA to provide the minimum standard of treatment to the Claimant's investment.[576] Furthermore, the Claimant alleged that, in breach of Article 10.3 of the Oman-USA FTA, Oman treated the Claimant less favourably than it would treats national investors in like circumstances.[577]

However, on 27 October 2015, the Tribunal issued the following award:

> 1. The Tribunal rejects all of the Claimant's requests for declaratory and compensatory relief.
>
> 2. The Tribunal orders that the Claimant shall pay to the Respondent forthwith the sum of US$ 5,667,410.24, which comprises the Respondent's reasonable costs and

573 *Al-Tamimi* (n 11) paras 47-48.
574 *Al-Tamimi* (n 11) Request for Arbitration (5 December 2011), para 5.
575 Ibid Award, para 167.
576 Ibid para 181.
577 Ibid para 195.

expenses incurred in connection with this arbitration, including the cost of their legal representation, expert witness and consultants' fees, disbursements associated with this proceeding, and the Respondent's share of the ICSID arbitration costs and lodging fees paid.

3. Interest shall be payable on the costs listed at 2 above from 60 days after the date of issue of this Award, calculated at the 91-day US Treasury Bill rate and compounded quarterly.

Prior to all this, the investor began his investment activities in Oman in 2006 and on behalf of two companies, Emrock Aggregate & Mining LLC (Emrock), and SFOH Limited (SFOH), Mr Al-Tamimi established an investment in Oman and through two lease agreements with an Omani state-owned company, Oman Mining Company LLC (OMCO) to operate a limestone quarrying and crushing concession on a parcel of Government-owned land.[578]

On 22 August 2007, OMCO instructed Mr Al-Tamimi by letter that Emrock and SFOH could begin quarrying operations on 1 September 2007, after receiving the initial environmental permit from the Omani Ministry of Environment and Climate Affairs (MECA) and the Certificate of Quarrying Operation from MoCI. On 22 August 2007, OMCO sent letters to Emrock and SFOH reminded Mr Al-Tamimi that he was allowed to mine only "quarry strata seams and beds of limestone" and that he was restricted to the "exploitation of limestone rock products only". The Claimant therefore started quarrying operations at the Jebel Wasa quarry on 1 September 2007.[579]

On 28 August 2007, OMCO wrote to Mr Al-Tamimi declaring that Emrock was violating the OMCO–Emrock Lease Agreement by "processing material originating in the alluvial deposits located in the area's streams". On 22 September 2007, MoCI issued a notice to OMCO that its experts had observed during a site visit that the Claimant was working beyond the borders of the restricted site. On 29 September 2007, OMCO wrote to Mr Al-Tamimi warning that Emrock was engaging in blasting outside of OMCO's concession. MECA issued two additional breach notices to

578 Ibid para 49.
579 *Al-Tamimi* (n 11) para 62.

OMCO on 7 October 2007 and 24 October 2007. Then, on 25 December 2007, MECA issued an infringement report and fined OMCO OMR 2,000.[580]

On 21 April 2008, MoCI issued OMR 10,000 fine against OMCO for claimed failure to "observe the boundaries of the leased site as previously determined"[581] and required that the Claimant stop such operations immediately. Mr Al-Tamimi claimed that he voluntarily ceased all production in the wadi at this time. OMCO paid the OMR 10,000 fine to MoCI and sought compensation from the Claimant. The Claimant offered to compensate OMCO but only if it would provide him with copies of the permits it had obtained.[582]

On 20 July 2008, OMCO decided to terminate the OMCO–Emrock Lease Agreement by sending letter to Emrock. Then, on 2 June 2008, OMCO informed the Claimant that it considered the OMCO–SFOH Lease Agreement as "null and void", because of the Claimant's failure to register SFOH in accordance with the Omani laws.[583] In addition, on 17 February 2009, OMCO terminated the Lease Agreements by sending two letters to Emrock stating the termination of the lease agreement on a number of grounds.[584]

Eventually, on 23 May 2009, the Royal Oman Police arrested the Claimant at the request of MECA for "allegedly conducting operations outside of his permitted boundaries, operating without the necessary permits, and removing material from the dry riverbed to the west of the Jebel Wasa mountain range".[585] Later, on 8 November 2009, the Mahda Court of First Instance sentenced Mr Al-Tamimi "on two misdemeanour counts: (a) stealing sands and stones without a permit; and (b) violating Omani environmental law by engaging in quarrying and crushing operations without the requisite permissions".[586] Then, "on 6 June 2010, the Ibri Court of Appeal issued a judgment overturning Mr Al-Tamimi's conviction on both misdemeanour counts".[587]

---

580 *Al-Tamimi* (n 11), para 65.
581 Ibid para 67.
582 Ibid.
583 Ibid para 63.
584 See ibid Request for Arbitration (5 December 2011) fn 31.
585 *Al-Tamimi* (n 11) Award, para 63.
586 Ibid para 78.
587 Ibid para 79.

3.7.2 The Impact of the Case on Oman's Foreign Investment Law and Policy

While the full picture of the impact of the *Al-Tamimi* case, especially in the domestic arena may need more time to emerge, since the award is relatively recent, certainly the involvement of the Omani government as a party in the case since the case was filed in 2011 is expected to lead to specific impacts and policies by the Omani policymakers, especially on the issues related to the case. This case is special, not only because it is the first arbitration case that Omani government faces, but also because the case raised and examined the Oman's practice in significant foreign investment issues, such as expropriation, international minimum standards and national treatment.

It can be argued that the clear impact of the *Al-Tamimi* case on Oman's foreign investment law and policy is that it raised awareness among policymakers in Oman of the need to reduce the vague areas in the foreign investment system and enhance its efficiency. Consequently, this led the Omani government to speed up its efforts to provide more protection and to improve the national legal system to attract foreign investment by requesting the World Bank's help to work on the DNFIL.

It is hoped that the DNFIL with the rights it provides, may help to improve the efficiency of the legal protection offered for foreign investment and will increase foreign investor confidence by enhancing consistency and removing possible conflict with international agreements and arrangements.[588] This is mainly for three reasons. First, the new law is assumed to take into consideration all Oman's commitments under existing international agreements, especially the WTO and FTAs. Second, it is expected to overcome some of the challenges in the current FCIL related to discrimination, vagueness and restrictive provisions. Finally, the draft of the new law has addressed some specific weaknesses of the current law, and provides for 100% foreign ownership, removal of a minimum capital requirement and an absolute right to refer disputes to international tribunals.[589]

It can be said that Oman's step of elevating the protection provided under Omani national law to that under Oman's BITs and FTAs is part of a progressive approach of offering better protection than existed previously.

588 Ernst & Young, 'Oman-proposes-new-foreign-capital-investment-law' (*Tax Insights*, 25 January 2016) <http://taxinsights.ey.com/archive/archive-news/oman-proposes-new-foreign-capital-investment-law.aspx> accessed 3 March 2016.

589 Ernst & Young (n 588).

Therefore, in one sense it is similar to the approach of seeking absolute protection of foreign investment in international foreign investment law, taken by other states and institutions, since both are going forward. Such an approach is apparent in provisions of the 2012 US Model BIT, and in the European Commission's proposal in 2015 to create a new (WTO) dispute settlement body-style Investment Court with an appellate body in relation to the negotiations with the US concerning the Transatlantic Trade and Investment Partnership (TTIP).[590] Subedi sees these as examples of a shift in attitude towards offering extensive protection to foreign investors.[591]

States concluding BITs or IIAs with an Investor-State Dispute Settlement (ISDS) Mechanism represented a significant development in international law, especially international investment law.[592] This is because, by allowing foreign investors to sue them before international courts and tribunals, host states are accepting an exception to their sovereign immunity.[593] Singapore is an example of this approach as it makes a distinction between state sovereignty and the foreign investor's right to take legal action against the government. When a Singaporean government agency enters into a contract with a foreign company, this is treated similarly to a contract concluded between two private entities,[594] according to Article 37 of the Constitution of the Republic of Singapore which empowers the government to make contracts and to sue and be sued. In addition, the State Immunity Act of Singapore emphasizes this by stating clearly that:

> A state is not immune as respects proceedings relating to a commercial transaction entered into by the State; or an obligation of the State which by virtue of a contract.[595]

Or where the

> State has agreed in writing to submit a dispute that has arisen, or may arise, to arbitration, the State is not immune

590 Subedi (n 7) 2.
591 Ibid.
592 Ibid 4, 5.
593 Ibid 4.
594 Shan (n 372) 75.
595 State Immunity Act of Singapore 2014 ss 5.1 (a, b).

as respects proceedings in the courts in Singapore that relate to the arbitration.[596]

In another sense, although Oman's current international approach is different, the standard of protection provided by Oman under the DNFIL seems to be similar to that taken by other developing countries. For example, in order to prepare themselves for the termination of their BITs, a number of countries, such as Bolivia, Ecuador and South Africa, have passed national laws to offer standards of protection to foreign investors similar to those provided by BITs. Importantly, the new Bolivian Investment Promotion Law provides that any disputes will have to be resolved under Bolivian law.[597]

Subedi notes that growing opposition to the ISDS mechanism under the IIAs is being voiced not only by developing countries but also their developed counterparts[598] since this new form of state practice is expected to contribute towards creating new norms or modifying existing norms of customary international law regarding the absolute protection of foreign investment.[599] Subedi argues that due to pressures coming from different directions, a paradigm shift is taking place within international investment law in favour of a more equitable, just and fair system.[600] There are numerous examples of this new pattern. In September 2013, many Latin American states agreed to take collective action against the ISDS mechanism under the IIAs and to introduce alternatives to this mechanism.[601] Developing countries, particularly India, Indonesia and South Africa, are leading a stand against the older generation of BITs.[602]

According to Subedi, many developing countries, particularly disadvantaged ones, have reached the conclusion that BITs are detrimental to their national interests and have started to reject signing BITs with unclear principles on protecting foreign investors. For example, the Constitutional Court of Ecuador stated that all BITs are unconstitutional and the country has started issuing its own laws for the protection of foreign investment.[603] Because of the growing caution and scepticism

596 State Immunity Act of Singapore 2014 s 11 (1).
597 Subedi (n 7) 21.
598 Ibid 17-25.
599 Ibid 20.
600 Ibid 22.
601 Ibid 14.
602 Ibid 19.
603 Ibid 21-22.

towards the ICSID mechanism, many countries have started systematically terminating BITs that offer access to ICSID for foreign investors.[604] Therefore, some scholars assume that history may be repeating itself with a return to the Calvo doctrine, or there may be a process of fundamental change in the landscape of international investment law.[605] It is not yet clear whether Omani policymakers share similar concerns about the ICSID mechanism.

Shan identifies a third international trend that aims for a balanced approach, which is more or less similar to the latest approach, arguing that while states will continue liberalising their investment systems and providing protection through BITs and IIAs, they will be more willing to exercise their sovereign rights to regulate foreign investment. Therefore, states will insist on maintaining their regulatory discretion when negotiating or renegotiating BITs or other IIAs.[606] This trend started to emerge due to the huge number of arbitration cases filed against states after 2000. While 71 of the 102 regulatory changes made in 2009 were in favour of foreign investors, restrictive legal changes have increased more rapidly. It is expected that this trend of liberalising the investment regime and preserving the host state's necessary power to regulate foreign investment will continue until a balanced liberal investment regime is achieved.[607]

In supporting the need for a balanced trend, it is recommended that it is vital to apply coherence and discipline to both international investment arbitration and the European Commission's proposal for a new and transparent system for ISDS: the Investment Court System. According to these proposals, the judges of these courts will be highly qualified and publicly appointed, comparable to those in the WTO Appellate Body and the ICJ.[608]

Overall, it is clear that the *Al-Tamimi* case has influenced Oman's foreign investment law and policy by prompting Omani policymakers to make the national foreign investment law a reliable source of foreign investment protection. Whether this will be followed by revising the Oman's BITs and whether Oman will establish its own model of BITs are not clear yet.

604 Subedi (n 7) 25.
605 Ibid 20.
606 Shan (n 372) 75.
607 Ibid.
608 Subedi (n 7) 34 The proposed Investment Court System would consist of a first-instance Tribunal and an Appeal Tribunal.

What is clear is that the international trends in state practice and the lack of fundamental reform indicate that neither the ISDS mechanism nor the BIT/IIA regime may continue for long in their current form.[609]

3.8 Conclusion

This chapter argued that while all foreign investors in Oman are generally protected by international customary law, the protection provided under Oman's international agreements varies. International agreements signed by Oman provide three levels of guarantees. The first level is the obligations on Oman under the WTO agreements. The second is under Oman's BITs and the GCC FTA with Singapore, which contain more or less similar standards of protection. The third and the strongest level of protection is under the GCC Economic Agreement and Oman-USA FTA.

It is argued that Oman applied fully both principles, national treatment and MFN under the GCC Economic Agreement and Oman-USA FTA compared with other Oman's international Agreements, such as the WTO agreements, BITs and the GCC-Singapore FTA, which contain exceptions to the principles. In addition, the principle of international minimum standards in the Oman-USA FTA is a much more reliable instrument in a case of arbitration, compared with the international minimum standard under Oman's other BITs.

In addition, it can be said that the more an investment agreement defines the basis and conditions of compensation, the more effectively it will reduce disagreement between parties and avoid a disappointing interpretation by the international tribunal, as demonstrated by the Oman-USA FTA and some BITs, such as those with Germany and the Netherlands. Nevertheless, the provisions of protection from expropriation included in Oman's BITs and its FTA will potentially play an important role in considerably enhancing the protection of foreign investment in Oman from expropriation.

While in most cases, exceptions in Oman's international agreements work as hiding rooms, there must be a balance between the protection of foreign investor rights in the case of money transfer and keeping the financial interest of the country secure and protection of the national interest. It is argued that the interaction of the narrower WTO protection

609 Subedi (n 7) 33.

rules with the broader measures of investor protection under BITs and, especially under FTAs, will achieve astonishing results.[610] Therefore, it can be argued that this combination of Oman's foreign investment commitments under the WTO, GCC, BITs, FTAs with USA and Singapore, and other international agreements will lead to significant foreign investment protection in Oman.

It can be argued that ICSID has proved to be a specialized and workable system of investor- state disputes. In addition, the fact that Oman is a member is a useful step further toward providing protection for foreign investors in the Sultanate as it is clear in the *Al-Tamimi* case. However, other mechanisms such as the DSB under the DSU and the ICJ generally are not suitable tools for individual foreign investors to take action against Oman.

While the *Al-Tamimi* case draw the attention of the Omani policymakers to improve the foreign investment legal system, it can be said that the full picture of the impact of the case on national law and policy awaits developments in the international arena, especially from developing countries.

The Oman international commitments cannot work alone and will not be effective in protecting foreign investment unless combined with a proper national legal system and practice. Therefore, the next chapter will examine Oman's commitments under Oman's national legal system.

610 Ewing-Chow (n 315) 550.

Chapter 4: Guarantees and Weaknesses in the Omani Legal Framework

4.1 Introduction

This chapter focuses on the guarantees and challenges for foreign investment in Omani law. The aim here is to analyse the various national legal norms that regulate foreign direct investment in Oman and investigate their effects on investment. These guarantees of protection are to be found in the Basic Law, the FCIL, the NDFIL, Labour Law and other related legislation. According to AlSameraie the national legal framework on foreign investment is the formal expression of the national policy and approach toward foreign investment.[611] To provide the fullest form of protection for foreign investment in international and regional agreements, there is a need for a compatible domestic law in the host country.

It is said that the 1994 FCIL removed restrictions on entry to the Omani market, including obstacles to ownership in most sectors, such as the amendment of FCIL by Royal Decree 16/1996 eliminated minimum capital requirements. In addition, FCIL provides guarantees regarding the transfer of money and profits. Moreover, companies with foreign participation may be exempted from corporate tax and customs duties during the first five years after establishment.[612]

The value of unilateral guarantees is controversial. It is argued that the protective measures included in national laws are of less importance for foreign investors since they are unilateral.[613] It is believed that foreign investors are not satisfied by the national laws and regulations provided by host states, mainly because the latter can unilaterally change any guarantee provided under their national laws.[614] Moreover, according to Sornarajah, since this is a constitutional matter, guarantees given by one government are not binding on its successors, especially when their ideology is different.[615] This is because the host state is completely free

611 Duraid AlSameraie, *Foreign Investment Legal Challenges and Guarantees* (1st edn, Center for Arab Unity Studies, 2006) 28.

612 Mellahi, Guermat, Frynas and Al-Bortmani (n 3) 4.

613 Nwogugu (n 97) 61.

614 Nicholas DiMascio and Joost Pauwelyn, 'Nondiscrimination in trade and investment treaties: worlds apart or two sides of the same coin?' (2008) 102 Am J Intl L 48, 55.

615 Sornarajah (n 8) 99, 100.

to amend or change investment law, on the basis of its sovereign rights over its territory and its right to choose its own economic and social system. This factor has had significant impacts on the history of the relations between sovereign countries and foreign investors, since they fear discriminatory treatment by the host state.[616]

Although non-commercial risks can be determined broadly or narrowly, according to the literature on the Convention Establishing the Multilateral Investment Guarantee Agency, foreign investors evaluate guarantees in terms of four non-commercial risks: guarantees of currency transfer; guarantees against expropriation; guarantees of repudiation of a contract, and guarantees from war and civil disturbance.[617] Sornarajah maintains that if domestic legislation provides a guarantee of dispute settlement provisions, this could provide vital protection for foreign investors.[618] In addition, as AlSameraie notes, any legislative changes made by the host state that lessen the level of protection provided for foreign investment will decrease the trust of foreign investors in the host state and consequently will negatively affect the state's ability to attract future foreign investment.[619] Undoubtedly, the obligations placed on Oman as a member of the WTO, its BITs and other international conventions all influence its commitments in national level toward the protection of foreign investment.

It is argued that the effectiveness of the guarantees included in investment laws largely depends on the permanence and enforceability of these provisions and if these are lacking, then this creates an insecure investment environment for foreign investors.[620] Therefore, in this chapter, Omani laws and practice will be evaluated in relation to international law standards and case law.

The first part of this chapter will examine how the Omani legal framework deals with the foreign investment risk of expropriation, focusing on the following issues: the legal protection from expropriation provided under the Omani system, concerns caused by indirect expropriation, the value of the guarantee, guarantees of compensation in Omani legislation property

616 DiMascio and Pauwelyn (n 614) 55.

617 T M Ocran, 'International Investment Guarantee Agreements and Related Administrative Schemes', (1988) J Intl L 341, 344-345.

618 M Sornarajah, 'Protection and Guarantees of Investment' (2000) 26 Commw L Bull 1290, 1290.

619 AlSameraie (n 611) 22.

620 Nwogugu (n 97) 61.

and intellectual property rights protection, the role of consumer protection, and the associated challenges.

The second part will analyse guarantees of non-discriminatory treatment. This will be done by examining the legal basis for non-discriminatory treatment in Omani law, the incentive of taxation and customs duties, the role of tax incentives, activities in which investors cannot invest, the guarantees provided by Free Zones (FZs), Duqm Special Economic Zone (DSEZ) and Knowledge Oasis Muscat (KOM), and the guarantees of transferring benefits.

The third part will examine the laws relating to industrial regulations. It will consider trade union regulations in Oman, the guarantees for companies wishing to bring workers to Oman, the challenge to employment regulations and the challenges posed by the Omanisation policy and the minimum salary for Omanis. Eventually, the guarantees of political stability will be analysed by examining the basis of political stability and the uncertainties associated with the handover of power in the Sultanate.

The analysis in this chapter is based mainly on three kinds of materials. The first consists of Omani legislation, both primary sources and secondary sources, beginning with existing Omani legislation ministerial decisions, and the implementation of those regulations. The second is the World Bank Group investigations and findings, and other materials, such as the outcome of meetings held by the Diwan Royal Court with lawyers, auditors and senior managers of foreign companies in Oman. The third is interviews carried out by the researcher in order to ascertain the actual situation on the ground of the guarantees and weaknesses in the Omani legal framework.

4.2 Guarantees against Expropriation

4.2.1 The Legal Basis for Protection Against Expropriation under Omani Law

Property expropriation is the most important risk from which foreign investors need to be protected.[621] The prohibition of expropriation in Oman's national laws can be found mainly in two laws: the Basic Law and the FCIL. Article 35 of the Basic Law, foreigners and their property, offers protection to all foreigners legally present in the Sultanate and to their property.[622] However, the protection offered by this article is that specified in Omani law. In addition, Article 11 of the Basic Law provides that expropriation is prohibited except under three conditions: it must be for the public interest; it must be according to the due process of law and it must be accompanied by provision of fair compensation.[623] Confiscation of property is also prohibited under Article 11 of this law except in the case of a judicial decision.[624] Hence, according to this article, if confiscation of property by the Omani government occurs without a judicial decision and does not fall within the cases specified by Omani laws, it will be illegal. Consequently, the foreign investor has the right to fair compensation if such an action takes place.

Article 12 of FCIL states that:

> The said projects may not be confiscated or expropriated unless for the public interest and against equitable compensation.

Therefore, both laws agree on the prohibition of expropriation except under the two conditions, that the action is in the public interest and that fair compensation is provided. Although the condition of due process

621 Sornarajah (n 618) 1297.

622 Basic Law of the State 1996, art 35 states that: „Every foreigner who is legally present in the Sultanate shall enjoy protection for himself and his property in accordance with the Law".

623 Basic Law of the State 1996, art 11 states that: "No property shall be expropriated except for the public interest in cases stipulated by the Law and in the manner specified therein, provided that the person dispossessed shall be fairly compensated".

624 Basic Law of the State 1996, art 11 states that: "General confiscation of property is prohibited. The penalty of specific confiscation shall only be imposed by virtue of a judicial decision and in such circumstances as prescribed in the Law".

is not stated in FCIL, it must be applicable to all expropriation cases in Oman because of the precedence of the Basic Law over all national laws. In addition, all the conditions should be met and the absence of one condition will violate the Basic Law.

Importantly, the DNFIL contains stronger protection with regard to expropriation because the provisions are intended to enhance clarity and reflect international good practice.[625] Article 19/1 adds the condition of non-discrimination, besides the conditions of the public interest and the due process of law.[626] This addition is an important step towards reducing the threat of expropriation and guaranteeing fundamental investor rights according to international standards and obligations.[627]

Sornarajah argues that there is a great deal of doubt about the value of unilateral commitments concerning the protection against expropriation.[628] The amount of legal protection provided for foreign investment is extremely dependent on what a host state considered to deserve legal protection under its legal system.[629]

However, although the tribunal in *Saluka Investments v the Czech Republic* recognised the legitimate right of the host state to regulate domestic matters in the public interest,[630] it concluded that the host state is obliged to treat foreign investors fairly and equally.[631] When expropriation is made without due process it will be discriminatory and a breach of commitments. Hence, this may amount to a "compensable taking".[632] Nevertheless, foreign investors have to prove that due process

625 World Bank Group, Trade & Competitiveness, Unpublished Proposal for the Draft of New Foreign Direct Investment Law (DNFIL) for Oman (July 2015), 4.

626 Art 19 of the Draft states that:" It shall not be permissible for the capital invested or the investment project to be expropriated in whole or in part, save for the public benefit in the cases stated by law and in the manner therein provided for, without discrimination as between those therein addressed and on condition that the person expropriated be appropriately compensated".

627 World Bank Group (n 625) 7.

628 Sornarajah (n 8) 99-101.

629 De Luca (n 79) 73.

630 *Saluka Investments BV v the Czech Republic* (Partial Award) 17 March 2006 UNCITRAL Arbitration, para 305. The tribunal stated that: "No investor may reasonably expect that the circumstances prevailing at the time the investment is made remain totally unchanged in order to determine whether frustration of the foreign investor's expectation was justified and reasonable, the host State's legitimate right subsequently to regulate domestic matters in the public interest must be taken into consideration as well".

631 Subedi (n 7) 201.

632 Sornarajah (n 8) 402.

has been violated by the host state. In the case *Concrete Pipe & Products of California v. Construction Labourers Pension Trust for Southern California*, the US Supreme Court stated that: "the burden is on one complaining of a due process violation to establish that the legislature has acted in an arbitrary and irrational way".[633]

It may be argued that since due process is a condition under the Omani Basic Law, this will automatically ensure the non-discrimination factor. So, what is the point of adding the condition of non-discrimination in the DNFIL? It can be argued in counter that due process is not linked fully to non-discrimination. In other words, the availability of due process in a case may not ensure non-discrimination in that case, because a similar case may be treated favourably. In addition, the inclusion of a non-discriminatory clause will make it much easier for foreign investors in Oman to prove discriminatory cases during the dispute settlement process by comparing with similar cases. Furthermore, the availability of both conditions under Omani legislation is much better than one, as it will be much easier for foreign investors to prove their case.

The opportunity given to foreign investors to rectify any breach of FCIL within a specified period of time can be seen as a feature of protection of foreign investment. According to Article 16 of the FCIL, violation of the provisions of FCIL is a justifiable reason to withdraw a licence, but before this can be withdrawn, a process must be followed. The foreign investor must first be notified of the nature of the violation; if he or she fails to rectify the violation within one month from the notification, the Minister of Commerce may then withdraw the licence if the CFCI recommends this. It remains unclear, however, whether the Minister can withdraw the licence without this recommendation from the CFCI. The members of the CFCI are not independent, since they are under the supervision of the Minister of Commerce. However, the weakness in this process from the foreign investor's side is that the Law does not grant any right to appeal the Minister's decision before the court.

International law was designed to deal with what is known as direct expropriation, but such actions are unusual today as states are aware of the need to attract foreign investment. The law is ambiguous concerning more recent developments in the field of foreign investment and according to Sornarajah, regulatory expropriation is an emerging problem. Developing

633 *Concrete Pipe & Products of California v Construction Laborers Pension Trust for Southern California* (Judgment) US 602 (1993) para 637.

countries seek the maximum benefits from foreign investment for their economies, so they now have protected foreign investment that enters their countries within a regulatory structure. Therefore, those countries regard regulatory interference as non-compensable takings, as is the case in developed countries.[634]

4.2.2 Concerns Caused by Indirect Expropriation

Indirect expropriation arises when a state applies measures that considerably deprive investors of their private property.[635] A typical example of indirect expropriation would entail the host state denying the presence of an investment and consequently refusing to compensate the foreign investor.[636] The World Bank considers that the notion of protection against expropriation also covers damages arising from government actions that may affect control over, eliminate or reduce ownership of the insured investment. Moreover, it also covers a series of acts that, over time, have an expropriatory effect, such as "creeping" expropriation.[637] However, because treatment standards must be tested by tribunals, some recent BITs made no distinction between direct and indirect expropriation.[638] Subedi notes that international law does not differentiate between direct or indirect expropriation when it comes to making adequate reparation or paying compensation and the host state is obliged to pay compensation in both situations.[639]

Whereas FCIL did not deal with indirect expropriation, Article 19/2 of the DNFIL specifies that protection also extends to the effects of expropriation, by stating:

634 Sornarajah (n 618) 1297.
635 Shan (n 372) 50.
636 Dolzer and Schreuer (n 91) 92.
637 Multilateral Investment Guarantee Agency (World Bank Group), 'Investment Guarantees' <https://www.miga.org/investment-gurantees> accessed 14 March 2015.
638 Antonietta Di Blasé, 'Intellectual Property in Investment agreements and public concerns', Giorgio Sacerdoti (ed), *General Interests of Host States in International Law* (CUP 2014) 208.
639 Subedi (n 7) 155.

> Expropriation as provided for in paragraph (1) of this article shall include nationalization, dispossession, forcible seizure and any other measure of like effect[640]

Gutbrod et al. assert that any significant interference with the property rights of a foreign investor by the host state that might considerably reduce its value, is enough to raise a case of indirect expropriation.[641] However, Article 19/2 of the DNFIL also makes it clear that a negative effect on the value of the foreign property does not, per se, constitute expropriation by stating:

> Any measure which adversely affects the economic value of the capital invested or the investment project is not in itself sufficient for the measure to be considered expropriation.

It is observed that this clarification addresses the inadequacy regarding investor rights in FCIL and raises these to international standards, including guarantees against expropriation.[642]

Two elements need to be taken into consideration here. First, the accepted criterion for distinguishing between expropriation and legitimate administrative regulation is the severity of the effect on the owner's legal status, namely the ability to use, enjoy, control and freely dispose of his investment. However, it may be debated whether this severity should be the sole determining factor since[643] the scope of national policy would be reduced to zero if the reduction in property value were to determine indirect expropriation. A host country would be confronted by foreign investor claims for compensation every time it changed its policy. In addition, this would limit international law on foreign investment to acting as an insurance policy against bad business decisions.[644]

Although international law recognizes that claims of indirect expropriation cannot be established on the basis of actions aiming to protect "legitimate public welfare objectives", it is not clear what objectives

640 Notwithstanding the difference between expropriation and nationalization in terms of their legal definition, they both result in the taking of private property.

641 Max Gutbrod, Steffen Hindelang and Yun-I Kim, Protection against Indirect Expropriation under National and International Legal Systems (2009) 2 Göttingen J of Int L 291, 302.

642 World Bank Group (n 625) 7.

643 Gutbrod, Hindelang and Kim (n 641) 300.

644 Ibid 301.

can be regarded as legitimate.[645] In *Al-Tamimi*, Mr Al-Tamimi accused Oman of creeping indirect expropriation, arguing that Oman, "through OMCO and other instrumentalities of the Omani government, has plainly and completely deprived Mr Al-Tamimi of his investment in the Quarry", and rendered him "unable to exercise any of the mining or leasehold rights he had acquired and invested in so heavily".[646] These measures by the Omani government were:

> Termination of the OMCO–Emrock and OMCO–SFOH Lease Agreements; the arrest of Mr Al-Tamimi; the police coercion of Mr Al-Tamimi to sign an undertaking to refrain from further production at the Jebel Wasa quarry; the prosecution of Mr Al-Tamimi; and the forced dispersal by the police of Mr Al-Tamimi's workforce and physical assets.[647]

Two issues need to be raised here. First, to establish an indirect expropriation there should be a clear link between the action of the host state and the indirect expropriation. In other words, the indirect expropriation must be a result of the host state's action. For example, with regard to the prosecution of Mr Al-Tamimi, the tribunal stated: "It is clear that it did not constitute or contribute to the loss of the Claimant's right to operate at the Jebel Wasa quarry, and accordingly did not permanently deprive the Claimant of any property rights"[648] The second issue is that Oman's implementation of its private property laws does not establish indirect expropriation.[649]

The second element of consideration, the amount of interference needed to hold the host country liable for indirect expropriation, is controversial.[650] A crucial means of differentiating between direct or formal expropriation and indirect expropriation is whether the measure in question has affected the legal title of the owner. Nowadays direct expropriation has become rare because countries are hesitant to threaten their investment climate by taking the radical step of openly taking foreign property. An official act of expropriation would cause lasting damage to the state's reputation

645 Subedi (n 7) 199-200.
646 *Al-Tamimi* (n 11) para 349.
647 Ibid para 350.
648 Ibid para 367.
649 Ibid para 368.
650 Gutbrod, Hindelang and Kim (n 641) 301.

for hosting foreign investment. Although indirect expropriation leaves the title of the investor untouched, it prevents him from utilizing the investment in a meaningful way.[651] It is this grey area that makes indirect expropriation a challenging issue.

4.2.3 The Value of the Guarantee

Does the guarantee provided under Omani laws against expropriation provide the protection needed for foreign investment? Two arguments can be raised in this regard. According to Sornarajah, a unilateral guarantee against expropriation must be backed by the jurisdiction of a foreign arbitral tribunal created through a treaty commitment, as a guarantee without full compensation has no international effect. Unilateral guarantees against expropriation cover foreign investors, including individuals and entities such as multinational corporations that do not have a personality in international law, meaning that the guarantees provided in domestic laws can be viewed as no more than strategies to attract foreign investment.[652]

Article 14 of FCIL only allows referral of disputes between foreign investment projects and third parties to international tribunals if they are protected by a BIT. However, this shortcoming is addressed in the provisions under Chapter Seven of the DNFIL, which deals fully with dispute settlement matters and allows referral to international dispute resolution upon agreement of all parties.[653] According to Articles 25 and 26 (1,2) of the DNFIL, a foreign investor has the right to resort to ad hoc or institutional arbitration. The process of dispute settlement detailed under Articles 24, 25 and 26 of the DNFIL provides a better guarantee. It is worth mentioning that in *Al-Tamimi*, Mr Al-Tamimi, in his claim of indirect expropriation against Oman, did not refer to any provisions of FCIL. Rather, his claim was totally based on the Oman-USA FTA. This suggests that it is unlikely that foreign investors in Oman will base their claims of expropriation upon FCIL.

However, it may be argued that unilateral acts of states, related to international concerns, have some binding force, even in the case of regime changes in the host state if, for example, they include referral to an international tribunal in case of expropriation.[654] Inclusion of such a

651 Dolzer and Schreuer (n 91) 92.
652 Sornarajah (n 8) 100-101.
653 World Bank Group (n 625) 10.
654 Sornarajah (n 8) 100.

clause provides protection for foreign investors. Subedi maintains that since the national law of the host country is the applicable law in the case of investment contracts, whether these are for overseeing engineering projects, constructing infrastructure, managing privatisation programmes, or operating of public services, tribunals should consider domestic laws in deciding international law disputes.[655] The tribunal may therefore have to investigate the obligations of the host state under its national law.[656] An example where the international tribunal took the national laws and policy into consideration was in *Southern Pacific Properties (Middle East) Ltd v Arab Republic of Egypt*,[657] where the tribunal argued that since Egyptian policy in investment legislation is to grant better security to investment, there is a reason "for an international arbitral tribunal to exercise jurisdiction over the dispute".[658]

Countries face the challenge of balancing development of their internal, economic and environmental policy with their commitments toward providing an attractive environment for foreign investors.[659] Thus, the admission of a foreign investment and granting of licences are conditional; failure to meet those conditions justifies state intervention that may lead to the withdrawal of these licences. If the legal procedures are followed in such cases, the legality of such measures under domestic legislation will be certain. This raises the question whether intervention in such circumstances by the host state can be regarded as expropriation under international law. It is believed that since the foreign investor was admitted on condition that domestic laws were obeyed, it would not be regarded as an expropriation. However, the conclusion on the issue will be different.[660]

Sornarajah observes that the new trend in modern international law is to regard taking by the host country as lawful unless it can be proved otherwise by the other party. However, host states must exercise this right on the basis of two conditions: that it is non-discriminatory and on the basis of public interest. Those conditions are consistent with international

655 Subedi (n 7) 216.

656 Ibid 173.

657 *Southern Pacific Properties (Middle East) Ltd v Arab Republic of Egypt* (Award) 1992 (ICSID Case No ARB/84/3).

658 This is based on the provision of Egyptian investment law which states that: "Projects may not be nationalized or confiscated assets cannot be seized, blocked, confiscated or sequestrated except by judicial procedure" cited in Sornarajah (n 8) 100.

659 Subedi (n 7) 200.

660 Sornarajah (n 8) 115.

customary law and are applied in all BITs.[661] However, others, such as Bolivar, add a further condition: that the taking should be followed by prompt, just, and adequate compensation.[662]

Beyond the case of *Al-Tamimi*, there have been no reports of expropriation in the Sultanate[663] and its increased interest in attracting foreign investment and technology transfer has made expropriation unlikely.[664] However, the World Bank recommended that Oman needs to develop and implement modern expropriation law.[665] The existence of a guarantee against expropriation in the national legal system is important in determining the legality of a taking and the significance of damages caused by the expropriation.[666] Sornarajah emphasises that when unilateral guarantees are violated, such guarantees can work as a secondary tool to exercise "arbitral jurisdiction and awarding damages to the foreign investor".[667]

4.2.4 Compensation for Expropriation

The norm of full compensation is usually included in national foreign investment laws, since this is most attractive to foreign investors.[668] Omani legislation has provided that foreign investors have the right to be fairly compensated in the case of expropriation. Article 11 of the Basic Law states that:

> No property shall be expropriated [...] provided that the person dispossessed shall be fairly compensated.

This article obliges the Omani government to provide fair compensation to the individual whose property has been expropriated and it applies to

661 Sornarajah (n 8) 208.

662 Omar E Garcia-Bolivar, 'Past and Present Legal Guarantees for Protection of Foreign Investments in Venezuela' (2012) 18 L & Bus Rev Am 173, 180.

663 Bureau of Economic and Business Affairs, *2012 Investment Climate Statement-Oman* (ICS 2012) <www.state.gov/e/eb/rls/othr/ics/2012/191213.htm> accessed 2 March 2015.

664 Ibid 2012.

665 World Bank Group, 'Investment Reform Map- Sultanate of Oman' (unpublished paper, Muscat, April 25 2015) 6.

666 Sornarajah (n 8) 100.

667 Ibid 101.

668 Ibid 424.

corporations also.[669] The obligation under the Basic Law is important in providing protection for foreign investment. In addition, this obligation is emphasised by Article 12 of FCIL, which states that:

> [T]he said projects may not be confiscated or expropriated unless for the public interest and against equitable compensation.

These two articles raised the issue of what constitutes fair or equitable compensation AlSameraie argues that such compensation should be sufficient, immediate, and effective, but neither of these laws includes these conditions.[670] In addition, the words "fair and equitable compensation" used in Omani laws, seem to be similar to "just compensation", which is usually interpreted to mean the same as the 'Hull Formula' under the USA national legal system. However, this interpretation is definitely not an agreed interpretation in all other domestic laws.[671] Article 19/4 of the DNFIL remedies the weakness in FCIL and complies with international standards and obligations,[672] stating that:

> The compensation provided for in paragraph (1) of this article shall be considered to be appropriate if it is adequate, effective, and prompt.

It is pointed that although, at times, compensation may be paid incrementally, this practice shows that Oman is willing to offer compensation for any expropriations it makes.[673] Sornarajah argues that countries with a history of expropriation are keen to provide guarantees of compensation intended to reduce the risk sensitivity resulting from past nationalisations; those with a low risk of expropriation do not need to issue such guarantees.[674] However, this is not always the case, as some countries offer such guarantees to reflect the depth of their commitment towards foreign investment.

669 The original text in Arabic used the word „*Ahad*" which generally refers to individuals but in this case also includes private ownership generally.

670 AlSameraie (n 611) 159-163 also examines the arguments about the meaning of sufficient, immediate and efficient compensation.

671 Shan (n 372) 53.

672 World Bank Group (n 625) 7.

673 ICS (n 663).

674 Sornarajah (n 8) 99.

According to AlSameraie, expropriation is illegal unless it includes compensation for the property owner.[675] It is recognised that unlawful nationalisation establishes an obligation to pay restitutionary damage, while lawful taking entails paying compensation.[676] Nevertheless, it is argued that the challenge with laws that contain a promise of full compensation is the lack of uniformity on the standard of compensation.[677] Unlike the FCIL, which does not specify the standard level of compensation, Article 19/5 of the DNFIL attempts to do this by stating:

> The quantum thereof shall reflect the market value as it is prior to the date of issue of the decision to expropriate, or the date when the threat of expropriation become publicly known, whichever is the earlier. Payment of the compensation awarded shall be made without any restrictions, and the amount of the compensation shall bear interest at the prevailing rate in the Sultanate as from the date mentioned in this paragraph until payment is made in full.

However, compensation for expropriation of foreign investment is a controversial area, since different legal systems adopt diverse approaches to property protection, making it difficult to extract common principles. It is argued that because of the different terms used under national laws, compared with the mostly standardised compensation under investment treaties, makes compensation under the treaty standard clearer, and possibly higher, than the national law standards.[678] Nevertheless, it is believed that unilateral guarantees, along with bilateral investment agreements, play an important role in providing guarantees for foreign investment in host states.[679]

675 AlSameraie (n 611).
676 Sornarajah (n 8) 364.
677 Ibid 424-425.
678 Shan (n 372) 53.
679 Sornarajah (n 8) 99.

4.2.5 Property and Intellectual Property Rights Protection

4.2.5.1 Protection of Property Rights

Both moveable and real securitized interests in property are recognised and enforced in the Sultanate.[680] Oman applies a free market economy that respects and protects individual ownership. Article 11 of the Basic Law states that: "The national economy is based on justice and the principles of free economy". According to Article 1 of Royal Decree 12/2006, foreign investors have the right to own or invest in properties in Integrated Tourism Complexes (ITCs). Article 3 of the same Decree provides that foreign-owned land in these ITCs should be invested within four years; otherwise, the Ministry of Housing (MoH) has the right to withdraw the land. In this case, the owner should be compensated with a sum equal to the land price at the time of buying or selling, whichever is lower. It is obvious that this four-year period is intended to ensure the seriousness of investors and to urge them to invest in the location. However, Article 4 of the Decree provides that the four-year period mentioned can be extended for a further two years following a recommendation by the Ministry of Tourism (MoT).

Three important features of protection and incentives for foreign investors appear in Royal Decree 12/2006. First, according to Article 3, the owner has the right to appeal against the expropriation decision before Omani courts. The Omani government has the right to expropriate but as stated in Article 6 of the Decree, fair compensation must be provided. It can be argued that since the appeal will be heard before a national court, the supervision of the judiciary over such a decision is an important guarantee to enable foreign investors to defend their rights. This right is much better than the expropriation decision being final. Article 7 of the Decree raises a second important issue for foreign investors since, after the death of a foreign investor, the law applicable for transferring ownership of the property would be the national law of the foreign investor. This is intended to avoid any conflict between the foreign investors' national laws and the Omani legal system in transferring the property ownership. Finally, Article 8 of the Decree provides an incentive for foreign investors who own property in Oman by offering them the right to a residence visa for themselves and their primary (first level) relatives.

---

680 *Oman, Investment and Business Guide: Strategic and Practical Information* (International Business Publication 2013) 73; ICS (n 663).

The only other exceptional case of land ownership outside the ITCs is that of GCC citizens, who have the right to be treated as Omani nationals[681] but this ownership is subject to certain conditions. The preamble of Royal Decree 21/2004 on Organising the Ownership of Lands of GCC Citizens in Oman makes it clear that this right is acquired on the basis of Article 3 of the GCC Economic Agreement, which declares that GCC citizens should be treated as nationals in the different GCC member states, and have the freedom to own land. According to Article 1 of the Decree, GCC citizens are allowed to own land and property in Oman, like Omani citizens. However, land ownership should not exceed four years, during which the GCC citizen must invest by building on it; otherwise, the Omani government has the right to withdraw the land but must provide compensation equal to the land price at the time of buying or selling, whichever is lower.[682] Even in the case of expropriation in the public interest, Article 4 of the Decree makes it clear that this should be on an equal footing with the treatment of Omani nationals.

The first issue which arises from this discussion of ownership for all foreign investors, including GCC citizens, is whether it is fair to provide compensation equal to the land price at the time of buying or selling, whichever is the lower, as provided in Article 3 of the Decree 12/2006, and Article 2 of the Decree 21/2004. Although the owner has the right to appeal against this decision, he is still restricted by conditions regarding the price he is to be offered. It can be argued that a fairer price for a foreign investor would be the highest price of land at the time of selling or buying or at the time of expropriation. This is because it is usual for land prices to increase every year. This argument can be challenged as well that foreign investor suppose to know the regulation in this case and avoid putting him or herself in such situation.

A further question that may arise is whether granting certain nationalities (GCC citizens) preferential treatment in relation to land and property ownership can be considered discriminatory treatment. This issue of preferential treatment to some nationalities has been discussed earlier, as it is the government's right to grant certain nationalities special treatment on the basis of international treaties, and this treatment is granted to GCC nationals on the basis of a regional agreement among the members of the GCC.

681 ICS (n 663).

682 Royal Decree 21/2004 on Organising the Ownership of Lands of GCC Citizens in Oman, art 2.

The Omani British Friendship Association (OBFA) highlighted two weaknesses resulting from ITCs. Firstly, title deeds and visas for property owners within ITCs are unclear.[683] Second, the recent revocation of various ITCs has created uncertainty regarding property investment.[684] However, although the reason for these revocations is not yet clear, and may have been due to the violation of provisions related to the requirement concerning investment in the property within the four-year period, expropriation was not identified as a challenge for foreign investors in the Sultanate by any of the sixteen professionals interviewed as part of this study.[685]

Although Oman allows foreigners to buy landed property in ITCs, these areas are limited. Therefore, Oman needs to attract investment in real estate by allowing foreigners to purchase apartments, in order to encourage vertical expansion and it seems that it faces difficulties due to limited local investors and buyers. One Omani policymaker interviewee pointed out that to attract foreign investment to Oman it is important to allow full ownership of real estate for all foreign investors and in all areas in the country.[686]

4.2.5.2 Protection of Intellectual Property Rights

It is important for Oman to achieve the level of protection applied in international standards as this will encourage foreign investment and lead to technology transfer.[687] Therefore, Omani laws related to intellectual property rights must be in accordance with the international standards applied in the TRIPS agreement and they must be backed up by an enforcement mechanism. The security of the intellectual and physical

683 Omani British Friendship Association (OBFA), 'Barriers to Trade and Foreign Investment in Oman' Joint Working Group, 10 February 2013, 7.

684 OBFA (n 683) 7.

685 Interviews were held in Oman from July to October 2014.

686 Interview with policymaker 3 (Muscat, Oman, 19 August 2014). In Singapore, for example, which has a very high population density of 7,697/km2, under the terms of the Residential Property (Amendment) Act 2010, c 274, foreigners may buy different kinds of residential property including any apartment within a building, any unit in an approved condominium, or any unit in an executive condominium which is at least 10 years old; restricted areas are limited.

687 Jabir Filaifel, WIPO National Seminar on Intellectual Property Rights (February 15 and 15, Muscat) <I:\orgarab\shared\tina\New_docs\Muscat_February_13_and_14_05\feb_15 & 16\ar\wipo_ipr_mct_05_5.doc, (NA)WIPO/IPR/MCT/05/5> 10 accessed 20 October 2015.

property of foreign investors in the host state is needed to guarantee the success of foreign investment.[688]

Nawafleh maintains that developed countries have used BITs and Bilateral Trade Agreements as instruments to build wider and better protection for intellectual property than that which existed under the WTO TRIPS Agreement.[689] Therefore, Oman has modified its intellectual property rights laws as a result of domestic economic reforms and its commitments under BITs, the TRIPS Agreement (WTO) and the FTA with the USA. This resembles the situation that applies in most developing countries.[690]

The fact that Oman seeks to attract multinational corporations and its commitments as a WTO member have challenged the Omani legislators to improve the conditions of intellectual property rights to reach international standards of protection. It is argued that the aim of many companies in engaging in foreign investment in the host country is to protect their intellectual property rights.[691] The case of *Plain Tobacco Packing*[692] is an example of when foreign investor can bring a case against a state before an international tribunal on the basis of a BIT or FTA with regard foreign investors' intellectual property rights.

It can be argued that the intensive efforts made by Oman in recent years to establish comprehensive legal protection for intellectual property rights have significantly developed protection for intellectual property rights. This culminated in the promulgation of two laws: the Industrial Property Law (Royal Decree 67/2008) and the Law for the Protection of Copyright and Neighbouring Rights (Royal Decree 65/2008). The first is a set of measures designed to protect owners of patents, trademarks and topography, and to afford protection from unlawful competition.[693] The

688 Abdullah Nawafleh, 'Development of Intellectual Property Laws and Foreign Direct Investment in Jordan' (2010) 5 J Intl Com L & Tech 142, 143.

689 Ibid 149.

690 Carlos A Primo Braga and Carsten Fink, 'The relationship between intellectual property rights and foreign direct investment'(1998) 9 Duke J Comp & Intl L 163, 163.

691 Nawafleh (n 688) 143.

692 *Philip Morris Asia Limited (Hong Kong) v The Commonwealth of Australia*, cited in Di Blasé (n 638) 208.

693 Curtis, 'Restructuring an entity: The right to transfer employees from a group of entities under Omani Law' (*Oman Law Blog*, 20 December 2014) <http://omanlawblog.curtis.com/2014/12/restructuring-entity-right-to-transfer.html> accessed 2 March 2015.

second aims to provide protection for creative works of literature, science and the arts.[694]

Oman is obliged to apply Article 3/1 of the TRIPS Agreement by not discriminating in treatment given to its own citizens and to nationals of other WTO member states with regard to the protection of intellectual property.[695] According to Article 41.1 of the TRIPS Agreement, Oman is required to ensure that enforcement procedures are available under its domestic law "so as to permit effective action against any act of infringement of intellectual property rights covered". These enforcement procedures must include "expeditious remedies to prevent infringements and remedies which constitute a deterrent to further infringements". Although the development in related laws has been able to provide foreign investors with the necessary degree of intellectual property protection, Oman needs to ensure that it continues to review and amend its intellectual property rights laws. One foreign investor interviewed stated that intellectual property rights in Oman are well defined.[696]

In addition, Oman needs to have tools at its disposal to guarantee effective enforcement and transparent application. Nawafleh maintains that even though a WTO member state may provide adequate provisions in its legislation, the enforcement mechanism that is applied may fail; in this case, the country will be in violation of its commitments under the TRIPS Agreement and could eventually be subject to trade sanctions.[697] Therefore, Oman should consider that the two elements, having intellectual property rights that match international standards and implementing these effectively, must be made to work together.[698] The next subsections will analyse the protection of foreign investment under Oman's copyright, patent and trademark related laws.

---

694 Ibid.

695 The Agreement on Trade-Related Aspects of Intellectual Property Righs (TRIPS) 1994, para 3/1 states that: „1 Each Member shall accord to the nationals of other Members treatment no less favourable than that it accords to its own nationals with regard to the protection3 of intellectual property".

696 Interview with foreign investor 2 (Muscat, Oman, 28 August 2014).

697 Nawafleh (n 688) 153.

698 Singapore has strengthened the enforcement of intellectual property rights by establishing a specialised crime division known as the Intellectual Property Rights Branch devoted to investigation and suppression of intellectual property rights violations in Singapore. This may help to explain Singapore's ranking as: number one in the world for IP protection in the World Economic Forum, *Global Competitiveness Report 2009-2010* <http://ww3.weforum.org/docs/WEF_GlobalCompetitivenessReport_2009-10.pdf> accessed June 26 2014.

4.2.5.3 Protection of Foreign Investment under Oman's Copyright Law

Oman's Copyright Law is intended to provide automatic protection for foreign investors' scientific work, original artistic work (including paintings, sketches and musical compositions), computer programs, books, lectures, and articles, upon their creation.[699] It can be argued that the Copyright Law offers robust protection for foreign investors of two kinds. First, Oman applies the terms of protection of copyright in accordance with international standards. For example, according to Article 26 of the Copyright Law the term of protection for economic rights is "the life of the author and seventy years starting from the beginning of the Gregorian calendar year following the year of his death" Moreover, under Article 31 of the Law, the economic rights of performers are protected "for ninety-five years starting from the first day of the Gregorian calendar year following the year during which the recorded performance was legally published for the first time". Likewise, according to Article 14/5 of the TRIPS Agreement, the term of the protection afforded to performers and producers of phonograms "shall last at least until the end of a period of 50 years computed from the end of the calendar year". It is clear that the Omani Copyright Law specifies the Gregorian calendar Oman may in some cases use the Hijra calendar, for example, in some cases in Omani Family Law. However, it is the approach in all Omani business laws to use the Gregorian calendar. It is essential here to link this point with Oman's commitments under the TRIPs Agreement. It is interesting that Article 14/5 of TRIPs did not define which calendar is to be used; the reason might be that the Gregorian calendar has become an internationally agreed calendar.

Oman is bound by relevant international agreements as a signatory of the WIPO Copyright Treaty, in force since September 2005,[700] and signatory of the Berne Convention (1971) since July 14, 1999.[701] Under Articles 9, 10 and 14 of the TRIPS Agreement it must apply the Berne Convention-related provisions. In addition, Oman is a signatory of the Paris Convention (1967) in force since July 1999,[702] which calls on TRIPS

699 Curtis (n 693).

700 Maximilian Bossdorf, Christian Engels and Stefan Weiler, *EU GCC Invest Report 2013: Promotion of Mutual investment opportunities and creation of a virtual European structure in the GCC* (2013) 64.

701 World Intellectual Property Organization 'Member States' <www.Wipo.int/members/en/> accessed 9 October 2015.

702 Bossdorf, Engels and Weiler (n 700) 64.

members to apply the related provisions as specified by Articles 15 and 16 of TRIPS.

Added protection can be found in the enforcement mechanism provided by the Copyright Law. This can only be by defining the scope of protection and prohibited actions in relation to copyrights that are provided under Articles 2, 3, 4 and 40 of the Law. This is important to provide a clear meaning of the infringement of copyrights and to determine acts that constitute copyright infringement.

Importantly, the law specifies two elements regarding the application of protection for the owner of copyrights and neighbouring rights. Firstly, civil and administrative procedures and remedies are determined in Articles 43 to 48. For example, Article 43 defines the mechanism that should be used to calculate compensation along with the Executive Regulations used to determine the amount of compensation due. The standard of compensation included under this article in a case of infringement is an important guarantee of a foreign investor's copyrights.[703] The second element relates to the criminal procedures and penalties specified under Articles 49 to 56. In order to ensure compliance with the Copyright Law, civil and criminal penalties can be applied against those who violate the Law, which also supports copyright protection for foreign investors' intellectual property.[704]

4.2.5.4 Protection of the Patent Rights of Foreign Investors

Since the level of protection of patent rights offered by host states is a serious issue for foreign investors making a decision about where to invest, the Omani Law on Industrial Property Rights offers three advantages of

703 Copyright Law 2008 art 43 states that:
"1 - Without prejudice to any other compensations prescribed by any other law, the Court shall order anyone convicted of committing acts of infringements against any of the financial rights of the Author or of the holders of Neighboring rights to pay to the rights holder the following:
a) Compensations sufficient enough to cover for the damages to the right holder attributed to the infringement;
b) The amount of profits gained by the infringer and attributed to the infringement, and which was not taken into consideration when estimating the compensations referred to in the previous paragraph
For the implementation of the provisions of this paragraph, the right holder is each and every exclusive licensee, and also the unions and association representing the right holders, as per prevailing laws."

704 These include a term of imprisonment lasting from a minimum of three months to a maximum of three years or fine raning from RO 2,000-10,000.

protection of patent rights:[705] First, the Law complies with international standards since Oman has a signed a number of international agreements to enforce patent protection. These include The Hague Agreement, in force since March 2009, the Patent Cooperation Treaty, in force since October 2001,[706] and the Paris Convention. In addition, according to Article 12.1.A of the Law on Industrial Property Rights, patents are protected for twenty years[707] in compliance with TRIPS Agreement Article 33.

However, Article 13.B of the Law on Industrial Property Rights raises an issue concerning the full rights of the patent owner. This article accords the Minister of Commerce the right to decide to exploit an invention for a government agency or a third person, without the agreement of the owner of the patent. Although the article notes that the provisions of the WTO General Council should be taken into account when applying this right, the fact that since it is "without the agreement of the owner of the patent" may weaken the protection of patent rights. In addition, the protection of patent rights may be weakened under national laws benefiting from the exceptions under TRIPS Agreement rights given to Member States. Therefore, such exceptions are controversial because of their impact in foreign investors' rights. For example, Article 27.2 of the TRIPS Agreement grants Member States the right to exclude the patentability of certain inventions under the reason of protecting public interest or morality.[708]

Second, in certain specified cases, the right to the patent belongs to the employer, which represents an important issue for foreign investors, particularly those in the information technology (IT) sector. If an employee has the right to claim the ownership of a program, this may discourage foreign investors. Therefore, Article 4 (3, 4) of the Law on Industrial Property Rights grants the employer the right to the patent in specific cases. Consequently, IT corporations and foreign investors are expected to benefit from these rights specified in Article 4 (3, 4) as follows:

> 3 – Where an invention is made in execution of an employment contract the purpose of which is to invent, the

705 The Patents Law 2000 (promulgated by Royal Decree 82/2000) has been replaced by Law on Industrial Property Rights 2008 (Royal Decree 67/2008, art III).

706 Bossdorf, Engels and Weiler (n 700) 64.

707 TRIPS, art 27 2 states that: „a patent shall expire 20 years after the filing date of the application for the patent".

708 Di Blasé (n 638) 194-195.

right to the patent shall belong, in the absence of contractual provisions to the contrary, to the employer [...]

> 4 – Where an invention is made by an employee but not in execution of an employment contract, and when for making that invention the employee used materials, data and/or know-how of the employer, the right to the patent shall belong, in the absence of contractual provisions to the contrary, to the employer [...]

Therefore, it is clear that the article grants the employer ownership of the patent in the two specific cases mentioned in the article. In addition, it is clear that the availability of one of the above cases is enough to grant the employer the right to the patent.

A third feature of the protection afforded by this Law is that it provides tools to apply its provisions effectively. Article 11 specifies the infringement acts which may occur by a third party whether the patent is for a product, process, plant or plant variety and others. Defining infringement acts is important to enable foreign investors who have exploited their patented invention to take action in cases that are detailed comprehensively and determined by this article. In addition, Article 24/3 grants the registered owner of an industrial design the right to establish court proceedings, not only in case of actual infringement but also when this is thought likely to occur.[709] Most importantly, in a case of infringement of those rights provided by the Law, remedies including injunctions and compensatory damages are possible by bringing a case before Omani courts, as stated by Articles 66-72 of the Law.

While the above analysis may ensure the regulation side of the protection of the patent rights of foreign investors, the effectiveness of these guarantees in practice needs deep investigation. Nevertheless, the Omani government has taken steps, such as in 2011, to implement the Intellectual Property Rights of American pharmaceutical and software manufacturers.[710]

709 Law on Industrial Property Rights 2008, art 24 3 states that: „The Registered owner of an industrial design shall have the right to institute court proceedings against any person who infringes the industrial design by performing, without his agreement, any of the acts referred to in subsection (1) or who performs acts which make it likely that infringement will occur".

710 ICS (n 663).

4.2.5.5 *Protection of the Trademark Rights of Foreign Investors*

Article 39/1 of Royal Decree 67/2008 provides that the owner of a registered trademark shall have protection through the exclusive right to prevent others from using without his consent, "identical or similar signs, including trade names and geographical indications, for goods or services related to those" which have been registered, if any confusion is likely to happen on account of such use.[711] However, the words "identical or similar signs" may raise debate between the foreign investors who own the trademark and others on what is the degree of similarity needed to raise the right for or against foreign investors. An example of this occurred in a recent case of *Alqudra Holding Company v. Registrar of Trade Marks MoCI* before Muscat Court of Appeal. The claimant was a foreign investor who applied to the registrar at the MoCI to register the trademark of ALQUDRA but the registrar refused on the basis that there was a similarity with another trademark, ALSTOM, arguing that the similarity appeared in the letters Q and O of the two trademarks, and was likely to lead to confusion. On 24 March 2016, the Court issued a verdict that the decision of the registrar (no.47652) with regard to the claimant (Alqudra Holding Company) was null and void.[712] The court found that there were clear differences between both trademarks and confusion between them was unlikely.

However, foreign investors can benefit from two elements of protection under the Law: first, the power of the judiciary can be used to ensure effective protection of the trademark owner's rights. They can challenge in court the Registrar's decision to refuse registration or make acceptance conditional, within thirty days, as provided by Article 11 of the Law.[713] The above *Alqudra Holding Company* case is a clear example of how the owner of a trademark can benefit from the judiciary in Oman against a governmental body. In addition, the owner of a registered trademark shall have the right to bring action against any person who infringes it by using it without his approval, or involvement in acts that make an infringement of the trademark likely to occur as provided by Article 39/2. The courts

711 According to the Preamble of Royal Decree 67/2008 the Trademarks Law 2000 has also been replaced by the Law on Industrial Property Rights 2008.

712 *Alqudra Holding Company v Registrar of Trademarks (MoCI) case 628/2014*, Commercial Circuit (Court of Appeal - Muscat) Judgment, 24 March 2016 Oman.

713 Law on Industrial Property Rights 2008, art 11 states that: „Each decision issued by the Registrar refusing registration or making acceptance conditional, may be contested by the applicant at the commercial court within thirty days from the date of notification of the applicant The court may sustain, cancel or modify the decision".

may also be involved in protecting a brand's reputation. For example, a brand name could be damaged if it is copied or used by another company supplying lower quality goods or services. Therefore, Article 42/1/A and B grants the interested party the right to take action to request the court to invalidate the registration of a mark if it is proved that there is a breach of the Law.[714] Further judicial protection is offered by the penalties applied for non-compliance regarding trademarks under Article 93 of the Law.

In this context, also, concerns may be raised by Article 40/1,2, which grants the MoCI the right to declare a trademark right exhausted:

> [W]hen that product is not available in the territory of Oman or is available in the territory of Oman with unreasonably low quality standards or in a quantity that is not sufficient to meet the local demand or at abusive prices or for any other reason of public interest.

The words "for any reasons of public interest" can be used in a very broad way that may breach the trademark rights of foreign investor. Therefore, more protection would be offered to foreign investors if such rights were kept under the judiciary's jurisdiction, or if the trademark's owner were allowed to appeal the Minister's decision before the Omani courts.

Further protection is guaranteed by the fact that the Law obliges the provisions of the law to be applied according to international standards. Article 100/1 of the Law obliges Oman to enforce the Law in accordance with conventions and treaties to which Oman is a party, and to provide citizens of those countries which are parties of the multilateral and bilateral conventions and agreements to which Oman is also party all rights with regard to trademarks and trade data.[715] Therefore, Oman would

714 Law on Industrial Property Rights 2008, art 42/1/A, B states that:
„(A) Any interested person may request the Court to invalidate the registration of a mark, within a period of five (5) years from the date of issuance of the registration certificate, or at any time if the registration was obtained in bad faith or on the purpose of harming a registered mark
(B) The Court shall invalidate the registration if it is proved that it has been issued in violation of the provisions of this Law. As such, the Registrar shall accord the invalidation and publish it in the *Official Gazette*".

715 Law on Industrial Property Rights 2008, art 100/1 states that: „The enforcement of the provisions of this Law shall not violate or contradict with the provisions of any of the multilateral or bilateral international treaties in respect of industrial property, that govern and regulate the rights of citizens of member state, and those equivalent, and to which Oman is a party, or shall be a party to".

be obliged by this article, in the application of this Law, to not discriminate against foreign investors and to provide foreigners with the same rights provided to Oman nationals. In addition, since joining the WTO, Oman has had to restructure its intellectual property (IP) legal system to conform to international standards.[716] For example, the term of protection of trademarks under Article 41 of the Industrial Law is ten years from the filing date of the application for registration, whereas, under Article 18 of the TRIPS Agreement it shall be not less than seven years. However, the protection under the TRIPS Agreement represents the minimum standard of protection.

4.2.6 The Weakness Caused by the Public Authority for Consumer Protection

The role of the Public Authority for Consumer Protection (PACP)[717] regarding its intervention in the pricing of goods and services is controversial. This is because on the one hand the PACP and related regulations were established to protect consumers' rights in the Sultanate.[718] On the other hand, Oman has a free market economy,[719] the laws and forces of supply and demand must be free from any intervention by any government authority and the prices for goods and services must be set freely by consent between sellers and consumers. Although intervention by PACP on prices may be supported by the majority of Omani consumers,[720] it has a negative effect on foreign investment when companies find themselves controlled by another body in their retailing policy.

In addition, one of the lawyers interviewed pointed out that the role played by PACP may lead to a lack of freedom in the Market, meaning that foreign investors do not have rights with regard to the market prices of their products.[721] Indeed, there are a number of cases where the practices of PACP have represented a challenge to foreign investment. For instance, four employees of the well-known multinational retailer Marks and Spencer (including an Omani female manager) were arrested and jailed

716 Oman has signed the Madrid Protocol, in force since October 2007 See Bossdorf, Engels and Weiler (n 700) 64.

717 PACP was established by Royal Decree 26/2011 to supervise the implementation of the Sultanate's general policy on consumer protection.

718 Consumer Protection Law 2014 (promulgated by Royal Decree 66/2014), art 2

719 See Mellahi and Guermat (n 227) 7.

720 This can be seen in the popularity of PACP actions especially on social media.

721 Written submission following interview with lawyer 1 (Muscat, Oman, 20 August 2014).

because the prices of some goods were increased without having PACP approval.[722] In another case recalled by an interviewee, the widespread retailer Select faced difficulties operating in Oman due to the restriction applied by PACP on their price capping.[723] When companies cannot increase the prices of their products without PACP approval, this creates problems.[724] PACP's actions were viewed as a barrier to investment in Oman and it was thought that consumers should decide whether or not they are prepared to pay increased prices.[725]

The legal basis for PACP's actions needs to be examined. It can be argued that the generality of some articles of the Law may cause challenges for foreign investment. According to Article 9 of the Consumer Protection Law, the only situations in which the chairman of the PACP can take temporary measures to curtail price increases are emergency cases, natural disasters, exceptional circumstances, extraordinary and special-nature market situations.

However, according to Article 13 of the Consumer Protection Law, the chairman of the PACP "may take the necessary measures and actions to guarantee consumer rights as stipulated in this law". Nevertheless, it does not define or specify these necessary measures and actions or what is meant by consumers' rights, leaving all these areas open to interpretation. These areas need to be clear to investors. In addition, the same article grants the chairman the right to stop any breach of "consumer rights or general health and safety rules related to the commodities or services". This article may represent a challenge to foreign investors due to its vague wording and lack of detail regarding what is covered by these areas, leaving these open to interpretation in an overly broad manner.

Article 37 may also create challenge for foreign investors since it states that:

> The public prosecution – pursuant to a prior request from the chairman or the authorized representative thereof – may issue a decision to temporarily shutter the premises or suspend the activity until the adjudication of the lawsuit and

722 Diwan of Royal Court, 'Barriers to foreign investment in Oman meeting' (unpublished paper, Muscat, 20 January 2014) 1.
723 Interview with lawyer 1 (Muscat, Oman, 20 August 2014).
724 Diwan of Royal Court (n 722) 1.
725 Ibid.

stakeholders may appeal the decision before the Court of Appealed Misdemeanors at the deliberation chamber.

Although closing premises or suspending commercial activity is viewed as a temporary measure pending the Court's decision, a closure or suspension period of this type would harm foreign investment. This could be done by amending Article 37 to have the suspension enacted by court decision instead of by the public prosecution. Overall, it can be argued that a balance needs to be sought in PACP regulations and practice between protecting consumers' rights and fully applying the policy of free market economy to achieve the country's target of attracting foreign investments.

4.3 Guarantees of Non-Discrimination

4.3.1 Legal Basis for Non-discriminatory Treatment in Omani law

Oman is bound to issue its national laws in accordance with its international commitments under the WTO and its other international agreements. For example, as a signatory to the WTO agreements, Oman is generally obliged not to discriminate either among its trading partners, or between its own and foreign products, services or nationals.[726] Subedi noted that the basis of non-discriminatory treatment provided for foreign investors in international law could be found under customary international law, BITs, investment contracts, WTO agreements and other regional and international tools.[727] The principle of non-discrimination forms the basis of a considerable part of traditional foreign investment law and is founded on the notion that foreign investors doing business in a host country should be protected from undue or unfair discrimination.[728]

The guarantee of non-discriminatory treatment is present in various areas of Omani national law. One example as discussed above concerns prohibition of confiscation or expropriation unless for the public interest and against equitable compensation under Article 12 of the FCIL. AlSameraie identifies two types of discriminatory treatment that can be exercised by host countries. The first entails expropriating foreign investments involved in certain commercial or industrial activities, but not those of national investors carrying out the same activities. The second

726 WTO (n 369).
727 Subedi (n 7) 178.
728 Ibid 177.

concerns expropriating certain foreign investments belonging to some nationalities but not others engaging in the same activity. In both these cases, the responsibility of the host country will arise in discriminating between foreign investments.[729] The host country may be considered to have carried out discriminatory treatment of foreign investors

While FCIL has not addressed the principle directly, the DNFIL clearly acknowledges the principle of non-discriminatory treatment. Article 14 of the DNFIL binds all Omani government bodies to grant foreign investors treatment not less favourable than that given to Omani nationals at all stages of their investment.[730] This is also emphasised under Articles 13 and 15 of the DNFIL. Therefore, after the promulgation of DNFIL, then any discriminatory treatment would be a breach of the Law, and a foreign investor receiving unfair treatment would have the right to take action on the basis of its provisions.

Nevertheless, two further guarantees of non-discriminatory treatment in Omani law are the exemption provided in respect of paying taxes and customs duties provided under Articles 9.1, 9.2, and 9.3 and foreign investors' right under Article 11 of FCIL to transfer abroad the imported capital along with the profits accrued from the project. Both will be examined here.

According to an interview with an Omani policymaker, a member of the CFCI at the MoCI, there are two main reasons why applications are rejected: firstly, when the source of the investors' capital is not known, since this raises security concerns, and secondly, when there is a clear indication that the Omani partner is not serious.[731] Although the first reason is understandable for security reasons, the second seems to be vague, as it is unclear how the seriousness of the Omani partner can be evaluated and decided.

However, five challenges can be found for the guarantee of non-discriminatory treatment under Omani laws. First, it is argued that the requirements relating to national ownership specified by Article 2 of FCIL limit market entry to Oman.[732] In addition, the condition of a

729 AlSameraie (n 611) 154.

730 Draft New Financial Investment Law, art 14 states that: "The foreign investor shall receive treatment no less favourable than that of a national investor in like circumstances The foreign investor and the national investor in terms of rights and liabilities as regards setting up the investment project, acquiring it, extending it, managing it, and conducting its activity".

731 Interview with policymaker 3 (Muscat, Oman, 19 August 2014).

732 The minimum is 30%, see World Bank Group, (n 665) 4.

minimum capital requirement of OMR 150.000 established in Article 2 of FCIL is another challenge that limits market entry to Oman.[733] It is believed that eliminating or reducing minimum capital requirements and instead using visas and work permits to control immigration would be a possible solution.[734] Several OECD countries handle this issue by requiring investors to obtain and update visas or work permits.[735]

The third challenge, is the lack of foreign investors' right to seek judgment by an international tribunal under FCIL,[736] as discussed earlier. Subedi noted that non-discriminatory treatment is guaranteed by the right of foreign investors to take action before international tribunals in cases of alleged discriminatory action by a host state. However, the DNFIL clearly guarantees this right upon the parties' agreement. Therefore, in a case of expropriation, a foreign investor can be compensated according to international standards regardless of the kind of expropriation he has experienced. As Subedi points out, this places foreign investors in an advantageous position compared with national investors and such an approach may mean that national companies face reverse discrimination in their own state, as mentioned earlier.[737]

Another challenge is the slow approval process for establishing a business in Oman. Although the one-stop shop for government clearances based in the MoCI exists, in practice, some investment projects still need clearance from other governmental bodies such as the MECA, MoM, and different Municipalities, meaning that approval of investment projects may take six months or more. Delays caused by red tape are exacerbated by a lack of clarity in procedures covering clearances.[738]

Finally, the latest challenge is the recent requirement imposed by the MoCI that foreign companies aiming to hold shares in a company incorporated in Oman must have been incorporated for a minimum period of three years. Moreover, the foreign company should have proof of its incorporation and should submit the latest audited accounts to prove its financial standing. Jones and Al Sabahi argue that these new conditions

733 World Bank Group (n 665) 4.

734 Ibid 11.

735 Ibid 11.

736 Ibid 10.

737 Subedi (n 7) 177-178.

738 Swiss Business Hub GCC, *Sultanate of Oman: Legal Provisions* (2015) 8 <www.s-ge.com/schweiz/export/de/filefield-private/files/784/field_blog_public_files/53243> accessed 4 March 2015; Ithraa, *Challenges facing investors establishing projects in the Sultanate and proposed solutions* (2015) 7.

not only make it difficult for foreign investors to establish a business in Oman but also this amounts to discriminatory treatment between foreign and national companies.[739] They note the requirement results from the increased number of shell companies in the Sultanate failing to sustain their share capital, since there are no limitations and restrictions on capital transfer. In addition, the authors explain, such companies are not using their capital to achieve their declared objectives, or to comply with Omanisation requirements. However, according to Jones and Al Sabahi, the majority of those foreign companies are small businesses and there is no justified reason to lose the available chances to invest in important infrastructure projects in Oman.[740] As a result, the World Bank Group have criticised FCIL for lacking some important investor rights and consequently inadequately addressing these rights.[741]

Two key principles must be considered when dealing with discrimination:[742] firstly, the basis of comparison for the supposed action of discrimination and secondly, whether it is necessary to prove that discrimination was intended, or if the fact that unequal treatment has occurred is sufficient to establish that discrimination has occurred. The question is how to define discriminatory action by the state. While one factor in deciding this question is whether the policy is lawful under other relevant rules of international law,[743] it is difficult to establish criteria that enable comparison of the activities of national investors with those of foreign investors. Is it essential that they are both conducting exactly the same business or merely in the same economic sector, regardless of the exact nature of their business?[744] In *Marvin Feldman v Mexico*, the phrase "in like circumstances" was understood to mean in the same line of business,[745] as examined in relation to *Al-Tamimi*, earlier. Therefore, it is argued that in specific cases, domestic policies in favour of national public interest can be a basis for providing less than national treatment.[746]

Dolzer and Schreuer argued that discriminatory action is independent of a violation of national law because this law itself may be the reason

739 Adrian Jones and Fatima Al Sabahi, 'Recent changes under commercial laws of Oman' (2013) Middle East Bus L Rev, 4.
740 Ibid.
741 World Bank Group (n 625) 7.
742 Dolzer and Schreuer (n 91) 177.
743 Ibid 183.
744 Ibid 180.
745 *Marvin Feldman v Mexico* (n 158) para 171.
746 Dolzer and Schreuer (n 91) 183.

for violating an international standard.[747] In *Ronald S Lauder v The Czech Republic*, the BIT that was applied provided protection against "arbitrary and discriminatory measures". The tribunal stated:

> For a measure to be a discriminatory, it does not need to violate domestic law, since domestic law can contain a provision that is discriminatory towards foreign investment, or can lack a provision prohibiting the discrimination of foreign investment.[748]

This is true; the national law largely is not a standard by which to evaluate the discriminatory action. Rather, the national law itself must be consistent with international standards and best practice.

However, Sornarajah argues that discriminatory investment policies in favour of national investors are justifiable and should remain in place in order to ensure the development of national economies. This argument is based on the fact that in the past, most developed countries benefitted from applying discriminatory policies in favour of their local investors to ensure their development, yet now deny the same policies to developing countries.[749] Nevertheless, countries aim to attract foreign investment must avoid any discriminatory measures. Therefore, Oman has established a number of incentives that may help to reduce discriminatory concern. These include incentives of taxation and customs duties, FZs, DSEZ and KOM.

4.3.2 The Incentives of Taxation and Customs Duties

Hurtado maintains that the financial policy of the host state is the most influential factor affecting decisions to invest in one state rather than in another.[750] In order to attract foreign investment, it is the policy of developing countries to provide various tax incentives for foreign investors, including exemption from income tax, tax credits or investment allowances, free economic zones, reduced tax rates or tax holidays for certain activities or for investment in specific areas considered vital to

747 Dolzer and Schreuer (n 91) 176.

748 *Ronald S Lauder v The Czech Republic* (Final Award) 3 September 2001 UNCITRAL Arbitration, para 220.

749 Sornarajah (n 8) 203.

750 Hugo A Hurtado, 'Is Latin American Taxation Policy Appropriate for Promoting Foreign Direct Investment in the Region?' (2011) 31 New J Intl L & Bus 313, 318.

the national economy of the host state.[751] Other financial incentives may come from granting full or partial exemption from customs duties for raw materials, building materials, plant and machinery.[752] Tax and customs duties incentives in the Omani laws and whether Oman applies discriminatory measures in tax and customs will be examined in the following section.

4.3.2.1 Tax Incentives

It can be argued that the approach taken by Oman to use tax as an incentive to attract foreign investment is based on two features; first, the equality of tax rates for Omani and foreign companies, aiming to reduce the chances to apply any discriminatory measures; and second, a low tax rate. The Omani tax regime is governed by the Income Tax Law issued by the Royal Decree 28/2009, and followed by the Executive Regulation 30/2012 issued in January 2012 by the Ministry of Finance.[753] According to this Law, foreign companies in Oman will be subject to three types of tax rate. The first applies, regardless of the percentage of foreign ownership, if a company's income exceeds OMR 30,000; it is taxed at a single rate of 12%. The second applies to a foreign company that establishes a branch in Oman. In this case, tax is payable at a single rate ranging from 5% to 30% on the basis of the entire amount of the branch's taxable income. Finally, there is a flat rate tax of 10% of gross income on certain types of income for foreign companies that do not have a "permanent establishment in Oman". These include rent for equipment, transfer of technical know-how, royalties, and management fees.[754]

In addition to the equality in the tax rate, guarantees of non-discriminatory treatment offered under Omani law with regard to tax incentives can be found in different areas of legislation. Firstly, Article 11 of the Basic Law defines three standards that should be respected with regard to levying of taxes: they should be just, lawful and without retrospective effect. It states that:

> –Taxes and general charges are based on justice and the development of the national economy.

751 See Ibid 327; Sornarajah (n 8) 103.

752 Nwogugu (n 97) 36.

753 Sectariat General for Taxation (Ministry of Finance) 'Tax system in Oman' <www.taxoman.gov.om/tax%20_system_inoman_features.html> accessed 24 May 2016.

754 Ibid.

-Imposition of public taxes, amending and cancelling the same shall be by virtue of a law and no person is exempted from paying all taxes or part thereof except in the cases specified in the Law.
-It is not permitted to impose a new tax, fee or any right with retrospective effect, whatever its type might be.

With regard to the first paragraph, on the principle of justice, as previously discussed, the idea of what is "just" is extremely complex and it may be difficult to be agreed upon because there are always two sides to every argument. However, the article accords foreign investors the right to take action if unfair taxes are applied on them. In the second paragraph, concerning the principle of due process in establishing laws related to taxes should be fully implemented by the Omani governmental bodies applying taxes; otherwise, it will be a breach of the Basic Law. The third standard will prevent any foreign investors from being victims, as a new law can be issued, but it cannot be backdated to a period when no such law existed. To do so would be unfair because it would impose liabilities that the company could not have anticipated and might have chosen not to incur.

Oman also offers foreign investors two other attractive taxation features. Oman does not impose any personal income, sales, inheritance, gift, or value added taxes.[755] In addition, Article 8.2 of FCIL grants foreign investors a tax exemption for five years from the date of either commencing production or carrying out the activity. This date can be extended for five more years in necessary cases.[756] However, if the net profits of any company are equivalent to more than 50 per cent of the capital paid up at the beginning of the exemption period, a renewal will not be available according to the executive regulations.[757] The term "necessary cases" in the article is vague and needs to be clarified, by setting out the basis, conditions or standards that allow for the five-year expansion. This is important to avoid any contradiction or inconsistency that may lead to

755 Mansoor Malik and Ravinder Singh, 'Taxation in Oman', 46 <www.amjoman.com/docs/MEED> accessed 18 March 2015.

756 Foreign Capital Investment Law 1994, art 8.2 states that: "Tax exemption shall be for a period of 5 years starting the date of commencing production or carrying out the activity, as the case may be This period can be renewed in necessary cases, for a period not exceeding 5 years However, a decision shall be issued by the Financial Affairs and Energy Resources Council for such renewals".

757 Malik and Singh (n 755) 46.

discriminatory treatment amongst foreign investors in the application of the extension.

Importantly, tax exemptions are accorded to entities engaged in mining, manufacturing, tourism, fishing, fish processing, fish farming, agriculture, animal breeding, public utilities, private sector schools, higher education institutes, private hospitals, training institutes, and export of manufactured and processed products.[758] Other activities, such as foreign shipping companies and airlines, are exempted from taxation on the ground of reciprocal treatment. Moreover, some activities do not qualify for any tax exemption, such as management agreements and construction.[759] According to Article 8.3 of the FCIL, application of tax exemptions falls under the supervision of the Ministry of Finance. However, after the promulgation of DNFIL this exemption will be abolished as all taxes issues will be under the Income Tax Law. According to a foreign investor interviewee, tax incentives are one of the major strengths a within the investment legal system and work well for foreign investment.[760]

However, it can be argued that the taxation incentive in Oman represents some challenges which may cause discriminatory treatment; The Tax Authority's view regarding tax holidays discriminates among foreign investors, as the Authority believes that the activities of Integrated Tourism Complexes (ITCs) are not covered by the term "promotion of tourism", which was used in the old tax law. The current Income Tax Law excludes "promotion of tourism" from the tax exemption provisions specified under Article 118.[761] Therefore, foreign investors in ITCs will not benefit from a tax holiday. However, this may be argued that there is no discrimination in this case since all foregn investors in ITCs treated equally.

Another challenge which may cause discrimination among foreign investors is that both "profits" and "gains" are vaguely defined.[762] Therefore, this may lead to inconsistency in application. For example, in most jurisdictions, things such as capital income resulting from the sale of

758 Bossdorf, Engels and Weiler (n 700) 64; US Department of State, 'Diplomacy in Action', 3 <www.state.gov/documents/organization/227428.pdf> accessed 10 March 2015.

759 Swiss Business Hub GCC (n 738).

760 Interview with foreign investor 1 (Muscat, Oman, 17 August 2014)

761 OBFA (n 683) 7.

762 Curtis 'Corporate Tax Matters in Oman' (oman Law Blog, 12 November 2013) <http://omanlawblog curtis.com/2013/11/corporate-tax-matters-in-oman.html> accessed 5 June 2015.

a capital or fixed asset, such as machinery or goodwill, are not regarded as income, profits, or gains for tax purposes.[763] Thus, "the Tax Authority may consider the proceeds received by a company from the sale of any company asset as taxable income".[764] In 2012, the Omani Supreme Court decided that "dividends received from foreign shareholding companies in tax years 2002-2004 were not taxable".[765] However, the situation is changed under the new Income Tax Law. According to Article 115, dividends are only exempted from taxable income for Omani companies.

Examining the guarantees and challenges addressed in this section, do any of these measures have the potential to be considered as discriminatory against foreign companies? The State has the right to apply incentives, as nothing in international law prevents countries from doing so. Nevertheless, the application of such incentives should be in a fair manner as the state may be accused of discriminatory treatment if it grants an incentive to desirable investors but not to others. Problems may arise mainly because of the vague definitions and ambiguity of some terms related to taxes and failure to consider some foreign investment areas such as ITCs with regard to taxes. While Sornarajah argues that if the discrimination is based completely on economic factors, there can be no legal objection to discriminatory treatment, legislation or practices that lead to discriminatory treatment between foreign investors could be challenged on the basis that they may distort international trade.[766]

4.3.2.2 The Real Role of Tax Incentives in Attracting Foreign Investment to Oman

The World Bank Group has argued that the incentives included in FCIL are generous, but it is unclear how effective they are in attracting foreign investment.[767] Sornarajah has made the general point that views are divided on the usefulness of the incentive of tax holidays in attracting foreign investment.[768] Hurtado also notes that there are a number of studies questioning the relation between tax policies and FDI, and argues that multinational companies consider three principal elements when deciding where to invest: advantages of location, ownership, and

763 Curtis (n 762).
764 Ibid.
765 Ibid.
766 Sornarajah (n 8) 103.
767 World Bank Group (n 625) 8.
768 Sornarajah (n 8) 103.

internalization.[769] Recent studies conclude that although the tax issue is not relevant when investors decide whether to invest in their own country, taxes can influence the investor's choice of location of investment abroad.[770] Griffith and Devereux's study on taxation within the European Union concluded that tax rate has an effect on where multinational companies invest.[771]

Nwogugu argues that incentives such as the five-year exemption from tax are less effective at attracting foreign investment because no profits are expected during this period of time.[772] In addition, Hurtado maintains that tax reduction and incentives to attract foreign investment may have negative consequences; there is no evidence, for example, that the benefits countries may gain from increased FDI due to low tax rates exceed the costs resulting from loss of tax revenues. He pointed out that most writers believe that this has not proved to be an effective factor in increasing FDI.[773] According to the World Bank, developing countries that reduce taxes to attract foreign investment may face a costly "race to the bottom",[774] as this tax burden is transferred onto consumption and labour, and there is "a net reduction in total revenue available to invest in social and physical infrastructure".[775] Both consequences would be harmful to the host state.

While up to date there are no specific studies defining the impact of the tax incentives in attracting foreign investment to Oman, Omani tax policy should try to strike a reasonable balance between not discouraging FDI and preventing creating "economic distortion".[776] Therefore, Oman needs to take this into consideration when it grants taxation incentives, calculating whether the foreign investment revenues it will bring in are greater than the money lost by reducing taxation or offering exemptions. Recent studies demonstrate that when combined with other factors viewed as attractive, tax elimination may play an important role in increasing

769 According to Hurtado (n 750) 322 „Ownership advantage refers to products or production processes that other firms do not have access to, such as patents or intangible elements like reputation for quality or brand names" and „internalization advantages derive from the firm's interest in maintaining its knowledge".

770 Hurtado (n 750) 322.

771 Griffith and Devereux cited in Hurtado (n 750) 322.

772 Nwogugu (n 97) 34-35.

773 Hurtado (n 750) 328.

774 World Bank cited in Hurtado (n 750) 328.

775 Hurtado (n 750) 328.

776 Ibid 319.

foreign investment.[777] Therefore, it is likely that tax incentives alone will not attract foreign investment to the Sultanate unless these are combined with other factors.

4.3.2.3 Customs Duties Incentives

A further financial incentive offered to foreign investors under Article 9.1 of FCIL is that they can be exempted for five years from customs duties on plant, machinery and necessary raw materials,[778] although Oman imposes a 5 per cent customs duty on most imported goods.[779] This exemption can also be extended for a further five years. However, according to a US Department of State report, this exemption provided on customs duties on "imports of equipment and raw materials required for production purposes" has been legally challenged by US and foreign competitors.[780] Nevertheless, it is not clear on what ground.

4.3.3 Activities in Which Investors Cannot Invest

FCIL did not exclude specific activities from the scope of investment. However, the MoCI issued a list of 25 commercial activities that foreign investors are not allowed to pursue in Oman. These activities are as follows: photocopying and typing services, translation services, transactions clearance, tailoring of non-Arab menswear, tailoring of Arab and non-Arab ladies' apparel, tailoring of sports clothing, tailoring of military uniforms, motor vehicle electrical repair and recharging of batteries, repairing and cleaning motor vehicle radiators, repairing punctured tyres, wheel balance, replacement of motor vehicle oils, repairing car air- conditioning repairing motor vehicle exhaust pipes, car cleaning and polishing, transport and sale of drinking water, labour provision offices, employment offices, other activities related to labour recruitment and provisions personnel, driving schools, washing of clothing, ironing of clothing, hair trimming and

777 Hurtado (n 750) 325.

778 FCIL art 9.1 states that Foreign Investment projects can be exempted from (paying) custom duties on plant and machinery imported by them for setting up the projects. They can also be exempted from (paying) custom duties on raw material needed in the manufacturing process which are not available in the local markets, for a period of not exceeding 5 years starting from the date of commencing production This exemption can be renewed once.

779 Malik and Singh (n 755).

780 US Department of State (n 758) 8.

cutting for men, hairdressing, facial massage and other beauty treatment for women, hair trimming and cutting for children.[781]

Although Article 5.1 provided that the CFCI shall be responsible to "make recommendations in respect of [t]he identification of the investment fields", the legal basis for excluding such activities is not clear. However, Bolivar argues that the State can legally reserve certain sectors for local investors or for its own development.[782] Nevertheless, it is necessary to consider whether such restrictions have negative effects on attracting foreign investment or whether they are important as means of protecting the national interest of the Sultanate. This consideration should be based on the size of these activities and the potential they have in the Omani market. Since such studies are not available to date it can be argued that this restriction is a way of protecting the Omani national market interest from being dominated and controlled by foreigners because of two reasons. First, these are generally small businesses that would provide opportunities for Omanis who are not highly qualified to establish enterprises. Second, Oman lies close to a number of highly populated countries such as India, Pakistan and Bangladesh, where such small businesses would be attracted, and lifting these restrictions would attract numerous small businesses operating in these areas.

4.3.4 Free zones, Duqm Special Economic Zone and Knowledge Oasis Muscat

Oman established FZs, DSEZ and KOM, a free zone for technology companies, with the aim of attracting foreign investment and achieving Oman's Vision 2020, a national development plan to eliminate dependence on the contribution of the oil sector to the country's GDP.[783] Today, Oman has three FZs: Sohar, Salalah and AlMazunah.[784] To provide a general legal framework for developing FZs, Oman promulgated Royal Decree 56/2002.[785] In addition, Royal Decree 119/2011 established DSEZ Authority, whilst Royal Decree 79/2013 issued the regulations for this SEZ. The DSEZ,

781 A list of the activities prohibited for foreign investors, issued by the MoCI was provided as a written submission by interviewee Policymaker 3 (Muscat, Oman, 19 August 2015).

782 Garcia-Bolivar (n 662) 179.

783 Oxford Business Group, 'Free zones and special economic zone to boost investment', <www.oxfordbusinessgroup.com/analysis/incentivising-growth-free-zones-and-special-economic-zone-boost-investment> accessed 9 June 2015.

784 Ibid.

785 Ibid.

strategically located by the Arabian Sea, is intended to be the key hub and gateway for the region.[786] As for KOM, which opened in 2003, this is under the supervision of the Public Establishment for Industrial Estates (PEIE) and has its own incentives to attract foreign investment but no special law has been issued to organise its work.[787]

It can be argued that the establishment of the FZs, the DSEZ and KOM in the Sultanate, together with their regulations, is a significant step forward in providing a better environment for foreign investment with non-discriminatory measures, since they provide a number of these features. First, both FZs and SEZ allow full foreign ownership (100%) and there are no minimum share capital requirements, as detailed under Article 4 of Royal Decree 56/2002, and under Articles 3/2 and 3/3 of Royal Decree 79/2013. Allowing full foreign ownership is an exception to the Commercial Companies Law (CCL) and FCIL. However, although KOM provides 100% foreign ownership it does specify the minimum capital investment required to establish an entity.[788]

Second, the FZs of Salalah and AlMazunah require a 10% Omanisation rate;[789] for Sohar Free Zone this rises to 15%.[790] It has been argued that even this minimum percentage of Omani staff in foreign companies operating in FZs may still be viewed as a challenge by foreign investors.[791] However, it can be argued to the contrary that these percentages will help to solve the challenge posed by the Omanisation requirement facing foreign investors. This is for two reasons; these percentages are easily achievable as they are relatively low and importantly, they are much lower than the usual rate (15%-100%). In addition, this small percentage is important for the national interest in that while these zones must operate on a significantly different basis, they must not irritate Omani nationals who can get access to them. However, the issue of Omanisation will be examined in the following sections in this chapter.

786 Oxford Business Group (n 783).

787 Oman has nine Industrial Estates and KOM was established through a public-private partnership as the Sultanate's flagship technology park. Knowledge Oasis Muscat, 'About KOM' <www.kom.om/About-KOM> accessed 11 October 2015.

788 Knowledge Oasis Muscat, 'Inceitves and services' <www.kom.om/Incentives-Services/Incentives> accessed 12 October 2015.

789 Oxford Business Group (n 783).

790 Sohar Port and free zone, 'Setting up bubsiness' <www.soharportandfreezone.com/en/setting-up-business/incentives> accessed 13 June 2015.

791 Healy Consultants, 'Oman Free Zones', <www.healyconsultants.com/oman-company-registration/free-zones/> accessed 12 June 2015.

Thirdly, another important incentive is the scope of jurisdiction and powers provided to DSEZ Authority by the Royal Decree 79/2013.[792] For example, under Articles 13, 14, 15, 16 and 17 of the Decree the Authority has the functions of MoCI, the MECA and the MoT in related matters. These significant powers are thought to be important in encouraging the establishment of foreign investment in the DSEZ by smoothing the bureaucratic procedures.

Finally, there are three kinds of financial incentives: tax exemption, free customs duties and unrestricted money transfer. Exemption from taxes and from submitting declarations of income set out in income tax provisions are accorded to the operating party and the working company in the FZs, as detailed in Article 3 of Royal Decree 56/2002 for the issue of FZs. Moreover, a 30-year exemption from taxes is provided in the SEZ under Articles 3/1 and 4 of the Royal Decree 79/2013. However, this article also excludes some sectors from this exemption on condition that they should be registered with the Authority and operate permanently within the borders of the zone. These are: banks, financial institutions, insurance and reinsurance companies, companies working in the field of telecommunications services, and those in the field of road transport, except road transport companies. Such conditions and exceptions seem unnecessary since companies cannot operate in the DSEZ without registration with the Authority and it cannot assure their permanence. The three FZs and the DSEZ are also exempt from customs duties, as detailed in Article 17 of Royal Decree 56/ 2002 and Article 5 of Royal Decree 119/2011. Furthermore, foreign investment in FZs and the DSEZ is exempted from restrictions on money repatriation, as provided by Article 13 of Royal Decree 56/2002, and Article 10 of Royal Decree 79/2013.

792 This includes the jurisdiction of the Secretariat General of the Commercial Registration with relation to implementing the commercial Registration Law for registering projects, the jurisdiction of the Ministry of Tourism in implementing the Tourism Law for issuing licenses for tourism projects, the jurisdiction of the MoCI for implementing the GCC Standard Industrial Regularization for Industrial registration and license granting for industrial projects, the jurisdiction of the Ministry of Manpower for applying the Labour Law, determining fees for expatriate recruitment and Omanisation rates for different projects, the jurisdiction of the Public Authority for Mining for enforcement of the Mining Law, and the jurisdictions of related authorities for implementing laws and regulations regarding environmental protection and food safety. See Sultanate of Oman, *Investment in Duqm, Special Economic Zones Authority* (Awareness and Media Department 2015) 10.

The main challenge with regard to the attraction of foreign investment currently is that this large number of independent entities, (DSEZ, FZs, Industrial Estates and other investment entities) are administered by different authorities and boards and this has produced a lack of coherent strategy for attracting investment.[793] For example, the OBFA found a lack of clarity concerning what the FZs and PEIE offer, and what is available generally if a project is of national importance.[794] It has also been observed that there is a lack of understanding between the MoCI and KOM about certain incentives for foreign investment[795] and that responsibilities for these areas are split among too many Ministries and Ministers.[796] A World Bank Group study concluded that foreign investors believe Oman lacks a clear strategic vision.[797] This will be addressed in further depth in Chapter Six.

FZs also pose some specific challenges, such as that it is obligatory to rent a site in the FZs to be able to invest [798] and that foreign companies must renew their licences annually when submitting their annual financial statements to the FZ authority.[799] In addition, since the FZs are still under construction, they lack many facilities and customer services are poor.[800] As these zones were only established relatively recently, it is hoped that this development problem will be solved over time.

4.3.5 Guarantees of Freedom to Transfer Money

The guarantee of freedom of money transfer from the host state is vital to the creation and enhancement of foreign investors' companies, as without this guarantee the investment would be useless for them.[801] This section examines whether there are restrictions on transferring money into or out of Oman. It also determines whether this is on a non-discriminatory basis and is in accordance with internationally accepted criteria.

793 World Bank Group (n 665) 8.
794 OBFA (n 683) 3.
795 Ibid.
796 World Bank Group (n 665) 8.
797 Ibid.
798 Healy Consultants (n 791).
799 Ibid.
800 Ibid.
801 Nwogugu (n 97) 39-40.

The free economy policy applied in Oman and declared in the Basic Law[802] enables foreign investors to remit abroad, in any convertible foreign currency, foreign capital invested.[803] FCIL ensures protection for the transfer of all payments related to investments. However, it is argued that this existing right under Article 11 of FCIL is addressed inadequately. Nevertheless, Articles 16 and 17 of the DNFIL increase the protection of the right to repatriation of funds to international standards.[804] Compared with the current law, the DNFIL contains more guarantees with regard to reducing financial obstacles. For example, Article 16 of the DNFIL ensures the right of foreign investors and the investment to "convert currency of the Sultanate into a freely convertible currency in order to make payment relating to the investment project".

Despite this difference in the guarantee between FCIL and the DNFIL, the inefficiency mentioned above under FCIL is not clear in practice; rather Oman places no reporting requirements or restrictions on private capital movements into or out of the Sultanate, including money transfer abroad of interest, branch profits, dividends, equity or debt capital, royalties, service and management fees, and personal savings. In addition, there is no plan to change money transfer policies in the Sultanate.[805] A bank account can be opened by anybody holding a residence visa or an investor visa, then funds can be exported or imported.[806] Oman does not require a currency declaration, so currencies can move in or out of the country without restrictions.[807] However, before approving a transaction involving foreign bank transfers, Omani banks require complete documentation of the source of funds.[808] Omani financial institutions, governed by the Central Bank of Oman, constitute a strong and effective supervisory system that is well capitalized.[809]

However, generally, it seems that there are two cases when a host country can apply restrictions on money transfer. First, Dolzer and

802 According to Basic Law of the State, Art 11: „the national economy is based on justice and the principles of free economy".

803 Bossdorf, Engels and Weiler (n 700) 64.

804 World Bank Group (n 625) 7.

805 ICS (n 663).

806 Just Landed, 'Currency: The Omani Riyal and international transfers' <https://www.justlanded.com/english/Oman/Oman-Guide/Money/Currency> accessed 30 June 2015.

807 Ibid.

808 ICS (n 663).

809 Ibid.

Schreuer have argued that in order to protect national policies of the host state is it necessary to monitor large currency transfers into the state and out of it, in order to control its currency and its foreign capital. Sudden short-term capital inflows, especially capital flight, may cause instability in domestic financial markets, as experience has shown.[810] Therefore, in some cases the right to transfer is restricted to specific types of transfers. The main rules ensure the right of free transfer of money resulting from investment, or allowing all transfers "in connection with an investment" or "related to an investment".[811]

Second, according to Sornarajah, the host state commitments to freedom of money transfer cannot be obligatory in a country at times of financial crises.[812] States have the right to exercise their sovereignty by controlling economic sources and property within their territory to ensure the development of their economic, political and other goals.[813] Sornarajah maintains that the rise of different situations of financial crisis makes the provision of absolute rights of repatriation defeasible and calls for the application of the doctrine of clausula rebus sic stantibus. In his opinion, until the difficult situation improves, a host state has the right to apply the general doctrine of necessity and suspend treaty obligations to permit repatriation. He notes that the treaties of some countries, such as the UK, provide that in exceptional economic or financial circumstances the right of repatriation of profits may be restricted.[814] Consequently, although the liberalization of financial markets is beneficial for both host states and foreign investors, during times of economic crisis states may apply restrictions on the right to transfer.[815]

Nevertheless, apart from the eligible restrictions under Oman's international agreements, Omani laws particularly Omani Basic Law, FCIL and the Omani Banking Law issued by Royal Decree 114/2000,[816] did not introduce any restrictions on money transfer, whether in an economic crisis or on the basis of national interest. Article 11 of Omani Basic Law provides that: "Private property is protected. No-one shall be prevented from disposing of his property within the limits of the Law". In addition,

810 Dolzer and Schreuer (n 91) 191.
811 Ibid 193.
812 Sornarajah (n 8) 207.
813 Ibid 364.
814 Ibid 207.
815 Dolzer and Schreuer (n 91) 193.
816 Banking Law 2000, arts 102 and 117.

Article 11 of FCIL states clearly that: "The investors in the investment projects shall be free [...] to transfer abroad the imported capital along with the profits accrued from the project."

4.4 Law Relating to Industrial Regulations

4.4.1 The Regulation of Trade Unions in Oman

The legal basis for the establishment of trade unions in the Sultanate is Article 108 of Royal Decree 74/2006 amending the Labour Law issued by Royal Decree 35/2003. This article allows workers to establish labour unions to defend their rights, protect their interests, represent them in all matters relating to their work affairs and improve their material and social status.[817] This development is important to safeguard workers' economic rights and ensure that a safe working environment is provided for them.[818] In addition, Article 12 of the Basic Law of the State emphasises that the aim of issuing the related laws is to protect workers and employers and manage the relationship between them. For instance, this article prohibits imposition of compulsory work on anyone unless it is specified by law.[819] Nevertheless, the clause "unless it is specified by law" may be controversial as it may weaken the protection under this article. This is because there is no guarantee that domestic regulation will not impose certain compulsory works.

Article 109 of the Labour Law urges trade unions in the Sultanate to establish an organisation to act as their representative in national, regional and international events[820] and the creation of the General Federation of Oman Trade Unions (GFOTU) in the Sultanate was a significant step

817 Labour Law 2003, art 108 states that: "The workers may form from among them labor unions to safeguard their interests, defend their rights and improve their materialist and social status and to represent them in all matters relating to their affairs".

818 Edwin Babeiya, 'Trade Unions and Democratization in Tanzania: End of an Era?'(2011) 4 J Pol & L 123, 123.

819 Basic Law of the State, art 12 states that: „The State enacts Laws for the, protection of the employee and the employer and regulates the relationship between them [...] It is not permissible to impose any compulsory work on anybody except by virtue of Law".

820 Labour Law 2003, art 109 states that: "The different labour unions shall together form the General Federation of the Sultanate of Oman workers, to represent them in local, regional and international meetings and conferences. The labour unions may form labour associations from among them".

toward ensuring greater respect for labour rights.[821] The Labour Law ensures the independence of trade unions and the GFOTU by prohibiting any means of interference in their work, as emphasized by Article 110.[822] More specifically, it prohibits employers from dismissing or punishing workers because of their union activities[823] as stated clearly in Article (110 Bis):

> It shall not be allowed to apply the dismissal penalty or any other penalty on the workers' representatives in the Labour Unions or Labour Associations or the General Federation of the Sultanate of Oman's workers for the activities they practice in their Labour Unions in accordance with this law and the ministerial decisions implementing it.

The International Trade Union Confederation (ITUC) has claimed that the Omani government maintains control over union activities, arguing that the Omani authorities can refuse the constitution of a union on the basis of arbitrary reasons and that compulsory requirements effectively limit their ability to exercise the right to strike. For example, the MoM may refuse to register a trade union if it is not persuaded that the requirements for registration have been met.[824]

While it could be argued that the way of objecting to the establishment of trade unions is clearly defined under Article 8 of Ministerial Decision 570/2012 issued by the Minister of Manpower and this should help to reduce the interference of the authority in the establishment of trade unions, it would be more protective to grant supervision of ministerial decisions to the judiciary. Nevertheless, as part of Oman's commitments under international treaties, new amendments in the Labour Law remove the requirements that union leaders must be able to speak and write Arabic

821 International Trade Union Confederation (ITUC), 'Oman: A New Trade Union Centre is Born' (19 February 2010) <www.ituc-csi.org/oman-a-new-trade-union-centre-is.html?lang=en> accessed 17 June 2015.

822 Labour Law 2003, art 110 states that: "The labour unions, labour associations and the General Federation of the Sultanate of Oman's Workers shall have an independent corporate body as from the date of registration at the Ministry and they shall have the right to freely practice their activity without interference in their affairs or influencing them".

823 ITUC, *Internationally-recognised core labour standards in the Sultanate of Oman* 3 <www.ituc-csi.org/IMG/pdf/TPR_Oman Final.pdf> accessed 18 June 2015.

824 Ibid.

and that unions must inform the MoM at least one month in advance of union meetings.[825]

It can be said that the provisions on establishing trade unions represent progress in improving the protection of workers' rights in Oman, reflected in Omani laws and court practice. For example, the Omani High Court ruled in 2006 that foreign employees could change employers without first receiving the consent of their original sponsor.[826] This is a positive progress, as previously foreign employees had to get the consent of their original Omani employer. However, it is argued that if trade unions are very active within a country, this is likely to impact negatively on foreign investment because of concerns among multinational enterprises that certain union activities may reduce the profitability of their investments.[827] This will be discussed further later.

4.4.2 Guarantees Provided Regarding Bringing Employees to Oman

Permission to bring foreign workers to Oman is important to enable foreign investors to run their business with well-qualified and cheap labour. The Labour Law and its subsequent amendments were reformed in line with market liberalisation and to deal with all aspects of the employee-employer relationship. However, it is believed that employment issues in the Sultanate are a major concern for foreign investors and unless the country can provide clear, well-targeted legislation to create a business-friendly environment, particularly with respect to labour laws, foreign investors will choose to go elsewhere.[828] For example, if the MoM is blocking the process of bringing employees, it will negatively affect foreign investment, no matter how good the other guarantees are.

It can be argued that the Omani government opted to ease the process of bringing employees to the Sultanate, so that foreign investors could benefit from guarantees provided under its legal provisions on the matter. According to Article 18 of the Labour Law, companies or employers wishing to use non-Omani workers must seek permission from the MoM. In addition, before permission is granted, specific conditions must be

825 Ibid.

826 Ibid 5.

827 Roxana Radulescu and Martin Robson, 'Trade Unions, Wage Bargaining Co-ordination and Foreign Direct Investment' October 2006, <https://community.dur.ac.uk/> accessed 16 June 2016.

828 Interview with lawyer 1 (Muscat, Oman, 20 August 2014).

met, namely, that Omanis are not available who can be employed for the required positions or professions, that the employer has achieved the prescribed percentage of Omanisation; and that the specified fee has been paid.[829] The MoM must apply the same standard procedure for both foreign and local investors.

Regulations in the DSEZ offer a better guarantee of the freedom to employ foreign workers. Article 19 of the Royal Decree 79/2013 obliges the MoM to issue the necessary permits for foreign labour within five working days from the date on which the applications were submitted. According to this article, if no decision has been made within this period, the application "shall be deemed as approved".[830] This means that the relevant Omani authorities should not hinder the completion of the process of bringing foreign labourers because of the approval of MoM. Moreover, the DSEZ Authority and the MoM signed a Memorandum of Understanding in 29/06/2015,[831] in order to implement this Article. A policy maker interviewee declared that this provision is now being applied effectively[832] which should help to solve what was a difficulty for foreign investors.

Articles 47 and 48 of the Labour Law grant employers the right to reorganise and restructure their business and the workforce for technical, economic and structural purposes.[833] The Omani High Court held that:

> [A]n employer has the absolute power and authority to reorganise its business, be responsible for the management

829 For further information on transferring employees in line with Omanisation, see Curtis (n 693).

830 Royal Decree 79/2013, art 19 states that:
„A manpower department shall be set up in the Zone by a decision from the Minister of Manpower to issue the necessary permits for the foreign labor, according to procedures that are expeditious and efficient that shall be issued by the Board in coordination with the Ministry of Manpower.
In all cases, the period of issuing these permits shall not exceed five working days from the date which the applications were submitted The lapse of such period without a decision regarding the application shall be deemed as approval and in the case of rejection, the decision must be justified".

831 Times News Service, 'Oman's Ministry of Manpower signs pact to issue expat labour permits in five days' *Times of Oman*, (Muscat, 29 June 2015) <http://timesofoman.com/article/62230/Oman/Government/Omans-Ministry-of-Manpower-signs-pact-to-issue-expatriate-labour-permits> accessed 30 June 2015.

832 Interview with policymaker 4 (Muscat, Oman, 3 August 2014)

833 Curtis (n 693).

> of the same for the realisation of profits therefrom and to assume responsibility for any failure of its business.[834]

Undoubtedly, under the Omani legal system, if employers decide to "restructure" and drop their workforce to cut costs, the rights and responsibilities of both employers and employees including foreign workers, will be dealt with according to their work contracts provisions in the Omani Labour Law. However, no formal criteria have been introduced by the Oman Labour Law to be followed regarding the restructuring and reorganization of a business. Accordingly, if the shareholders of different entities, for example, A and B, decide to restructure their ownership to incorporate a new entity, employees of A and B may be transferred to the new entity. Nevertheless, it is recommended that the employers in entities A and B seek the consent of each employee to be transferred in order to avoid any legal claims and safeguard the employer's future interests. Article 47 of the Labour Law states that:

> With the exception of the cases of liquidation, bankruptcy and the final authorized closure, the contract of work shall remain existing and the successor shall be jointly liable with the previous employer for discharging all the obligations prescribed by law subject to the established priority of the worker's rights.

Therefore, in the case of merger of firms, the employment contract remains in force and both firms share joint responsibility for safeguarding the workers' existing rights.[835]

One challenge that may be faced by foreign investors is the obligation regarding Omani workers. According to Article 48 bis of the Labour Law, Omani employees must be automatically transferred to the new contractor on the same terms and conditions as with the previous contractor, when there is a transfer of an employment contract on a project from one contractor to another, and the work to be carried out remains the same.[836]

---

834 Ibid.

835 Ibid.

836 Labour Law 2011, art 48 bis states that:
„The employer shall employ the same Omani labor that was working in the project reverted to his ownership partially or fully They shall receive the same previous benefits and financial incentives as long as work exists and continues".

Therefore, in this situation, if an employment contract is transferred to a foreign investor, then that company will be obliged to employ Omani workers under the same conditions and terms as the previous contractors, whereas the article does not oblige foreign employees to be transferred in the same manner as Omani employees.

A lawyer interviewee observed that in practice, there are difficulties in transferring workers from one contract to another[837] and these mostly concern foreign employees. Therefore, foreign investors who intend to use expatriate labour should take into consideration two things: the necessary approval from the MoM prior to the transfer, and that this does not negatively affect the Omanisation percentage, either with the previous or the new employer.[838] However, the first is more challenging than the second for foreign investors, as elaborated above. Article 18 of the Labour Law specifies the conditions that must be met in order for labour cards to be issued to employees. These include:

> Omanis are not available for employment for the required positions or professions for which the labour clearance is sought;
>
> The Employer has achieved the prescribed percentage of Omanisation.

Given that there are two conditions, this raises the issue of whether both conditions must be met at the same time by a foreign company in order to obtain labour clearance. While in practice it is not clear how strict the MoM in applying this article,[839] it seems that companies must meet both conditions, which may be difficult for foreign companies in some cases, especially from a business perspective.

Despite the protection afforded, there are three challenges to bringing foreign workers to the Sultanate. The first is the quota of Omanis who must be employed; this point will be examined in detail later. Second, under Article 11 of the Foreigners' Residence Law issued by Royal Decree 61/95, an employment visa will not be issued to any expatriate who has previously worked in Oman but has not completed two years from the date

837 Interview with lawyer 1 (Muscat, Oman, 20 August 2014).

838 Curtis (n 693).

839 Several attempts were made to arrange an interview with the Director of the Legal Department at MoM but this did not prove possible.

of their last departure.[840] This article is controversial and it is believed it may have a negative effect on the Omani labour market because it deprives companies of workers who have acquired much-needed local knowledge, experience and skills. For example, new middle-level and senior level workers need at least six months to obtain a driving licence.[841] The law also affects expatriate workers since it may effectively force them to work with the same employer, even if the working conditions are not good because if they wish to leave a company to work elsewhere, once the employer has released them, they will not be able to return to Oman for two years. In addition, the regulation may reduce company expansion, since the only way of interviewing most overseas labour is by telephone, which means companies cannot know their actual skills and may find themselves forced to fire employees who fail to meet expectations.[842] In contrast, companies are in a better situation to know their prospective employees if they are already working within the country.[843] Therefore, opponents of this policy argue that it impacts negatively on Oman's image with the international business community.[844]

Others argue conversely, that the two-year ban will help to reduce hidden businesses in the Sultanate.[845] In addition, it will help companies to maintain a more stable workforce, since previously workers frequently moved between companies and there was a great deal of poaching. The current legislation means companies wanting experienced workers must now hire them from outside the country. Another view trying to balance between the mentioned views saying that the ban should be based on criminal offences; a professional who has committed no such offences should have full rights to use his experience.[846]

840 Foreigners' Residence Law 1995, art 11 states that: „Foreigners may not be issued a work entry visa if he has previously worked in the Sultanate until two years has lapsed since his last departure The Inspector General may waive this period if it is in the public interest".

841 Times News Service, 'Oman expatriate labour ban: Two-year ban to end poaching of foreign workers' *Times of Oman* (Muscat, 11 May 2014) <http://timesofoman.com/article/34219/Oman/Oman-expatriate-labour-ban-Two-year-ban-to-end-poaching-of-foreign-workers> accessed 22 June 2015.

842 Ibid.

843 Ibid.

844 In 2014 when the *Times of Oman* article was published Oman was ranked 47th in the *Doing Business 2014: Economy Profile* by the World Bank and 77th for ease of starting up a business.

845 Times News Service (n 841).

846 Ibid.

There are two exceptions to the two-year ban: if workers either re-join their previous employer or obtain a no objection certificate from their current employer. In the latter case, the foreign worker is allowed to work in another company even if the initial contract is not completed. However, in this case the challenge which may be faced by the employer who issues a no objection certificate is that this will result in them losing an expatriate visa from the company quota, presumably meaning that they can only replace the departing employee with an Omani. On the contrary, if they refuse to issue the no objection certificate, then the company can hire another expatriate or retain the same employee.[847]

The third challenge relates to decisions prohibiting transfer of foreign workers into certain sectors and jobs. The MoM issued three Ministerial Decisions in one year (550/2013, 617/2013 and 618/2013) that prohibited temporarily bringing foreign labour to Oman in various sectors and jobs. This was viewed as a response to significant increases in foreign labour in the Sultanate and as an attempt to create employment for Omanis.[848] However, these decisions may impact negatively on the foreign investment environment in Oman. Although Ministerial Decisions 550/2013 and 617/2013 do not apply to international companies, they may negatively affect the performance of other foreign investors as they will be unable to bring in foreign workers but Omani labour will be unavailable for certain jobs.[849] Another difficulty caused by these decisions is that they do not exclude well-qualified and skilled workers, only those who are unqualified.[850] Moreover, issuing three decisions in one year is an indication of the quick changes in regulation, which need to be considered carefully to keep the regulations related to foreign investment more stable.

Some foreign investors have raised concerns about the difficulties in obtaining labour clearances from the MoM[851] and it has been said that this practice is intended to make foreign investors recruit from local job seekers.[852] Notably, the MoM has been accused by policymaker, lawyer, and

847 Fahad Al Ghadani, 'Oman expat labour law: No plan to defer two year ban on expatriate return', *Times of Oman* (Muscat, 15 June 2014) <www.timesofoman.com/News/35261/Article-Oman-expat-labour-law-No-plan-to-defer-two-year-ban-on-expatriate-return> accessed 9 March 2015.

848 Ithraa (n 738) 3.

849 Ibid .

850 Ibid.

851 Written submission from interviewee lawyer 1.

852 Diwan of Royal Court (n 722) 4.

foreign investor interviewees of not being conducive to foreign investment, by failing to provide approval for expatriate labour clearances.[853]

However, it can be argued that notwithstanding the mentioned challenges, official statistics show that the Omani market has attracted a large number of foreign workers, which may be evidence of how easy it is to bring in foreign labour. According to the Omani Centre for Statistics and Information (OCSI), on 20 of May 2016 the number of foreigners in the Sultanate was 2,024,460, including 1,763,710 foreign workers until April 2016, although there are only 2,418,931 Omani nationals.[854] This means that foreigners constitute about 45% and foreign workers about 40% of Oman's total population. Therefore, these statistics are real proof of the ease of bringing foreign labour into the country and that it is encouraging foreign investment.

4.4.3 Challenges Posed by the Omanisation Policy

While hiring a specific percentage of Omani citizens in companies may be a challenge for foreign investors, it has become a high priority for the Omani government.[855] Pursuant to Article 11 of the Labour Law and the Ministerial Decision 321/2009 by the MoM, companies working in Oman are subject to "Omanisation" requirements. According to the Decision, the Omani government established targets for Omanisation of the private sector in six fields as follows: information technology, transport, travel and tourism, oil and gas, consultancy offices and contracting. The Omanisation quotas vary from one job to another, between 15- 100%.[856] It is the responsibility of the MoM to specify the percentage of Omanisation needed in each sector of economic activity.[857] The percentages of Omanisation are reorganized from time to time according to national development and economic needs.[858] However, a lawyer interviewee highlighted the challenges faced by foreign investors wishing to obtain

853 This point was made by a number of interviewees including policymaker 1, foreign investors 1 and 3, and lawyers 1 and 2.

854 National Centre for Statistcs & Information <www.ncsi.gov.om> accessed 12 June 2016.

855 US Department of State (n 758) 22.

856 See Ministry of Manpower Ministerial Decision 321/2009.

857 Hanka Jahn, 'Omani Labour Law – Recent Changes and Amendments' (*Lex Arabiae*, January 2012) <http://lexarabiae meyer-reumann.com/issues/2012-2/vol-xvi-january-2012-1st-issue/omani-labour-law-recent-changes-and-amendments/> accessed 9 March 2015.

858 US Department of State (n 758) 23.

labour clearances as a result of the Omanisation policy.[859] One foreign investor also complained that the MoM had rejected his applications for expatriate labour clearances unless he employed Omanis from the MoM's list of job seekers.[860]

The changing rate of the Omanisation requirement is a challenge.[861] However, it can be argued that the problems is not in the changing rate is per se, but the way of changing the rate. This is a real challenge when the change of quotas is quick because there is a need to make it consistent and not conflicting with the stability and consistency of the regulation. For example, due to the Arab Spring protests in 2011, this percentage was increased as the Omani government aims to employ more Omanis every year.[862] In addition, in 2014, the Omanisation quotas in certain occupations were increased by a MoM Ministerial Decision.[863] The affected areas included construction, carpentry, cashiering, metalworking, brick making, debt collection, shop-keeping, and janitorial services.[864] Therefore, it is argued that quotas cause uncertainty among foreign investors, as they are likely to be increased.[865] This has occurred already in Salalah, in the South region of Oman.[866]

Although the MoM has a scheme for rewarding or punishing companies according to whether or not they achieve the Omanisation quota,[867] it is observed that in practice, it is rare for fines to be enforced if the company shows good faith in attempting to achieve the target.[868] However, the most challenging measure that may be taken by the MoM against companies that fail to hire qualified Omanis to meet the Omanisation targets, is

859 Interview with lawyer 1, (Muscat, Oman, 20 August 2014).
860 Diwan of Royal Court (n 722) 1.
861 World Bank Group (n 665) 5.
862 US Department of State (n 758) 22.
863 Ibid.
864 Ibid.
865 World Bank Group (n 665) 12.
866 Ibid.
867 In order to reward companies that achieve the Omanization target, they are provided with a green card, when they deal with the MoM. In addition, if companies agree to hire Omanis worker, the MoM is ready to help then with training Omanis for highly demanding positions. However, the MoM has the authority to impose fines on those who fail to make Omanisation targets. Penalties range from OMR 250 to OMR 500 for each Omani employee short of the target. Penalties double if requirements are not met within a time limit of six months.
868 US Department of State (n 758) 23.

refusal to issue expatriate labour clearances, unless qualified Omanis are not available.[869] According to the Omani High Court, it is fair and acceptable if a company has dismissed an expatriate employee in order to replace him or her with an Omani national.[870] Allowing only one fixed term contract per worker is the approach hold by Omani Courts.[871] The positions to be filled and the industry in question determine the percentage of Omanis to be employed.[872] While the position of the Omani courts may be based on the Labour Law, much consideration is needed to the application of these provisions, especially when the foreign worker is already employed and his or her right should be protected according to the contract with the company.

It is argued that the quota of Omanisation, even with a small percentage of 30%, is still difficult for foreign companies to meet, especially where there is a lack of the qualifications and productivity needed among Omani workers.[873] Therefore, it is claimed that the government policy of Omanisation has hindered investment in Oman and it is a real challenge for foreign investors.[874] A policymaker interviewee suggested that a better approach to Omanisation would be through a one-year holiday from Omanisation,[875] or through a transitional plan. For example, foreign investors should be required to show within a specific number of years that they have recruited Omanis and participated in training them. It is believed that it is difficult to expect foreign investors' companies to achieve the Omanisation rate from the first days. The difficulty is shown by some cases when jobs have been announced for 8 months and the company has received very few applications.[876]

One may argue that the Omanisation policy is an important national security programme, especially as unemployment is one of the main concerns that may cause instability in the country.[877] The actual problem

869 Ibid 22.

870 High Court Principles from High Court Judgements 2007/2008, High Court 113/2007, Labour Circuit, issued in 12 November 2007, 767.

871 US Department of State (n 758) 21.

872 Curtis (n 693).

873 Disadvantages of Oman company registration, <www.healyconsultants.com/oman-company-registration/#disadvantages> accessed12 June 2015

874 Bossdorf, Engels and Weiler (n 700) 85; Diwan of Royal Court (n 722) 1.

875 Interview with policymaker 4 (Muscat, Oman, 30 October 2014).

876 Diwan of Royal Court (n 722) 1.

877 This was clear during the Arab spring demonstrations when the employment issue was one of the main issues of these demonstration.

with attraction of foreign investment might be not with the quota of Omanisation, which varies, but with the availability of qualified and skilled Omani workers. For example, one foreign investor claimed that he was unable to recruit Omanis because half of the Omani candidates did not attend the interviews and the majority of applicants were not suitable for the jobs.[878] According to a survey conducted by the International Labour Organisation (ILO) in 2011, 66% of respondents believed that the current labour legislation is a challenge to enterprise growth. The survey showed that only 13% of respondents felt that the national workforce had the needed skills. In addition, in 2012 a survey by Oman American Business Council reached a similar conclusion, that the quality of the workforce is the biggest challenge in doing business in Oman.[879]

Human resources, including availability of labour with training and technical skills, are important in the investment decision.[880] Therefore, it is argued rightly that Omanisation can only be achieved without discouraging investment if the government takes actions needed to ensure Omanis are well prepared to enter the workforce.[881] It also needs to amend its Omanisation scheme in accordance with best international practice by using work permits, visas and positive incentives to achieve Omanisation targets.[882]

4.4.4 The Challenge of the Minimum Salary for Omanis

The increased cost of Omani labour is another challenge that was raised by some interviewees.[883] According to the Ministerial decision 222/2013, the minimum wage for an Omani worker is OMR 325.[884] This development of obliging companies to apply minimum wages for Omanis is combined with the Omanisation requirement.[885] It is found that the factor of availability of labour supply has a strong effect on the location of foreign direct investment.[886]

878 Diwan of Royal Court (n 722) 1.
879 US Department of State (n 758) 23.
880 Hurtado (n 750) 319.
881 World Bank Group (n 665) 12.
882 Ibid.
883 Interview with lawyer 1 (Muscat, Oman, 20 August 2014) and foreign investor 1 (Muscat, Oman 17 August 2014).
884 This is about $841.75.
885 US Department of State (n 758) 22.
886 Mellahi and Guermat (n 227) 1, 8.

However, the link between low wages and the attraction of foreign investment is controversial. Some argue that the lower the cost of labour, the more attractive the country, whereas, the higher the cost of labour, the weaker the country's ability to attract foreign investment.[887] It is believed that low wage costs in developing countries and high production standards are significant in attracting foreign investors searching for cost efficiency.[888] Therefore, there is a clear link between stronger worker rights and higher labour costs, which are expected to have a negative effect on attracting FDI.[889] Nevertheless, it is argued that there is no evidence that countries with low labour standards have attracted more FDI; instead, the opposite is the case.[890]

It can be argued that, as has been seen with the challenge of Omanisation, the decision to impose a minimum salary is not a problem by itself. However, the combination of three elements, the minimum wage condition, the Omanisation rate requirement, and the lack of well-qualified workers in some sectors, would be a real challenge. This is because foreign companies find themselves obliged to achieve a certain rate of Omani workers, drawn from a specific list, and at the same time are not allowed to pay them less than a specified salary. The challenge for companies caused by this combination of the two requirements may lead foreign investors to seek places with cheaper labour. However, it is argued that the negative effect of the wages increase on FDI is likely to be offset by other positive effects of stronger freedom of association and collective bargaining (FACB) rights to attract FDI to the country.[891]

4.5 Guarantees of Political Stability in Oman

Political stability is mainly an internal issue that plays an important role in attracting foreign investment. If a country lacks political stability, it will significantly decrease the inflow of FDI.[892] Political risk is ranked as the second most important constraint to FDI in developing countries after

887 Ibid; David Kucera, 'Core labour standards and foreign direct investment' (2002) 141 Intl Lab Rev 31, 62.
888 Hurtado (n 750) 319.
889 Kucera (n 887) 62-63.
890 Ibid 63.
891 Kucera (n 887) 62.
892 Mellahi and Guermat (n 227) 1, 8.

the challenge of macroeconomic instability.[893] The World Bank Group's Multilateral Investment Guarantee Fund (MIGA) defines political risks to include "war, revolutions, government seizure of property and actions to restrict the movement of profits or other revenues from within a country".[894] Some of these issues have already been examined earlier in this chapter and this section addresses them from a legal perspective.

Political stability in Oman may become a controversial issue. On the one hand, it can be argued that Oman has a number of strong elements for political stability. It is a member in many international organisations and a signatory of significant number of multilateral and bilateral treaties, as has been discussed earlier. Clearly, this has its effect on Oman's commitments internationally and in the development of its domestic legislation, in addition to the guarantees provided by the agreements themselves, especially the significant number of BITs signed by Oman. In addition, experience shows that Oman has the ability to respond wisely to public needs and internal challenges by amending the related domestic laws. For example, in response to the Arab Spring in 2011, significant changes were made in the government's membership and amendments of laws necessary to maintain stability including the Basic Law.[895]

On the other hand, the handover of power in Oman may become a challenge for attracting foreign investment. It is argued that Oman has an uncertain future.[896] This is because it is the only monarchy in the world that does not have a known successor.[897] It is argued that the death of the Sultan could lead to political instability and cause market uncertainty.[898] To investigate this claim, a number of questions need to be raised; what are the scenarios for transfer of power? What would be the effect of those scenarios on the protection of foreign investment in the Sultanate?

Article 5 of the Basic Law specifies the conditions of eligibility for the succession. A successor must be male, a descendant of Sayyid Turki bin

---

893 Multilateral Investment Guarantee Agency, *World Investment and Political Risk 2013*, 18, Available at <www.miga.org/documents/WIPR13.pdf>accessed 28 June 2015; Yackee, Political Risk and International Investment Law, 479.

894 Kathryn Gordon, 'Investment Guarantees and Political Risk Insurance: Institutions, Incentives and Development' in *OECD Investment Policy Perspectives* (OECD 2008) 92, <www.oecd.org/finance/insurance/44230805.pdf> accessed 29 June 2015.

895 There has been change in number of provisions in the Basic Law, the Law of Judiciary Power and other laws as a response to demonstrations in 2011.

896 Disadvantages of Oman company registration (n 873).

897 Ibid.

898 Ibid.

Said bin Sultan, Muslim, mature, rational and the legitimate son of Omani Muslim parents.[899] Article 6 of the Basic Law states that:

> The Royal Family Council shall, within three days of the throne falling vacant, determine the successor to the throne.
> If the Royal Family Council does not agree on a choice of a Sultan for the Country, the Defence Council together with the Chairman of *Majlis Al Dawla*, the Chairman of *Majlis Al Shura*, and the Chairman of the High Court along with two of his most senior deputies, shall instate the person designated by His Majesty the Sultan in his letter to the Royal Family Council.

According to this article, there are three possible scenarios: first, the Royal Family Council would agree on choosing the individual named in the Sultan's letter, within three days after the Sultan's death. The second scenario is that the Royal Family Council will disagree on choosing the successor nominated by the Sultan in his letter. Therefore, this assumes that the Royal Family Council may agree or not within three days in choosing a successor. The question which may be raised by this article is, who are the members of the Royal Family Council? The membership of the Royal Family Council is not known publicly. Another question is, is it possible for the Royal Family Council to agree on a successor different from the one named in the Sultan's letter? Although the Basic Law does not express it, it seems that in practice it is impossible for the Royal Family Council to agree on a successor not specified in the Sultan's letter, as its role specified by Article 6 is merely to agree or not on the person designated by the Sultan in his letter.

The third scenario, according to this article, is that if the Royal Family Council does not agree in choosing the Sultan, then the Defence Council together with the Chairmen of State Council and Alshura Council and the Chairman of the High Court along with two of his most senior deputies shall appoint the one chosen by the Sultan in his letter to the Royal Family Council. It is clear that this scenario is a fallback position to avoid any

899 Basic Law, art 5 states that: "The system of governance is Sultani, hereditary in the male descendants of Sayyid Turki bin Said bin Sultan, provided that whomever is to be chosen from amongst them as successor shall be a Muslim, mature, rational and the legitimate son of Omani Muslim parents".

disagreement or clashes on the successor. It is obvious that this article assumes that the Sultan has written a letter, naming the designated person.

It can be argued that there are two challenges for foreign investors with all of these three scenarios. The Sultan possesses exclusive power according to the Omani Basic Law, but because of the mechanism specified under Article 6, the successor and his approach toward foreign investment will not be known to foreign investors until the death of the Sultan. Another challenge is that the country may be left for about three days without knowing who is to be Sultan, which may become a challenging situation for foreign investment. It is important for the stability of the country and better attraction of foreign investment that the successor be known in advance and before the death of the Sultan.

Nevertheless, it is clear that the Basic Law through the handover of power has established a new approach compared with what is generally applied in the region. It is clear that the successor is already named in the Sultan's letter and his succession will be ratified either by the Royal Family Council or by the other bodies. In addition, Article 8 makes it clear that the Government should perform its functions as usual until the power is shifted to the new successor.[900] Importantly, it is obliged to adhere to the international and regional charters and treaties by Article 10 of the Basic Law.

4.6 Conclusion

While the guarantee against expropriation under Omani Basic Law is relatively better than the FCIL, both laws provide weak protection, mostly because of the absence of the right of referring to international tribunal. However, the DNFIL is expected to address this challenge, as it contains such a right. Compensation for expropriation seems not a challenge in Oman, as long as foreign investor is able to prove the expropriation.

It is clear that the prohibition of landed property for foreign investors out of ITCs except for GCC citizens and the limited ITCs areas affected negatively the attraction of foreign investment to Oman. It is argued that Oman's obligations under the TRIPs Agreement (WTO) are applied consistently in all Oman's national intellectual property rights laws.

900 Basic Law, art 8 states that: „The Government shall continue to perform its functions as usual until the Sultan is chosen and exercises his authority".

However, the exceptions accorded to the WTO's Member States need to be balanced carefully between safeguarding the Omani national interests and at the same time protecting the core intellectual property rights of the owner in order to attract foreign investment.

It is further argued that to provide better intellectual property rights for foreign investors, Oman needs to do three things, first, to allow intellectual property owners to appeal against the administrative decisions before the national courts. Second, to improve the enforcement mechanism for protecting intellectual property rights, benefiting from the experience of some countries. For example, Singapore has strengthened the enforcement of intellectual property rights by establishing a specialised crime division devoted to the investigation and suppression of intellectual property rights violation in Singapore within its Police Force, known as the Intellectual Property Rights Branch.[901] Third, to eliminate the vagueness in some areas, such as has been analysed with the word "similar".

While money transfer by foreign investors is guaranteed by Omani laws, there is a lack of clarity as to the legal basis in national laws for any restrictions which may be applied by Oman in cases of transferring large amount of money or in a national financial crisis. It is argued that to balance between protecting foreign investment and national interests it is important to facilitate entry for skilled and qualified foreign workers.

Three further shortcomings to foreign investment caused by Omani regulations have been examined this including, the Consumer Law and policy, the Omanisation scheme and the minimum wage condition. It is believed strongly that certain amendments may help to establish a balanced approach in the Consumer Law provisions, between protecting consumers' rights and fully applying the policy of free market economy to eliminate unnecessary measures against companies. In addition, it is believed that to address the challenges of the Omanisation scheme and the minimum wage condition, it is important to look at the issues in a broader way by linking them with other factors such as the lack of well-qualified workers rather than dealing with each issue separately. Furthermore, although ignorance as to the successor may worry foreign investors, it is clear that the successor is already named in the Sultan's letter and his succession will be ratified either by the Family Council or by the other bodies.

---

901 World Economic Forum, *Global Competitiveness Report 2009-2010* <http://ww3.weforum.org/docs/WEF_GlobalCompetitivenessReport_2009-10.pdf> accessed June 26 2014.

With regard to the guarantee of non-discrimination, the World Bank Group recommended that a possible solution for the requirements relating to national ownership specified by Article 2 of the FCIL, would be to eliminate or reduce the local ownership requirement, as is already the case for GCC and US nationals who have 100% ownership rights.[902] In addition, Omani national ownership could be maintained through a short negative list for certain sensitive sectors.[903]

It is recommended as well that the issue of incentives in the Sultanate needs to be tackled in two ways. The short-term priority is to conduct an inventory of Oman's investment incentives, identify which kinds of incentives are effective and refocus on these to achieve the country's goals. The medium-term priority involves incentive reform.[904] This can be achieved through consultation and coordination among many governmental bodies, including the MoCI, Ministry of Finance and its Directorate for Taxation, the Ministry of Tourism (MoT), the Ministry of Foreign Affairs, and the Council of Ministers.[905] This will be analysed further in Chapter Six. Nevertheless, there is no doubt that the establishment of FZs and the DSEZ in the Sultanate, with their regulations, is a significant step forward to providing the protection and guarantees needed to foreign investment.

Overall, the evaluation in this chapter suggests that the NDFIL will go a long way towards remedying existing weaknesses in Oman's treatment of foreign investors, bringing it into line with the best international standards. Even this, however, is not sufficient in itself; much will depend on the quality, consistency and effectiveness of the new law's implementation and enforcement. Moreover, under any FDI rules, it is possible that disputes will arise from time to time. In the next chapter, therefore, the appropriateness and effectiveness of Oman's dispute settlement system for issues related to foreign investment will be analysed.

902 World Bank Group (n 665) 6, 11.
903 Ibid 11.
904 Ibid 9, 10.
905 Ibid.

Chapter 5: Guarantees and Weaknesses in the Omani Dispute Settlement Mechanism with regard to Foreign Investment Disputes

5.1 Introduction

This chapter evaluates the extent to which the judiciary and arbitration in Oman provide appropriate vehicles for settling investment disputes by analysing the challenges and guarantees available in both these mechanisms in Oman. The host state needs an effective national dispute settlement mechanism since this serves as the means by which its obligations under BITs and international conventions and treaties are enforced.

With regard to litigation, investment related disputes within Oman are resolved through Oman's Administrative Court, and through the commercial and labour circuits of the Omani courts. These courts have jurisdiction over the decisions made by the Omani authorities, and commercial, tax and labour cases. This chapter begins, therefore, by examining the Omani litigation system covering foreign investment. It will analyse the reform of the Omani judiciary, the basis for its independence, Omani court practice, and the levels of confidence in the Omani national court system.With regard to arbitration, Oman has modernised its laws by adopting the UNCITRAL Model Law of Arbitration.[906] As mentioned earlier, Article 14 of FCIL allows for referral of any dispute between foreign investors and third parties to a national or international tribunal, by mutual agreement. Arbitration is also recognised as a way to settle investment disputes in all Oman's BITs[907] and the Oman-USA FTA.[908]

906 M I M Aboul-Enein, 'The development of international commercial arbitration laws in the Arab World' (1999) Arbitration 1, 3.

907 For example, according to Oman-Germany BIT 2007, art 10/2 (b) if a dispute arises between a foreign investor and a state and it cannot be settled within a period of three months, international arbitration may be sought alternatively or consecutively when requested by the investor. Oman-Sweden BIT 1995, art 8/2 refers the dispute between a signatory state and a citizen of the other signatory state to ICSID.

908 Oman-USA FTA 2009, art 10 15 states that: "1 In the event that a disputing party considers that an investment dispute cannot be settled by consultation and negotiation: (a) the claimant, on its own behalf, may submit to arbitration under

Oman's legal framework, including the Arbitration Law and related laws, provides for the enforcement of arbitral awards in the Sultanate. In addition, it is a party to the UN New York Convention and the ICSID.

The second part of the chapter will focus on whether the Arbitration Law and mechanism in Oman provide an appropriate environment for the resolution of disputes concerning foreign investment.

Therefore, it will analyse the following issues: the extent to which arbitration is supported by the Omani courts, how arbitral awards are enforced in Oman, and finally, whether the public policy element of arbitration adopted by Omani courts is in accordance with international standards, in other words, is it in broad or narrow interpretation.

5.2 The Omani Litigation System regarding Foreign Investment

5.2.1 The Reform of the Omani Judiciary

In order to provide a reliable legal environment for foreign investment, the reform of the judiciary since 1970 in the Sultanate has attempted to strike a balance between modernizing the system whilst at the same time recognising the cultural heritage of Omani society. Oman is different from other countries in the region, in that the Sultan is the head of a hierarchy that relies "upon Shari'a of the *Ibadhi* School"[909] and this Islamic school of law was traditionally reflected in Oman's legal system.[910]

Legal reforms in Oman went through three main developments. The first, beginning in 1970, involved establishing three judicial bodies; the Shari'a Courts, the Committee for the Settlement of Commercial Disputes (CSCD), and the criminal courts. The Shari'a Courts, which are under the

this Section a claim".

909 *Ibadhi* is a "distinct school of thought of Islam, neither Sunni nor Shi'ite, that emerged in the early Islamic period and remains today in small pockets of Africa and is dominant in Oman". See Islam in Oman <www.islam-in-oman.com> accessed 26 Mai 2016; W M Ballantyne, 'The states of the GCC: Sources of law, the Shari'a and the extent to which it applies' in W M Ballantyne, *Essays and addresses on Arab law* (reprint, Routledge 2000) 58.

910 *Ibadhi* is the dominating community crowned by the Royal family with a Sunni community and shi'a minority, See Hirst (n 235) 8; Carnegie Endowment/FRIDE, *Arab Political Systems: Baseline Information and Reforms: Oman* (2008) <www.carnegieendowment.org/arabpoliticalsystems> 6.

supervision of the Ministry of Justice (MoJ), dealt with civil and family cases, and handled the majority of judicial activity in Oman.[911] The CSCD was established in 1974 by Royal Decree 4 /1974 to deal with commercial disputes. It was replaced in 1981 by the Authority for the Settlement of Commercial Disputes (ASCD), a judicial body with a separate legal personality, and a greater degree of administrative independence from the MoCI. In 1984, a countrywide system of criminal courts was established, with a special administration for criminal justice.[912]

Secondly, in late 1999 a fundamental reform of Oman's judicial system was carried out by four Royal Decrees.[913] This was a significant legislative event that was a crucial step in establishing a unified and comprehensive legal system in Oman.[914] These brought the responsibility for all the courts under the umbrella of the MoJ, in order to harmonise the courts and determine their jurisdiction and hierarchy.[915] These regulations were issued after the promulgation of the Basic Law 1996 in order to codify all laws in line with its provisions.[916] Royal Decree 90/1999 issued the Judicial Authority Law and this sets out the different levels of courts in Oman as follows: (1) The High Court; (2) The Appellate Courts; (3) The Primary Courts.

In addition, Royal Decree 91/1999 established the Administrative Court and issued its law. This Court plays an important role as an independent judicial body with the exclusive power to review decisions issued by government bodies. These include issues relating to foreign investors' rights in cases of violation of laws or regulations together with misapplication, misinterpretation or misuse of Omani authority.[917] However, according to Article 7 of the Administrative Court Law the Court does not have jurisdiction over Royal Decrees or Orders, and sovereign matters. The latter expression, "sovereign matters", is vague and has the potential to cause difficulties in relation to the court's jurisdiction in certain areas, is due to the absence of a definite definition. The concerns

911 Hirst (n 235) 8.

912 Ibid 11.

913 A A Khan and C S Laubach, 'Oman: Further development of Oman›s legal system' (2000) 15 Arab LQ 112, 112.

914 The judiciary power <www.caaj.gov.om/word_sultaneng aspx accessed 19 November 2015.

915 Khan and Laubach (n 913) 112.

916 Carnegie Endowment/FRIDE (n 910) 6.

917 Khan and Laubach (n 913) 113.

is the risk to foreign investors from broad interpretation of "sovereign matters".

Royal Decree 92/1999 established the Public Prosecution Authority as an independent body and issued its law whilst Royal Decree 93/1999 formulated the High Judicial Council. Its aims are to set up the general policy of the judiciary and to ensure its independence and continued development.[918]

It is believed that these four Royal Decrees ensure both a high degree of consistency in applying and interpreting the law, and a commitment to attaining and maintaining the independence of the judiciary.[919] Therefore, their enactment was seen as an encouraging development for foreign investors because they represent a progressive approach toward the development and maintenance of a reliable and modern legal system.[920] Moreover, under the new court system established in 2001,[921] the jurisdiction of *Shari'a* courts has been restricted to family matters only, rather than dealing also with civil cases as occurred previously.

The final phase of the reforms consisted of amendments in 2011 and 2012 in the Basic Law and the Judiciary Power Law, to ensure greater independence of the judiciary. Royal Decree 25/2011 determined complete independence for the Public Prosecution, which is a part of the judicial authority in the Sultanate.[922] One of the most important reforms took place as a result of Royal Decree 10/2012, as this separated the judiciary from the executive power by reconstituting the High Judicial Council and excluding any role for the Minister of Justice, who was replaced by the Chief Justice.[923] The aim is to enable the different powers to function independently of each other and with maximum efficiency.[924] This will be analysed in the following section.

5.2.2 The Basis for Independence of Omani Judiciary

Two conditions need to be met to ensure that national courts are suitable for dealing with foreign investment disputes. The first is that the national legal system of the country concerned should be "up to international

918 Khan and Laubach (n 913) 113.
919 Ibid.
920 Ibid 113-114.
921 Carnegie Endowment/FRIDE (n 910) 6.
922 Bader Al Kiyumi, 'Report' *Oman Daily Observer* (Muscat, 7 May 2012).
923 See Sunil K Vaidya, 'Oman makes judiciary independent of executive Council reconstituted to eliminate interference', *Gulf News* (Dubai, 2 March 2012).
924 See Oman News Agency <http://omannews.gov.om> accessed 26 May 2016.

standards". The second is that the judicial system in the country should be fully independent, not only in the regulations but also in practice as well.[925] The legal system in Oman has been analysed in the previous chapter but here it is important to establish the extent to which Oman's judges are independent and have the authority to make, review and correct administrative decisions, particularly with regard to the violation of foreign investors' rights.

The fact is that the independence of the judiciary in Oman is a debatable issue. It can be argued that the elements necessary for the independence of the judiciary system in Oman can be found in a series of provisions and features. Regulations regarding the independence of judicial authority are set out clearly under Omani laws. In addition to acknowledging the rule of law in Oman, Article 59 of the Basic Law states that "The dignity, integrity and impartiality of the judges are the guarantee for the preservation of rights and freedoms" in the State.[926] Article 60 emphasises that the judiciary in Oman is independent.

Further important provisions highlighting the independence of the judiciary are to be found in Article 61 of the Basic Law, including "Judges are subject only to the Law", and "No party can interfere in law suits or matters of justice; such interference shall be considered a crime punishable by law". This wording makes it clear that interference by anyone in the judicial process is a crime and the affected party has the right to take action against any party that interferes in this process. This article is a real guarantee that the judiciary will not be subjected to interference. Nevertheless, it may be difficult to invoke this article, as it may be difficult to prove interference in the judicial process.

To ensure the transparency of the courts' process, Article 63 of the Basic Law provides that Court sessions are open to the general public, the only exceptions being "in the interest of public order or morals". Even in these cases, "the pronouncement of judgment must be in open session". Another strength of the judiciary in Oman is that if public officials reject the courts' judgements or impede its enforcement, this is considered a crime punishable by law and the party affected has the right to file a criminal case under Article 71 of the Basic Law. This strengthens the enforcement mechanism and the rule of law in the country.

925 Subedi (n 7) 267.

926 Basic Law, art 59 states that: "The supremacy of the Law shall be the basis of governance in the State".

However, it is argued that although in principle the independence of the judiciary in Oman is guaranteed by the Basic Law and the dismantling of the State Security Court in 2010, the executive branch still strongly influences the judiciary.[927] Subedi notes that fear of executive influence and intervention in court proceedings, or a kind of loyalty to the state, may mean that in many countries an independent judiciary cannot be taken for granted.[928] It has been suggested that the Omani national courts may discriminate against foreign investors.[929] Moreover, Newton Martin maintains that although laws in Oman are intrinsic in nature and applied effectively, there is a yawning chasm in the interpretation of these laws.[930] On 26 July 2016 *Azamn*, an Omani newspaper in the front page reported the interference of highly influential people in a inheritance case.[931] However, the newspaper did not provide any evidence to support its claim.

In addition, according to BTI, one of Oman's key weaknesses is its lack of a system of checks and balances; since the Sultan is the head of the Legislature, the Executive and the Judiciary, there is no separation of powers.[932] Indeed, this principle is not declared in the Basic Law, except with regard to the independence of the judiciary.[933] According to Article 42 of the Basic Law, among the functions discharged by the Sultan is "appointing senior judges and and relieving them of their posts" and he is the head of the Supreme Judicial Council. Nevertheless, the membership of the Judiciary Council was amended by Royal Decree 9/2012 and the Minister of Justice and the Inspector General of Police and Customs were replaced, reducing the credibility of allegations of influence upon judiciary

927 Carnegie Endowment /FRIDE (n 910) 6; BTI Project, *BTI 2014 Oman Country Report*, 9 <www.bti-project.org/reports/country-reports/mena/omn/index nc#chap3> accessed 24 November 2015.

928 Dolzer and Schreuer (n 91) 214.

929 Disadvantages of Oman company registration (n 873).

930 Henrietta Newton Martin, 'What Oman's legal system needs today', 29 June 2014 <https://www.linkedin.com/pulse/20140629144025-66699887-what-oman-legal-system-needs-today> accessed 24 November 2015.

931 *Azamn* Newspaper Thursday 26 July 2016, available at <www.azamn.com> accessed 05 August 2016.

932 BTI Project (n 927) 9.

933 In contrast, Singapore establishes its checks and balances within the Government; there are several layers of checks, including the Auditor-General's Office. In addition, its Constitution is based on the separation of the three powers, obliging each of these to act within their own sphere of constitutional power. See K Shanmugam, 'The rule of law in Singapore' (2012) Sing J Legal Stud 357, 360 and Chan Sek Keong, 'The courts and the ‚rule of law' in Singapore, a lecture delivered at the rule of law symposium' (2012) Sing J Legal Stud 209, 216.

power. Such accusations are not supported by clear evidence, except that the Sultan is the head of the Council and at the same time, he is the prime minister.[934]

Overall, although there has been significant progress in the independence of the Omani judiciary there are some areas that need to be addressed, such as having a strong and effective system of checks and balances and clear separation between powers. Subedi argues that currently the role and the aim of international law should be to encourage countries to improve their own national legal systems so that these are in accordance with international legal standards.[935] This will prevent a country being subject to international investment tribunals functioning under an "unpredictable set of rules and awarding excessive amounts of compensation to foreign investors for alleged breaches of the rules of foreign investment."[936]

5.2.3 The Practice of the Omani Courts

A clear and comprehensive view of the Omani judiciary can be gained by exploring the practice of the Omani courts. It is vital to examine the extent to which Oman's judges will exercise review and correct the government's administrative decisions. Traditional international law requires foreign investors to seek legal remedies offered by the host state's domestic courts, before an international claim can be taken to international proceedings, except when there is a prior agreement to make use of investor-state arbitration. According to Article 26 of the ICSID Convention, a state may "require the exhaustion of local administrative or judicial remedies as a condition of its consent to arbitration" but that option is "hardly ever used".[937] It is argued that the function of the principle of sovereign immunity is to reduce the possibility of actions being taken against the host state before national courts.[938] Foreign investors should be allowed to access the judiciary system and benefit freely from national courts in order to seek the available remedies.[939]

It can be said that the practice shows that generally the Omani courts can be a reliable tool in protecting foreign investment, as evidenced by a

934 According to the Basic Law, art 42 the Sultan discharges the function of presiding the Council of Ministers.
935 Subedi (n 7) 267.
936 Ibid 267-268.
937 Dolzer and Schreuer (n 91) 215.
938 Nwogugu (n 85) 61.
939 Ibid 62.

number of cases of this kind that they have dealt with. *Case No. 301/2013* issued by the Omani Administrative Court of Appeal [940] provides a significant example in which foreign investment rights were protected, highlighting Oman's commitment to enforcing the need for a clear and consistent rule of law. The MoCI had refused to grant clearance for a foreign investor to establish market and bakery activity on the basis that this kind of commercial activity requires premises to be not less than 1000m2. The foreign investor argued that he had received a previous clearance for the same commercial activities in another area of Oman in premises smaller than 1000m2. The court voided the MoCI's decision, ruling that the legal regulations and provisions lacked clear rules which covered foreign investors' activities in such cases in this sector.[941]

Case No. 164/2005 addressed the residential rights of a foreign investor in Oman after the immigration authority at the Omani Royal Police refused to renew the foreign investor's residential visa on the basis of security concerns. The court voided the decision on the grounds that Royal Police were unable to substantiate their claim. The court justified its ruling on the basis that a foreign investor and his investment in the Sultanate should be protected. The court added that such refusals must be supported by true evidence and the courts should review and have oversight of the authority's decision. This must follow the due process of law and be based on reasons that are undoubtedly serious and critical to national security.[942]

In addition, the previously discussed case of *Alqudra Holding Company* shows that a foreign investor can challenge an Omani government body before Omani courts and protect his or her trademarks right.[943] Furthermore, two judges interviewed observed that regardless of the conclusion of the High Court in the case of the Blue City,[944] the verdict of the Muscat Court of First Instance was in favour of the foreign investors against the Omani government, which demonstrates the efficiency and fairness of the Omani courts.[945] Moreover, in *Al-Tamimi* the Tribunal referred to Omani national courts in dealing with criminal aspects of Mr

940 *Case 301/2013* Administrative Court (Appeal Circuit - Muscat) Judgment, 30 April 2013 Oman.

941 Ibid.

942 *Case 164/2005* Administrative Court (Primary Court First Circuit) Judgment, 27 December 2005 Oman.

943 *Alqudra Holding Company* (n 712).

944 A well known foreign investment case in Oman in 2010, in which the planned investment was $15 billion.

945 Interview with judges 1 and 2 (Muscat, Oman 17 August 2014).

Al-Tamimi's case before Omani courts stating that: "Ibri Court of Appeal of 6 June 2010, [...] acquitted Mr Al-Tamimi of the two misdemeanour criminal charges on which he had previously been convicted by the Mahda Court of First Instance".[946] All these cases are evidence that with regard to foreign investors' rights, the Omani judiciary have oversight of the government's actions and will check actions that they consider to be unjustifiable in legal terms.[947]

However, two foreign investors interviewees raised two challenges in the practice of the Omani courts; the first, challenge is that if there is any case against foreign investor, the court will freeze everything belonging to the foreign investors.[948] It is clear that what is meant here is in the stage of enforcement of courts' verdicts. According to Article 361 of the Omani Civil and Commercial Procedural Law "execution shall be affected on the judgment debtor's properties by attaching the said properties with third parties and under his possession and sell the same by auction within the portion that settles his subject dept". Actually, there is a need to clarify two issues with regard to this Article, aiming for a quick and effective enforcement of courts' verdicts. First, it is a general article addressing all cases of judgment execution, regardless who is ruled against. Second, with regard to foreign investors, this article is a two-edged sword. It can be a challenge to foreign investors when the judgment is against them. However, it can benefit them if the judgement is in their favour, since the court will use these means of enforcement and consequently they can achieve their right easily.

Another challenge in Omani courts' practice, pointed out by another foreign investor interviewee, is the large number of cases which judges see in a day, about 60 cases.[949] This is a real challenge in the Omani practice, due to the limited number of judges compared with the increased number of cases.[950] No doubt this will negatively affect the quality of judges' work.

946 *Al-Tamimi* (n 11) para 355.

947 Another example of the supportive approach taken by Omani courts is that if a company suffers heavy losses, on certain occasions they have judged it justified for workers to be laid off US Department of State (n 758) 21.

948 Interview with foreign investor 1 (Muscat, Oman, 17 August 2014).

949 Interview with foreign investor 3 (Muscat, Oman, 24 August 2014).

950 According to the latest statistics to the end of 2015 the total number of judges in Oman are only 317, see <www.omanlegal.org/law/> accessed 05 August 2016. In addition, the author himself has faced these difficulties as a judge in the Omani Courts.

However, Oman has realised this challenge and it is on its way to solving it as the number of judges increases every year.

Nevertheless, there is evidence that in certain cases the outcome may not be favourable for foreign investment. An example is *Case No. 510/14* before the Administrative Court of Appeal, which concerned ownership of property by a foreign investor who had established a company with an Omani partner. In 1987 the company rented a plot of industrial land of 9640m2 from the Omani Government. In 1998 the Omani partner sold his shareholding in the company to another Omani citizen. The company then applied to the MoH for ownership of the land in the name of the new Omani partner. In 2008 the Omani government issued the title deeds to the Omani partner following a special Royal Order agreeing to grant this request made in his application. After the issue of Royal Decree 96/2010, which allowed companies to own land, the company applied to transfer ownership of the land to its name, asking the court to issue an order to prevent the Omani partner from free use of the land. The court refused the company's application on the basis that the Royal Order that had granted ownership of the land specified free ownership for the Omani citizen.[951] Regardless of whether the court reached the right conclusion or not, the challenge in this case is that this judgement would put the foreign investor in a difficult situation if the owner of the land decided to sell the disputed land. However, a foreign investor still has the right to take action for compensation if any action by the Omani partner causes damage to the foreign investment.

In certain cases, tribunals have required evidence that an effort has been made to obtain reparation through domestic courts, not as a matter of jurisdiction of admissibility but as part of the evidence that the relevant standard of international law had been breached.[952] In the *Waste Management v Mexico* case the tribunal stated that: "in this context the notion of exhaustion of local remedies is incorporated into the substantive standard and is not only a procedural prerequisite to an international claim".[953] In a similar manner, the tribunal in *Generation Ukraine v Ukraine* noted:

951 *Case 510/2014* Administrative Court (Appeal Circuit- Muscat) Judgment, 29 April 2014 Oman.

952 Dolzer and Schreuer (n 91) 215.

953 *Waste Management v United Mexico States* (Final Award) (Dismissing on Jurisdiction) 2 June 2000 (ICSID Additional Facility Case No ARB(AF)/00/3), para 97.

> [T]he failure to seek redress from national authorities disqualifies the international claim, not because there is a requirement of exhaustion of local remedies but because the very reality of conduct tantamount to expropriation is doubtful in the absence of a reasonable –not necessarily exhaustive– effort by the investor to obtain correction.[954]

5.2.4 Confidence in the Omani National Court System

The extent of confidence in the Omani national court system is important, because the host state's courts usually have to settle an investment dispute between a state and a foreign investor in the absence of an agreement to the contrary.[955] For example, Article 10/2 (a) of the Oman-Germany BIT provides that in a case of dispute between a foreign investor and a state, if the dispute cannot be settled within a period of three months and upon a request of the investor, the dispute may be referred alternatively or consecutively to a competent court in the state where the investment is made.[956] However, seeking domestic courts in the first place to settle investment disputes would raise issues such as the, legitimacy, transparency, and accountability of the system.[957]

The OBFA has highlighted a number of difficulties faced by foreign investors using the Omani judicial system, including significant delays and uncertainty about the implementation of the law by judges on issues such as employment and construction. Consequently, foreign investors lack confidence in the Omani court system and prefer their investment contracts to be governed by foreign law, settling disputes outside Oman.[958] In addition, one foreign investor interviewee pointed out that there is always a worry among foreign investors, about the process in Omani courts and on the dispute resolution process generally.[959]

Indeed, some believe that the judiciary in Oman more accurately act "only as the interpreters of law, aiding and delivering verdicts of what they perceive as justice".[960] Regardless of the usual suspicions and fears

954 *Generation Ukraine, Inc v Ukraine* (Award) 16 September 2003 (ICSID Case No ARB(AF)/00/9) paras 20, 30; *EnCana v Ecuador*, (Award) 3 February 2006 LCIA Case No UN3481, UNCITRAL, para 194.
955 Dolzer and Schreuer (n 91) 214.
956 Germany-Oman BIT 2007, art 10/2 (a).
957 Subedi (n 7) 267.
958 OBFA (n 683) 6.
959 Interview with foreign investor 3 (Muscat, Oman 24 August 2014).
960 Martin (n 930).

of foreign investors, it can be said that the cases examined in the previous subsection show that the Omani court system has displayed its strengths and can prove its ability to be trusted, but its weaknesses still need to be addressed. This will be tackled in Chapter Six.

To put the challenge of the confedence on Omani courts in a fair scale, it must be admitted that such concerns are not unique to Oman. International experience shows that, for a variety of reasons, foreign investors fear a lack of fairness in the courts of the host state. In addition, domestic courts may be obliged to apply national law even in cases where it conflicts with the international legal rules protecting foreign investor rights and some countries may not be signatories to the relevant treaties.[961]

Subedi maintains that countries with democratic systems and an independent judiciary are more likely to want their investment disputes to be adjudicated by their own courts and notes that this preference is reflected in the fact, for example, that the USA-Australia FTA does not contain a separate international dispute settlement mechanism. In contrast, most BITs between developing and developed countries contain provision for settlement of investment disputes by international tribunals, suggesting a lack of confidence in the judiciary systems of developing countries.[962]

Although Oman's policy of using Omani nationals as judges may be understandable, as OFBA's report highlighted, there is a need for better training before they are promoted to higher courts.[963] Interviews for this study conducted with two judges and a high level policymaker, suggested that with regard to foreign investment cases in Oman, the lack of training poses a significant challenge to the judiciary.[964]

In order to address this challenge in the Omani judiciary, there are two recommendations. The first is that it is important to establish special divisions in Omani courts dealing with foreign investment cases, in order to improve specialist judicial expertise. Two interviewees, both Omani judges, suggested that it would be helpful to have a special department in courts for foreign investment cases, similar to those established for financial crimes.[965] Subedi recommends that in order to achieve the confidence of foreign investors and ensure swift dispensation of

961 Dolzer and Schreuer (n 91) 214.
962 Subedi (n 7) 267.
963 OBFA (n 683) 6.
964 Interview with judges 1 and 2 (Muscat, Oman, 17 August 2014); Interview with a policymaker 1, minister (Muscat, Oman, 18 August 2014).
965 Interview with judges 1 and 2 (17 August 2014).

justice, countries should establish separate foreign investment courts or chambers within the Supreme Court, with a speedy mechanism for the settlement of investment disputes.[966] The second recommendation is that rulings made by Omani courts on foreign investment cases need to be published more quickly.[967] This is important to enable close measuring and evaluation of how Omani courts are dealing with foreign investment cases. However, as mentioned above, Chapter Six will discuss further related recommendations for the Omani Judiciary.

5.3 Arbitration of Foreign Investment Disputes in Oman

5.3.1 Support for Arbitration in Omani Courts

The support needed for arbitration by the Omani national judiciary system is significant in providing a healthy environment for arbitration of foreign investment disputes. Irrespective of the nature of the disputing parties and whether public or private law is applied to the contract, both Article 1 of the Arbitration Law issued by Royal Decree 47/97 and Article 14 of FCIL emphasize that arbitration clauses in any contract are valid.[968]

In addition, due to the sensitivity of international trade issues, more experienced judges are needed in such cases; therefore, Article 9 of the Arbitration Law differentiates between whether the arbitration concerns international commercial cases or not. The law makes the Court of Appeal competent in the former case and the commercial circuit of the Primary court in the latter. Importantly, another aspect supportive of foreign investment in Oman and consequently important for foreign companies is that even when the arbitration proceedings take place outside Oman, the Omani courts still have jurisdiction over cases that arise out of it. Article 9 states that:

> The Commercial Court shall have the jurisdiction to entertain the issues of arbitration referred to Oman judiciary as per this Law. However, in case of arbitration concerning international trade and commerce, the Appellate Circuit

966 Subedi (n 7) 267.

967 OBFA (n 683) 6.

968 Amel Abdallah, 'Arbitration in Administrative Disputes in Oman' (*Young ICCA Blog*, 13 June 2014) <www.youngicca-blog.com/arbitration-in-administrative-disputes-in-oman/> accessed 2 December 2015.

of the said Court shall have the jurisdiction to look into it, irrespective of whether the proceedings take place either in Oman or abroad.

However, the role that Omani courts play in arbitration is controversial. On the one hand, both the Arbitration Law and the practice of the Omani courts suggest that the intervention by Omani courts can be seen as a supportive tool of arbitration of foreign investment cases. Article 13/1 of the Arbitration Law clearly signals this intention, obliging the Omani courts to decline to hear a case when there is a valid agreement to arbitrate.[969] Abdallah notes that the Administrative Court dismissed a suit concerning a dispute between the Ministry of Oil and Gas and a construction company on 25 June 2006, on the grounds that there was an arbitration clause between the parties.[970] In fact, it seems this is the approach taken by Omani courts generally.[971] According to Al-Siyabi, the Arbitration Law was intended to strengthen the contractual features of arbitration in order to make this an independent dispute settlement mechanism that provided an alternative to the Omani judicial system.[972]

Abdallah observes that there was formerly a contradiction in Omani legislation concerning the validity of arbitral clauses in administrative contracts concluded with governmental entities between Article 1 of the Arbitration Law and Article 6 of the Administrative Court Law issued by Royal Decree 91/1999.[973] The latter provided that the Administrative

969 Arbitration Law, art 13 1 states that: "The Court, before which a suit is filed with regard to a dispute in respect of which an arbitration clause exists, shall dismiss the suit provided the defendants plead for the same prior to him having submitted any petition or defence in respect of the suit".

970 Abdallah (n 968).

971 Such verdicts have experienced by the author in both Sohar and Nizwa primary courts in Oman (2008 and 2011).

972 Mohamed Khalfan Ali Al-Siyabi, 'A Legal Analysis of the Development of Arbitration in Oman with Special Reference to the Enforcement of International Arbitral Awards' (PhD thesis, University of Hull, 2008) 208.

973 Arbitration Law, art 1 states that:
"Without prejudice to the provisions stipulated in the international treaties operative in the Sultanate, the provisions of this Law shall be applicable to any arbitration between persons under public or private law, irrespective of the nature of legal relationship on which the dispute is based, provided the arbitration takes place in the Sultanate or in case of international commercial arbitration taking place abroad, provided the parties to it have agreed to submit themselves to the jurisdiction of the provisions of this Law".

Court had conclusive jurisdiction in disputes involving such contracts,[974] whereas the former made provision for all disputes to be settled regardless of the subject or the basis of the dispute.[975] However, concerns raised by this inconsistency was one of the reasons that led legislators to amend the Law by Royal Decree in 2009, thus broadening the application of the Arbitration Law to include disputes arising out of administrative contracts.[976] At the same time, this increased the possibility of intervention by the judiciary in the arbitration process. Therefore, as long as an arbitral clause in an administrative contract complies with the provisions of the Arbitration Law, the clause will be valid.[977]

As a result of this amendment, the Court of Appeal at the Omani Administrative Court confirmed that an arbitral clause in a contract between the Omani Public Authority of Electricity and Water and a private company was valid.[978] The court declared that the meaning of "the conclusive jurisdiction of Administrative Courts, in disputes related to administrative contracts," stated under Article 6 of the Administrative Law, was intended to differentiate between the "scope of jurisdiction of administrative courts and of civil courts" but did not stop disputing parties in administrative contracts from using arbitration to settle their disputes.[979]

The most significant support is by the Omani High Court, which issued a decision that minutes of the arbitral tribunal should be considered as official records that have a *res judicata* effect.[980] In addition, it is argued that the Omani judiciary provides support for arbitration at three stages of the proceedings: prior to commencement of arbitration, during arbitration and finally in enforcing the arbitral award.[981] The latter will be examined in the next section.

Prior to commencement of arbitration, under Article 14 of Arbitration Law, the Court of First Instance or the Court of Appeal in Muscat has the right to issue interim measures to prevent any change in facts on the

974 According to Administrative Court Law, art 6, the Administrative Court has jurisdiction over disputes by parties concerning administrative contracts.

975 Abdallah (n 968).

976 Ibid.

977 Ibid.

978 Ibid the ruling was issued by Administrative Court (Appeal Circuit) 5 January 2009.

979 Abdallah (n 968).

980 *Case 1/2002,* High Court Decision 92, 28 May 2002 Oman.

981 Moosa Al-Azri, 'The Role of the Omani Judiciary in Supporting Arbitration' (2010) 2 J Arab Arbitration, 30.

ground that might lead to the loss of rights of the other party. This means that the judiciary can address one of the weaknesses of the arbitration system, namely, that it is not able to issue and enforce orders.[982] This was emphasised by the decision of the Omani High Court in November 2003 that:

> The existence of an arbitration agreement should not preclude the judiciary from using its authority to render the appropriate conservatory and interim measures under the procedural law that is applicable pursuant to the request of the parties.[983]

The importance of Article 14 here is that it defines the jurisdiction of the interim measures upon the Omani courts and solves the issue of division of powers between tribunals and courts, as the absence of this may cause a challenge of uncertainty.[984] For example, the lack of a clear division of powers between courts and tribunals led to vagueness in the case of *Channel Tunnel Group v. Balfour Beatty*.[985] In addition, although the issue of the interim measures may appear to constitute a challenge, since there is no clear definition of them in the law, it is clear that such measures should not affect the objective rights (the disputed rights) or change the legal position of the parties. Furthermore, the parties to the arbitration have the right to seek the competent court's assistance in case of disagreement on the composition of the arbitral tribunal, as provided by Article 17 of the Arbitration Law.

Omani courts may also intervene in a number of ways during the arbitration to rescue the arbitration process. According to Article 20 of the Arbitration Law, the president of the competent Court of Appeal has the power to force a member of the arbitration tribunal to be removed under certain conditions:

> In the event an arbitrator is unable to carry out his responsibility, fails or causes unjustified delay in the

982 Moosa Al-Azri (981) 31.

983 *Case 23/2003*, High Court Decision 171, 19 November 2003 Oman.

984 Raymond J Werbicki, 'Arbitral Interim Measures: Fact or Fiction?'in AAA (ed) *Handbook on International Arbitration* and ADR (2nd edn, Juris 2010), 102.

985 *Channel Tunnel Group v Balfour Beatty* [1993] AC 334 (HL) cited in Werbicki (n 984) 102.

> arbitration proceedings and is unwilling to resign from his office and the parties are not agreed upon his removal, the President of the Commercial Court may issue orders terminating his assignment on the basis of a request made by any of the parties.

The court may also intervene during the arbitration process by imposing a fine on any witnesses who fail to appear or to render their depositions, as provided by Article 37/1 of the Arbitration Law, which states:

> The President of the Commercial Court on the basis of a request from the arbitration board shall have the following authorities:
>
> 1 to impose a fine ranging from five to twenty Rials Omani against the witnesses who fail to appear or abstain from rendering their depositions. The said decision shall not be subject to appeal and shall be enforceable like any other final judgement.

However, this form of intervention by the President of the Court of Appeal must be initiated by the arbitration tribunal. Interestingly, although according to this article, the fine imposed by the court is final and will be enforced in the same manner as the court's decisions, the more important issue here is whether a fine of this amount would actually make any difference, as it is very low.[986]

In addition, under conditions specified in Article 45, the President of the competent Court of Appeal has the right to determine a time limit for the rendering of awards.[987] These conditions include it should be upon a request of one party, if the parties have not agreed on issuing the award within a specific period, and if the award is not rendered within 18 months.

986 This would be equivalent to $14-$55.

987 Arbitration Law, art 45 (2) states that:
"2- In the event, the arbitration award has not been passed within the period referred to in the preceding paragraph, either party to the arbitration may request the President of the Commercial Court to pass orders prescribing an additional period or have the arbitration proceedings brought to an end. In such a case, either party may file his claims before the Competent Court".

Whilst some view this possibility of intervention positively, Al-Siyabi argues that it could be seen as evidence of judicialisation of the arbitration process in Oman and consequently may negatively affect the confidence of foreign parties.[988] The powers given to the head of the Court of Appeal under Article 45 (2) may be seen as problematic in this context. This article grants this individual the right to terminate arbitral proceedings upon a request of one of the parties in dispute if the tribunal is unable to issue an award after 18 months.[989]

5.3.2 Enforcement of Arbitral Awards in Oman

Writing in the mid-1980s, Lane and Morton argued that it was generally believed it would be difficult to enforce foreign tribunal arbitral awards in Oman unless both the substantive and procedural law applied in the arbitration followed *shari'a* principles. However, they noted that this was not the case since arbitral awards obtained in foreign tribunals could be enforced in Oman.[990] They based this opinion on their analysis of a case involving a UK company (the claimant) that had submitted a request for arbitration against an Omani company (the respondent) to the ICC in May 1981.[991] The claimant was asking the Tribunal *inter alia* to order the release of funds "representing the proceeds of the promissory notes" that were being held in Oman. The Tribunal ruled that most of this amount, plus interest due, should be awarded to the claimant. The claimant then started proceedings in Oman to enforce the award before the ASCD. The Omani respondent challenged the claimant's request on the basis that the ICC had exceeded its jurisdiction and called on the ASCD to declare that vital parts of the award were void. However, following the hearing, it ruled that the award should be enforced.[992]

---

988 Al-Siyabi (n 972).

989 Arbitration Law, art 45 (2) states that: «If there is no agreement between the parties as to the time limit for making the arbitral award, and if the tribunal is unable to make the award within 18 months, upon the request of one of the parties, the president of the competent court of appeal can terminate the proceedings, or grant more time for the arbitration».

990 Terence Lane and William Morton, 'Enforcing a foreign arbitration award in Oman' (1985) 4 Intl Fin L Rev 33, 33.

991 Hearings were held in the Hague, London, and Copenhagen. See Lane and Morton (n 990) 33.

992 Ibid.

Oman is under international obligations to enforce arbitral awards, as a member of the WTO, a signatory to the New York Convention,[993] and to many bilateral treaties and the FTA with the USA, which allow the disputing party to seek enforcement of an arbitration provided by an international arbitration centre.[994] Oman is obliged to enforce arbitral awards issued within the GCC, since this is one of its membership commitments.[995]

Although the arbitral award may be subject to an internal annulment procedure through an ad hoc ICSID Committee,[996] arbitration awards are not subject to judicial review by national courts.[997] According to Article 54 of ICSID, both arbitral award parties are under obligation to recognize and enforce the arbitral award in their territories as though it were a final court judgment issued in the country in question.[998] Notably, the Omani Arbitration Law does not allow parties to challenge the enforcement decision made by the competent court.[999] Article 57 of the Arbitration Law states clearly that "the filing of a suit for nullification of an award shall not suspend/cease the enforcement of the arbitration award". Therefore, the filing of a suit for nullification of an award does not automatically lead to stay of enforcement of that award.[1000] However, it is permissible to appeal against a court decision that refuses enforcement of an arbitral award, as provided in Article 58/3:

> It is not be permissible to make an appeal/petition against the order passed for the enforcement of an arbitration award.

993 'Arbitration in Oman' (*GCC Arbitration*, 21 August 2012) <https://gccarbitration.wordpress.com/2012/08/21/arbitration-in-oman/> accessed 2 December 2015.

994 Oman-USA FTA 2009, art 10 25 9 states that: «A disputing party may seek enforcement of an arbitration award under the ICSID Convention or the New York Convention regardless of whether proceedings have been taken under paragraph».

995 Oman is a member of the GCC Arbitration Centre which is expected to ease and facilitate enforcement issues See Arbitration in Oman (n 994).

996 ICSID, art 52.

997 ICSID, art 53; Loibl and Evans (n 25) 747.

998 Loibl and Evans (n 25) 747- 748.

999 Al-Azri (n 981) 35.

1000 This Article allows the competent court to issue orders to suspend enforcement proceedings under three conditions: (a) the applicant in the suit petition requests this; (b) the request for suspension is based on valid and clear grounds; and (c) „the Court may issue orders for submission of a guarantee or financial security". Condition (c) is at the judge's discretion. See Al-Azri (n 981) 36.

> However, it may be permissible to appeal against the order issued rejecting the application for enforcement before the Commercial Court referred to in Article 9 of this Law, within 30 days from the date of its issue.

It is clear that the aim of this provision is to ensure the effectiveness of arbitration and to prevent courts from not enforcing arbitral awards.

The conditions for enforcement of awards set out by Omani laws are limited in comparison with those of the UNCITRAL Model Law. Conditions in the latter cover whether the agreement is valid according to the law of the state where the award was rendered, if none of the parties to the arbitration agreement lack capacity, or if the formation of the tribunal is contrary to the agreement of the parties or the law of the state where the arbitration is held.[1001]

It can be said, regardless of the issues that parties should consider, that arbitral awards are enforced in Oman and it is likely that the Omani Courts will not refuse to enforce arbitration agreements.[1002] For example, in April 2010, the Muscat Court of Appeal emphasised that an arbitral award issued in Denmark against an Omani company was enforceable in Oman on the basis of the New York Convention.[1003] According to a study undertaken in 2014 in which 37 attorneys, arbitrators, and legal consultants were interviewed about foreign arbitration, Oman was judged to be the third most friendly state towards foreign arbitral award enforcement among the GCC countries (6.25) behind Bahrain (7.44) and UAE (7.43).[1004] It was considered to be better than Kuwait (5.78), Qatar (5.74) and Saudi Arabia (3.44).[1005]

However, foreign investors seeking to enforce an arbitration agreement must consider a number of issues. The arbitration agreement should be clear about whether the parties intend to seek arbitration or not, since this may affect its chances of being enforced in Omani courts. In *Case No. 197/2010*, the Omani High Court refused to enforce an arbitration

1001 Moosa Al-Azri (n 981) 35.
1002 Arbitration in Oman (n 993).
1003 Arbitration in Oman (n 993).
1004 A M Almutawa and A F M Maniruzzaman 'Problems of enforcement of foreign arbitral awards in the Gulf Cooperation Council states and the prospect of a uniform GCC arbitration law: an empirical study' (3 February 2015), 24 <http://ssrn.com/abstract=2559590> accessed 22 February 2016.
1005 Ibid.

agreement on the basis that the parties' intention to arbitrate was not clear. The arbitration clause stated that:

> This pay order is irrevocable and shall be governed by Omani laws. All possible disputes between the parties in this particular irrevocable fee protection agreement will be settled at the tribunals in Oman, in the event of dispute the arbitration laws of the International Chamber of Commerce will apply [...][1006]

In addition, parties must consider the signing of the arbitral award as specified by Article 43 (1) of the Arbitration Law. Therefore, in Case *No. 57/2005*, an arbitral award was nullified by the Omani High Court because the award was only signed by the chairman of the three-member arbitral tribunal and its secretary. The court ruled that, according to "Article 43(1) of the Arbitration Law, the majority of members of the tribunal must sign and reasons why the minority did not sign must be shown in the award." [1007]

Parties should consider as well cases of annulment specified by the Arbitration Law. In order to ensure that the arbitral award is enforced, the law identifies issues that cause extreme damage.[1008] The Omani High Court

1006 Arbitration in Oman (n 993).

1007 Arbitration Law, art 43 (1) states that the award must: "Be rendered in writing and signed by the arbitrator. If the arbitral tribunal is greater than one, the majority must sign with reasons being expressly provided as to why the minority did not sign" See 'Arbitration in Oman' (n 993).

1008 According to Arbitration Law, art 53 grounds for annulment are as follows:
"1 if there is no agreement in respect of arbitration or if such an agreement is void, voidable or time barred;
2 if one of the parties to the arbitration agreement, at the time of execution of the arbitration agreement was incompetent or insane in accordance with the Law which governs his capacity;
3 if one of the parties to the arbitration fails to submit his defence due to him not being properly notified of the notice concerning the appointment of an arbitrator or arbitration proceedings or any other reason beyond his control
4 if the arbitration award has ignored the application of the Law agreed upon by the parties for application in respect of the subject matter of the dispute;
5 if the arbitration board is constituted or arbitrators are appointed contrary to the Law or the agreement between the parties;
6 if the arbitration award has settled issues which do not come under the purview of the arbitration agreement or has crossed the limits set out in the agreement[...];
7 if the arbitration award is null or the arbitration proceedings are void to the extent affecting the terms of the award.

has emphasised that "the grounds provided under Article 53 of Arbitration Law are exclusive and should not be expanded by analogy".[1009] The High Court has refused to annul arbitral awards on grounds not included under Article 53, such as, if the award did not mention the nationality, addresses and titles of arbitrators, or if the arbitrators had not appointed experts,[1010] because such matters are not considered as grounds for nullification under Article 53.[1011] However, the right to decide on the annulment of an award depends totally on the competent court, as the law grants this right to the court only.[1012] The Omani High Court emphasised this by stating clearly that "whether the ground of annulment is available or not it depends merely on the competent court, not the will of parties".[1013]

Although in practice arbitral awards cannot be enforced until a competent court issues an exequatur, Article 55 of the Arbitration Law makes it clear that the awards have a *res judicata* effect and should be enforced.[1014] However, the party that seeks to enforce the arbitral award has to verify the fulfilment of the following three conditions:

1. The award is not contrary to previous decisions rendered by the Omani Courts.
2. The award does not violate the public policy of Oman.
3. There has been valid notification of the award.[1015]

The High Court has emphasised the last condition by stating that "the period for filing a request for annulment of an award begins only after the award is notified to the other party"[1016]. According to Articles 252 and 253 of the Law of Commercial and Civil Procedure two more conditions should be taken into consideration by the parties if the arbitral award is rendered in a foreign state. These conditions are that: "the award must not violate

1009 *Case 1/2002* High Court Decision 92, 28 May 2002 Oman.
1010 Ibid The principles of the High Court 2004, Commercial circuit, paras 246, 247, 248.
1011 Al-Azri (n 981) 36.
1012 Ibid 37.
1013 *Case 1/2002* High Court Decision 92, 28 May 2002 Oman.
1014 Arbitration Law, art 55 states that: "Awards passed by the arbitrators in accordance with this Law shall be treated as a *res judicata* and shall be enforceable pursuant to the provisions laid down in this Law".
1015 As provided by Arbitration Law, art 58/2.
1016 *Case 24/2004* High Court Decision 39, 26 May 2004 Oman.

Omani law and the State where the award was rendered must accept the enforcement of Omani awards in its territory".

5.3.3 Public Policy and International Standards

Oman's approach to setting public policy is important since this may be viewed as a barrier by foreign investors, since it may be used to justify the annulment or refusal to recognise and enforce an arbitral award.[1017] This country's rights of refusal can be found under Articles 34 (2) (b) (ii)[1018] and 36 (1) (b) (ii) of the UNCITRAL Model Law,[1019] and Article V (2) (b) of the New York Convention.[1020] The tribunal in Radio Corporation of America v. China emphasised this clearly by stating that:

> It is a correct rule known and recognised in common law as in international law, that any restriction of a contracting government's right must be effected in a clear and distinct manner. Contracts affecting the public interest are to be construed liberally in favour of the public. [1021]

In *Al-Tamimi*, although OMCO argued that its suspension of the contract with Emork and SFOH was on the basis of the latter's violation of the contract, as mentioned ealier, the Tribunal found the measures taken by the Omani Government, especially MECA, to protect the national interest as justifiable. According to a survey carried out by Almutawa and

1017 Michael Pryles, 'Recent Singapore decisions on international arbitration' (2012-2013) 24 Nat'l L Sch India Rev 35, 36.

1018 UNCITRAL Model Law, art 34 states that: "(2) An arbitral award may be set aside by the court specified in article 6 only if: (b) the court finds that: (ii) the award is in conflict with the public policy of this State".

1019 Ibid art 36 states that: "(1) Recognition or enforcement of an arbitral award, irrespective of the country in which it was made, may be refused only: [...] (b) if the court finds that: [...] (ii) the recognition or enforcement of the award would be contrary to the public policy of this State".

1020 Art V of the New York Convention states that: "2 Recognition and enforcement of an arbitral award may also be refused if the competent authority in the country where recognition and enforcement is sought finds that:[...] (b) The recognition or enforcement of the award would be contrary to the public policy of that country".

1021 Shavarsh Toriguian, *Legal aspects of oil concessions in the Middle East* (Hamaskaine Press 1972) 43 See Mary B Ayad, 'International Commercial Arbitration Award Enforcement at the Crossroads of *Sharial* Law and *Ordre Public* in the MENA: Paving the Golden Path towards Harmonisation' (2009) 4, 10 J World Investment & Trade, 723, 747-748.

Maniruzzaman, an overly broad interpretation of public policy was found to be the most frequent reason for non-enforcement of arbitral awards in the GCC states.[1022]

However, according to the UNCITRAL Model Law every jurisdiction has the right to define and give effect to its own public policy.[1023] These differences among states in interpreting public policy may prove to be a barrier to recognition and enforcement of arbitral awards, especially when Omani courts can challenge an award on the basis of public policy on their own initiative, without this issue having been raised by any party.[1024] According to Article 22 of the Law on Civil and Commercial Procedures,[1025] "Except in the cases where the annulment is relating to the public policy, no other than the person in whose favour the annulment is raised for can use it...". Therefore, if a contractual stipulation is seen to run contrary to public order, then it must be set aside by the judge, even if the point is not raised by either party.[1026]

Article 11 of the Omani Arbitration Law is vague in relation to public policy. It states that: "It shall not be permissible to have arbitration in respect of the issues, which are not subject to reconciliation/compromise." It is known in Omani regulations that issues which violate public policy are not matters of reconciliation or compromise, and therefore, they exceptions from being subject to arbitration. Although most disputes concerning foreign investment are assumed to be arbitral in Oman, the lack of a clear definition of public policy means that how the arbitral decision is implemented may depend on the court's understanding of this concept.

Ayad notes that the difficulty posed by public policy generally is that it has no clear definition, with every state defining its scope differently.[1027] Therefore, under no circumstances can the concept of public order contradict with international public order.[1028] Ayad urges MENA countries to establish a definitive understanding of public order to eliminate

1022 Almutawa and Maniruzzaman (n 1004) 5, 6.

1023 Pryles (n 1017) 36.

1024 The Omani High Court made it clear that an annulment related to public policy can be raised by the court itself without needing to be raised by the party. See *Case 177/2013*, High Court, Commercial Circuit (Decision) 2 January 2013 Oman.

1025 Promulgated by Royal Decree 29/2002.

1026 'Arbitration in Oman' (n 993).

1027 A G Tweeddale, 'Enforcing Arbitration Awards Contrary to Public Policy in England' (2000) 17 Intl Construction LRev 159, 160.

1028 Ayad (n 1021) 749.

ambiguity. It is believed that a *lex petrolea* could be improved to establish a harmonized code of law on the doctrine of public order and consequently facilitate better enforcement of law.[1029]

Parties need to take into consideration that courts generally have three approaches when applying public policy.[1030] The first approach involves adopting a narrow interpretation of public policy, according to which courts are obliged to address the arbitral agreement in the same way as the arbitrator, by enforcing it unless it is against the law. The second approach adopts a broad interpretation of public policy, arguing that the role of the courts is to protect the public interest beyond the positive law. The third approach differentiates between foreign and domestic awards by applying the narrow interpretation of public policy to the former and a broad interpretation to the latter.

Whilst there is no provision in Omani law that defines the term 'public order', a judgment issued on 8 December 1993 defined this concept in the following way:

> Laws which relate to public order are those whereby it is intended to accomplish a public interest – political, social or economic – which relates to the higher order of society and which transcends the interest of individuals. All individuals must respect such interest and the accomplishing of it, and they may not negate it by agreements entered into between themselves even where such agreements accomplish interest for them, because private interests cannot prevail over the public interest.[1031]

A similarly clear definition of public policy can be found in Parsons & Whittemore Overseas Inc. v RAKTA, where it is stated that:

> [T]he Convention's public policy defence should be construed narrowly. Enforcement of foreign arbitral awards may be

1029 Ibid.

1030 Moosa Al-Azri, 'Prevention of Non-Compliance with Arbitral Awards: Some Proposals for Efficient Enforcement' (2005) 12 Tilburg LR 348, 360.

1031 Arbitration in Oman (n 993).

denied on this basis only where enforcement would violate the State's most basic notions of morality and justice.[1032]

On the basis of Article 53 (2) of the Arbitration Law, the Omani High Court concluded that the court might nullify an arbitral award only if its outcome contradicts with basic principles of Omani law.[1033] However, it should not be assumed that Omani courts would apply a specific approach of public policy, as currently this will depend on the individual judge's broad or narrow understanding of public policy. Although such definition by national courts' practice may become guidance for judges' practice and reduce the vagueness, it seems that different judges' understandings of public policy will continue due to the absence of a clear definition in Omani laws. Therefore, it is vital to apply a definitive and narrow approach to public policy. The narrower the approach taken by the Omani judiciary, the more it will be perceived as providing a business-friendly environment for foreign investment.

5.4 Conclusion

This chapter argued that significant progress has been made with respect to the independence of the Omani judiciary and the reliability of the Omani courts as means to settle investment disputes, aiming ultimately to create a reliable dispute settlement mechanism for foreign investment in Oman. However, it is argued that weaknesses in some areas such as the lack of a clear and effective system of checks and balances and shortage of well-trained Omani judges, negatively affected the confidence of foreign investment in the Omani judiciary system. It would be desirable to have special divisions in courts dealing with foreign investment cases or investment chambers within the High Court, together with a speedy mechanism for the settlement of investment disputes.

Notwithstanding the argument on the Omani courts' role toward arbitration, it is argued that the role given to and experienced by the Omani judiciary is supportive of the arbitration process. In addition, it is clear that arbitral awards are generally enforced in Oman, regardless of the

1032 *Parsons & Whittemore Overseas Co Inc v Societe General de l'Industrie du Papier (RAKTA)*, (Judgment) 508 F 2d 969 The United States Court of Appeals (2d Cir 1974).

1033 *Case 127/2000* High Court Decision, on Appeal 10/2000 Oman.

issues that those who are parties to arbitration should consider. Although the practice and *Al-Tamimi* show there is no broad approach to public policy in Oman, the lack of a clearly defined approach of public policy in the Sultanate raises a concern with regard to the approach that might be adopted by individual judges.

While the investigation in this chapter shows some weaknesses in the dispute settlement system in Oman, the next chapter tries to complete the whole picture which this appraisal aims to draw. Therefore, the following chapter will analyse the findings and the significant recommendations to protect and attract foreign investment in order to achieve better guarantees in the Sultanate.

Chapter 6: Findings, Recommendations and Conclusion

6.1 Introduction

It is argued in this chapter that by identifying the main legal weaknesses of foreign investment in Oman, it is possible to improve the level of protection that can be provided for foreign investment. Importantly, it examines the steps that Oman should take in order to ensure that it both safeguards its national interest and at the same time attracts foreign investment.

This chapter begins by exploring the findings of the main arguments that underpin this analysis. These relate to the increasing steadiness and consistency in foreign investment protection, the contribution of Omani law and practice to the development of international investment law, particularly the need for Oman to take a balanced approach, and the importance of the efficiency of national regulations and practice.

The chapter concludes with specific recommendations aimed at providing a better regulatory environment that will enhance levels of protection for foreign investment and increase the attractiveness of Oman to foreign investors. The recommendations include a specialised investment council with a unified policy, making it easy to do business in Oman, the need for training and a national arbitration centre in Oman.

The recommendations draw on comparisons between the experiences of Oman, Singapore and the UAE, especially the Emirate of Dubai. These two countries were chosen because Singapore is considered to be one of the most successful developing countries in terms of attracting foreign investment, while the UAE is a neighbouring member state of the GCC and was able to attract about 10 times more foreign investment than Oman in 2014.

In 2013, UNCTAD's Global Investment Report nominated Singapore as the eighth largest recipient of FDI in the world and third largest in Asia.[1034]

1034 Open Company Singapore. Com, 'Why Is Singapore Attractive for Foreign Investors?', Updated on 1 September 2015 <www.opencompanysingapore.com/why-is-singapore-attractive-for-foreign-investors> accessed 17 February 2016.

The investment inflow to the UAE in 2014 was $10.1 billion[1035] whilst that of Oman for the same year was only $1.180 billion.[1036] However, according to the World Bank, the inflow of foreign investment to Oman in 2014 was $739 million[1037] whereas for Singapore this was more than $67.522 billion[1038] and for the UAE $10.066 billion.[1039]

6.2 Findings

6.2.1 Toward a Greater Protection in Oman

It can be argued that there are evidences that Oman has begun to move towards a greater protection for foreign investment. First, the significant number of BITs that Oman has signed, its FTA with the USA and the DNFIL, together with the FTA between the GCC and Singapore, all of which were evaluated in Chapters Three and Four. Although investors from the GCC and USA can enjoy broader, more inclusive application of the principle of national treatment in Oman, the lack of such a guarantee for other WTO and BITs members still represents a challenge for investors from those countries.

It can be said that Oman has taken a steady and consistent policy toward improving the guarantees provided for foreign investors. This development of protection trends has been applied in both Oman's international agreements and its own national legal system. This is clear in the developments seen in BITs, culminating with the FTA with the USA and the GCC FTA with Singapore. Significant developments in Omani FDI laws have been identified, starting from the 1974 law, then the FCIL, and finally the DNFIL expected to be enacted soon, which contains standards of protection similar to those provided under Oman's BITs and FTA. Although it does not meet the purpose, this policy has kept Oman in a

1035 UNCTAD, *World Investment Report 2015: Reforming International Investment Governance*, 52 <http://unctad.org/en/PublicationsLibrary/wir2015_en.pdf> accessed 3 March 2016.

1036 UNCTAD, *World Investment Report 2015: Country Fact Sheet Oman* <http://unctad.org/sections/dite_dir/docs/wir2015/wir15_fs_om_en.pdf> accessed 3 March 2016.

1037 World Bank, 'FDI: net inflows', <http://data.worldbank.org/indicator> accessed 14 April 2016.

1038 At the time of writing, the 2016 report was not available. See World Bank (n 1037).

1039 World Bank (n 1037).

relatively successful situation with regard to the ability to attract foreign investment, as shown by the FDI inflows in the period 2008-2013.

Table 6.1: Oman FDI inflows, 2008-2013 (Millions of US dollars)

2008	2009	2010	2011	2012	2013
2952	1485	1782	1563	1040	1626

Source: World Bank Group, Investment Reform Map- Sultanate of Oman (unpublished paper, Muscat, 25 April 2015) [4]

Further evidence of this approach by Oman is that from 1970 onwards, Oman has never voided a foreign investment treaty or taken any backwards step in its policy toward the protection of foreign investment. Moreover, the dispute settlement provisions under Oman's BITs, Oman's USA FTA, and in addition, Oman's membership of ICSID, unquestionably strengthen the protection of foreign investors' rights by enabling claimants from other signatories to sue Oman, as is clear in the *Al-Tamimi* case.

It can be argued that the in-depth analysis offered of the *Al-Tamimi* case, especially in Chapter Three, reveals aspects of the protection of foreign investment within several Omani bodies. For example, the tribunal in the *Al-Tamimi* case inspected parts of the Omani foreign investment regime, particularly the areas of the rule of law of the Omani judiciary, the legal system and executive branch. The outcome of this investigation by the tribunal, particularly to the proceedings taken by Mahdha Primary Court and Ibri Court of Appeal show the predictability of the Omani judiciary system.

6.2.2 The contribution of Omani Law and Practice to the Development of International Investment Law

Following the above argument, how can a small country like Oman be expected to contribute to the development of international investment law? It can be said that the significant contribution of Omani law and practice to the development of international investment law is in supporting the trend of the need for a balanced approach. In other words, this study argues that BITs, FTAs and IIAs are not full guarantees without pain for Oman. Tanzi argues that although the purpose of BITs is to protect foreign investment, the approach to protection of foreign investment taken by arbitral tribunals is not only against the public interest of the host states, but also counter to the scope and aim of the body of international investment law itself.[1040] Regardless of the accuracy of this statement, Oman should strike a balance between protecting foreign investment and safeguarding its sovereign rights.

Oman needs to rethink how far it should go in the issue of defending its sovereignty and national interests. Thus, there is a need to take into consideration the argued changes in the landscape of international investment law by paying attention to the emergence of a protective approach to foreign investment. The simple way is to take the approach of increasing the gain of attracting foreign investment to Oman and at the same time minimising the pain which may accrue, especially by considering provisions related to the absolute right of international dispute settlement of other parties included in these BITs or FTAs.

Although the award in *Al-Tamimi* was in favour of Oman, this case should awaken Omani policymakers to some issues related to the appropriate approach toward providing protection for foreign investment. A clear example of the issues that Oman needs to consider under these international agreements is that the tribunals have the advantage and the power to interpret not only contracts and agreements, but also the Oman national laws. The tribunal in the *Al-Tamimi* case stated that:

> The provisions of the CCL[1041] cited above indicate that a company has no legal presence in Oman unless registered. Article 2 of the CCL, it will be recalled, provides that a company is "null and void" unless it "adopts one of the types listed". Article 4 of the CCL, moreover, provides [...]. The Tribunal accepts the Respondent's submission that the effect of Article 4 is to "require an Omani registration number to meet the threshold requirement of having a legal presence in the jurisdiction. Accordingly, registration is a condition

1040 Attila Tanzi, 'On Balancing Foreign Investment Interests with Public Interests in Recent Arbitration Case Law in the Public Utilities Sector' (2012) 11 Law & Prac Intl Cts. & Tribunals, 47, 73.

1041 Commercial Companies Law issued by Royal Decree 4/1974.

> precedent for any agreement entered into by the company to become effective.[1042]

The Tribunal in this case even interpreted other states' national laws. For example, it decided in the Jurisdiction *ratione personae*, that the ICSID tribunal interpreted the national laws of the USA and UAE regarding its application to the claimant's nationality.[1043]

Oman's sovereignty was another issue tackled by the Tribunal. Did the claimant have the right of access to conduct a site inspection on Omani land?[1044] The claimant applied to the Tribunal on 25 September 2012 for an order directing the respondent to grant the claimant's industry and damages experts' immediate access to the site of the former quarry that was the subject of this arbitration, for the purposes of conducting a site inspection. After a debate between both parties on this issue, the Tribunal ruled that:

> Having carefully considered both parties' positions, the Tribunal finds that the Claimant's request to conduct a site visit is, in general terms, justified and should be allowed. In particular, the Tribunal accepts the need for a site visit for the reasons given by the Claimant.[1045]

This ruling by the Tribunal shows the extent of the protection which can be provided by international tribunals for foreign investors, granting a foreign investor the full right to gather information needed to defend his case, regardless of the sovereignty of the country. The argument concerning state sovereignty is weakened when it is set against the protection of the other party's right to defend his or her case.

The *Al-Tamimi* case sounded a warning to the Omani government, taking into consideration that the amount of money the claimant claimed was more than half a billion US dollars. Another instance is the case brought by investors from Italy and Luxembourg against South Africa in 2007, claiming that their mineral rights had effectively been expropriated by provisions included in South Africa's Mining and Petroleum Resources

---

1042 *Al-Tamimi* (n 11) para 109.

1043 Ibid para 95.

1044 Ibid Procedural Order No 2 (28 September 2012).

1045 Ibid para 4.

Development Act 2002.[1046] This claim led South Africa to launch a process of review of its BITs that resulted in the termination of its BIT with Germany, despite their important trading relationship.[1047] On 23 June 2013, South Africa also served a notice of termination of its BIT with Spain.[1048]

Despite the common approach taken by international tribunals in interpreting and applying BITs in favour of foreign investors and containing the host state's regulatory power, especially in investment disputes related to public services sector,[1049] Tanzi argues that such an approach may be gradually mitigated, due to the increased criticism from international legal literature and State practice.[1050] In addition, Subedi notes that while the main aim of BITs is to protect foreign investment, this aim should be in harmony with promoting "economic development cooperation between the States Parties" as stated in 1965 ICSID Convention.[1051] Therefore, provisions designed to admit non-compensable regulatory expropriation have been included in an increasing number of BITs and IIAs, such as the 2012 US Model BIT.[1052]

Although it may be argued that granting such a right to individual investors is important, because they do not have access to the WTO dispute settlement mechanism,[1053] the *Al-Tamimi* case provides support to the existing trend in international arena for striking a balance between protecting foreign investors' rights and its own sovereign right. Therefore, Oman needs to consider the approach of the greater right to refer to an international arbitral as it is applied even by developed countries. The UK's general practice in negotiating BITs is to restrict the protections provided for foreign investors "to the post phase of the investment".[1054] For example, Article 2(1) of the UK-Mexico BIT in 2006 provides that "each

1046 Subedi (n 7) 26, 27.

1047 Ibid 27.

1048 Herbert Smith Freehills, 'South Africa terminates its bilateral investment treaty with Spain: Second BIT terminated, as part of South Africa's planned review of its investment treaties', 21 August 2013, <http://hsfnotes.com/arbitration/> accessed 15 April 2016.

1049 Tanzi (n 1040) 73.

1050 Ibid.

1051 The Preamble of the ICSID emphasised the: „need for international cooperation for economic development", See Tanzi (n 1040) 73-74.

1052 Subedi (n 7) 23.

1053 Ibid 31.

1054 Agreement between the Government of Great Britain and Northern Ireland and the Government of the United Mexican States, for the Promotion and Reciprocal Protection of Investments 2007, art 2 (1). The Agreement

Contracting Party shall admit investments in accordance with its laws and regulations".[1055] Harrison maintains that this article does not create any right of entry for foreign investors, apart from those rights provided in the national laws in each party, despite the fact that this provision is drafted as an obligation.[1056]

The lack of clarity in international investment law is caused mainly by the fact that there is no single global treaty. This gives arbitrators in investment tribunals the freedom to decide what the law is, on the basis of their understanding, even though many of them may not possess the requisite qualifications.[1057] For example, in *Al-Tamimi*, if the tribunal had decided that the OMCO's conduct was attributable to the Omani Government, the verdict may have gone against Oman.[1058]

Vadi argues that the constitutional balance needed between foreign investors' rights and legitimate state concerns must take into consideration the implications of international human rights treaties and concerns about exploitation of resources.[1059] According to Malkawi, although striking the right balance between the benefits of foreign investment and national security concerns can be challenging for host governments, this is necessary.[1060] Sornarajah argues that there is a space for balancing the rights between the need for protection and the treatment granted to foreign investors and the right of regulation by the host state.[1061] In this context, it can be argued that the need for an efficient and attractive national legal system for foreign investment should not prevent Oman from the consideration needed to its BITs and FTAs. In other words, it does not conflict with a cautious approach in international agreements.

In addition, the *Al-Tamimi* case is expected to be of special interest for international law lawyers, both practitioners and scholars, for a number of reasons; first, it took narrow and strict approach in the attribution of the

---

entered into force on 25 July 2007. <http://investmentpolicyhub.unctad.org/Download/TreatyFile/2009> accessed 15 April 2016.

1055 James Harrison, 'UK National Report' in Shan (n 372) 663, 679.

1056 Ibid 679.

1057 Subedi (n 7) 28, 30.

1058 *Al-Tamimi* (n 11).

1059 Valentina S. Vadi, 'When cultures collide: foreign direct investment, natural resources, and indigenous heritage in international investment law' (2011) 42 Colum Hum Rts L Rev 797, 888- 889.

1060 Bashar H Malkawi, 'Balancing open investment with national security: review of US and UAE laws with DP World as a case study' (2011) 13 U Notre Dame Austl L Rev 153, 191.

1061 Sornarajah (n 8) 231- 232.

governmental company action, particularly the attribution of the OMCO contract termination. The Tribunal states:

> There is no evidence that in making the decision to terminate the OMCO–Emrock Lease Agreement, OMCO was exercising, or indeed would have been authorised to exercise, any regulatory, administrative or governmental authority. There is, furthermore, no evidence that OMCO acted under direction from MECA, and the Tribunal is not satisfied in any event that this would meet the narrow test for attribution under the US–Oman FTA.[1062]

Saleem argues that the Tribunal did not rely on the international law rules but on Omani national laws, especially the Royal Decree 11/81 establishing OMCO. He points out that the Tribunal, considering that the main point on which Mr Al-Tamimi relied, claiming the termination of the two lease agreements by OMCO, to be expropriation, concluded that it could not be regarded as expropriation according to the Oman-USA FTA and international law. Rather it was merely a commercial dispute related to the contract between parties.[1063] Therefore, the Tribunal in *Al-Tamimi* took a different approach compared with similar cases, such as *Maffezini*.[1064] Therefore, this precedent may open the door for following cases to take a similar approach.

It can be argued that Tribunal based its conclusion on the words of the Oman-USA FTA particularly Article 10.1.2 which states:

> A Party's obligations under this Section shall apply to a state enterprise or other person when it exercises any regulatory, administrative, or other governmental authority delegated to it by that Party.

1062 *Al-Tamimi* (n 11) para 316.

1063 Saleem (n 414) 816.

1064 Saleem pointed out that in *Maffezini* the tribunal differentiated between two kinds of company actions; when the company gave advice to Mr. Maffezini the tribunal regarded it as not a governmental action belonging to the Spanish Government, but when one of a company's senior staff negotiated with Mr. Maffezini for the money transfer procedure the tribunal concluded that it was a governmental action, not a commercial action. See Saleem (n 414) 814.

The ruling of the Tribunal and its interpretation of all parties' action should be based on the FTA, since the Claimant raised his dispute on the basis of the Oman-USA FTA. Therefore, ignoring the FTA's words where they should apply is incorrect. The Oman-USA FTA sets out a narrow specification of the circumstances under which the actions of a state company may be attributed to the State.[1065]

Furthermore, the Tribunal has addressed a number of hot topics in customary international law, for example, the strict interpretation of the principle of fair and equitable treatment. This has been examined in Chapter Three. This case as well confirms that customary international law remains central to the application and interpretation of international investment treaties (FTAs or BITs). The Award particularly with its interpretation of the principle of minimum standard of treatment is an important contribution to the consolidation of established customary rules and to the clarification of the complex interplay between customary international law and international investment treaties.[1066]

6.2.3 The importance of Efficient National Regulation and Practice

This research study argues that the development of foreign investment-related laws in Oman is merely the first step in protecting foreign investment; these laws must also be supported by the necessary policies and practice.[1067] This point was illustrated in Chapter Four, which pointed out that restrictions on foreign investors can be found in the practices of a number of governmental bodies involved in issuing necessary permits. In addition, a lack of clarity, and consistency, and sudden changes in issues related to foreign investment, were noted. This, together with regulations imposed by some governmental entities, was shown to affect negatively the guarantees needed for foreign investment and to weaken the attractiveness of Oman for foreign investors.

Weaver maintains that the legal and judicial systems in developing countries usually lag behind their business development.[1068] Nonetheless,

1065 *Al-Tamimi* (n 11) para 318.

1066 See *Al-Tamimi* (n 11) para 374.

1067 For example, the combination needed between regulations and efficient national policies in similar issues, see Andrew Campbell, 'Insolvent Banks and the Financial Sector Safety Net - Lessons from the Northern Rock Crisis' (2008) 20 SAcLJ 316, 340-342.

1068 Griffin Weaver, 'The underutilized foreign investor' (2013-2014) 5 Creighton Intl & Comp. LJ 29, 36.

it seems that due to the early promulgation of FCIL (1994), compared with Oman's later commitments under the WTO (2000) and the Oman-USA FTA (2009), FCIL is behind Oman's international commitments, especially the FTA and the WTO.

The significant decline in oil prices by a two thirds during 2015 and 2016, from $100 per barrel in June 2014 to below $30 by early 2016,[1069] is expected to push policymakers in Oman to expedite the issue of the new law (DNFIL) and enhance the efficiency of foreign investment instruments, as a further move to minimise the state's dependence on oil. To date, in collaboration with the World Bank, the MoCI has completed the third draft of the DNFIL and the revision of the foreign investment map.[1070] On 25 January 2016, the MoCI presented the final stage of drafting the law.[1071]

Overall, it can be argued that to attract foreign investment and to provide better guarantees of protection, Oman will not be able to take restrictive steps in its international agreements to safeguard its own national interests, unless it has an efficient national system to gain the confidence of foreign investors in all related areas, including a dispute settlement mechanism. Having its own efficient national system is the only way Oman could reduce referral to international dispute settlement bodies in its agreements, by offering foreign investors a suitable alternative to seeking redress elsewhere. Undoubtedly, foreign investors will avoid countries where their money is not protected. Therefore, the functionality of Omani legal and judicial systems and the efficiency of Omani policy will play a significant role in foreign investors' decisions.

6.3 Recommendations

Although Oman has been able to attract a relatively reasonable amount of foreign investment, there is much more that can be done, taking into consideration its potential, as discussed earlier. These recommendations need to consider three factors together, namely, the need to attract foreign

1069 Sarah Townsend, 'Oman: where to now?' (*Arabian Business*, 29 January 2016) <www.arabianbusiness.com/oman-where-now--620154.html> accessed 22 March 2016.

1070 ONA, 'Foreign investment law to create jobs, woo investors to Oman', *Times of Oman* (Muscat, 25 January 2016) <http://timesofoman.com/article/76202/Oman/Government/Foreign-investment-law-to-create-jobs-woo-investors-to-Oman> accessed 3 March 2016.

1071 Ernst & Young (n 588).

investment, the need to improve Oman's economic development and at the same time to protect its sovereignty, and they should not conflict with any of these factors. Therefore, based on the findings of this research, some guidelines are suggested for Omani policy that would enhance guarantees of legal protection for foreign investment and eliminate the weaknesses that it faces.

It is proposed that Oman should establish a specialised Investment Council with a unified policy, should make it easier to do business in Oman, and should train in order to gain. Finally, it is argued that Oman needs to establish a national arbitration centre.

6.3.1 Establishing an Investment Council with a Unified Policy

Analysis shows that currently Oman has 12 governmental investment-related entities with different responsibilities but no organisation that has oversight of them all.[1072] Oman will not be able to maximise the performance of these entities unless it adopts a coherent strategy. Although many of these entities are under the responsibility of the Minister of the MoCI,[1073] other key entities such as DSEZ, Ithraa, Salalah FZ and Salalah Port, are overseen by different ministers and do not even report to the MoCI.[1074] Consequently, one of Oman's barriers to providing an attractive investment environment is that it does not have a comprehensive investment vision and strategic policy to attract FDI; due to this weak inter-agency coordination.[1075]

Singapore created the Economic Development Board (EDB) to manage its economy and promote the country to foreign investors.[1076] Although the EDB came under the purview of the then newly established Ministry of Trade and Industry,[1077] it continued its role of running the foreign investment system in Singapore.[1078] The government of Singapore has been able to influence almost all its national bodies in its pursuit of economic development.[1079] Although Singapore's small size helped it to

1072 See Appendix B.
1073 These include the Supreme Council for Planning, the Foreign Investment Committee, the One-Stop Shop and the Free Zones Committee.
1074 World Bank Group (n 665) 8.
1075 Ibid 4.
1076 Jean Ho, 'Singapore National Report', in Shan (n 372) 593.
1077 This occurred in 1979, Shan (n 372) 594.
1078 Ibid.
1079 Suppiah Murugesan, 'Judicial independence in a corporatist state: Singapore - a case study' (2012) 99 Lawasia J 110.

protect the operation of foreign investment from executive or legislative decentralisation,[1080] it is vital to have a centralised, coherent and unified policy.

In the UAE it seems that the role of the Federal Ministry of Economy is limited mainly to promoting the investment climate,[1081] whereas each Emirate has its own investment policy, operation and promotion bodies, belonging to the local governments.[1082] In Dubai, the Dubai Economic Council is only an advisory body to the government of Dubai, advocating sound economic strategies and policies,[1083] and does not act as an umbrella organisation for other investment bodies. In Dubai there are more than 20 FZs in 10 different main sectors,[1084] all of them operating as self-contained 'offshore' areas, where investors deal exclusively with the free zone authorities, handle with almost all aspects of business set-up and management. Even employee visas are obtained through these authorities. All these FZs are coordinated by the Dubai Freezone Council established by Dubai government to propose rules and policies for registration, licensing and observing activities within the FZs whilst at the same time aligning their activities and progress with the Dubai Strategic Plan.[1085]

There is no similar body coordinating FZs in Oman, with some under the MoCI, others under the Supreme Council for Planning (SCP), the Ministry of Tourism and the PEIE. Therefore, it is argued that the establishment of one umbrella organisation would enable the Omani government to gain a broader view of the policy needed in these zones. Malkawi argues that the existence of the FZs in the UAE has established two separate economies within the UAE, the FZ economy and the regular UAE economy.[1086] Dubai has proven the effectiveness of FZs, especially Jebel Ali FZ (manufacturing businesses) and the Internet City FZ (internet companies).[1087] It is believed

1080 Shan (n 372) 598.

1081 See UAE Federal Ministry of Economy <www.economy.gov.ae/English> accessed 29 March 2016.

1082 See for example Dubai FDI <www.dubaifdi.gov.ae> accessed 29 March 2016

1083 See <www.dec.org.ae/about/> accessed 7 April 2016.

1084 These include industrial, ICT, financial, media, education, logistic and others. See Dubai, 'Obtaining one-stop shop services from freezones', 11 November 2013 <www.dubai.ae/en/Lists/Articles/DispForm.aspx?ID=127&category=Businesses> accessed 27 March 2016.

1085 'Obtaining one-stop shop services from freezones'.

1086 Malkawi (n 1060) 188.

1087 Weaver (n 1068) 70.

the Dubai FZs were one important reason why the economic recession in 2009 was short-lived in Dubai.[1088]

The lessons derived from these experiences suggest there are a number of steps to be taken by Oman to address this challenge: first, to establish an agreed government strategy on the basis of Oman's FDI objectives.[1089] Second, an inter-governmental body (a fully specialised investment council) should be established to administer development, implementation, monitoring and review of a national investment policy.[1090] Third, in order to chart progress towards achieving the FDI strategy there is a need to establish a monitoring mechanism using Key Performance Indicators (KPIs).[1091]

Figure 6.1: Proposed structure for Investment Council

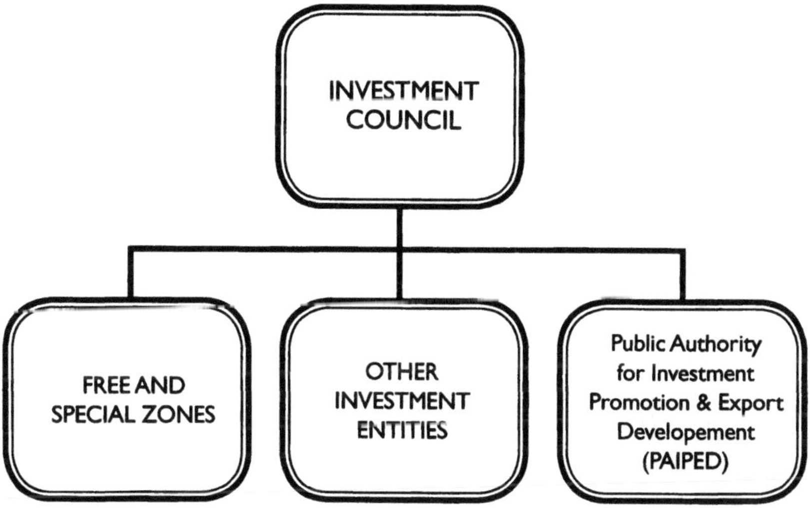

1088 Ibid 70.
1089 World Bank Group (n 665) 6.
1090 Ibid.
1091 These indicators should be under the responsibility of the investment council. World Bank Group (n 665) 6.

The recommended council needs to be chaired by the president or the vice president of the Ministerial Council[1092] and should consist of three main bodies; the first one would supervise all FZs and SEZs, including DSEZ, the FZs of Sohar, Salalah and Al Mazunah. The second body would be for foreign investment generally, excluding FZs and SEZs, such as PEIE Sohar Port, Salalah Port, and the One-Stop Shop. The third body would be PAIPED as a promoting body. All these three main bodies should report to the Investment Council, which would work as a policymaker.

It is important to mention that the Ministerial Council is not a suitable umbrella for policy or decision-making on foreign investment because it will slow the development and the progress of the policy of all issues related to foreign investment due to the burden upon the Ministerial Council.[1093] For example, there was a complaint that the Ministerial Council should not be the body responsible for approving the set-up of 100% foreign-owned companies because of the long time needed to get approval and the difficulty of access to investors.[1094] Although the SCP[1095] is better able than the Ministerial Council to address foreign investment policy, it is still not a suitable tool. This is because, although the role of the SCP is to develop the strategies and policies that are required to achieve sustainable development in Oman, this includes many areas such as education, health, and transport.[1096]

This study disagrees with the recommendation of the World Bank that PAIPED should report to MoCI and the SEZ, the FZs, Industrial Estates (IEs) and other investment entities be brought under the umbrella of one Ministry (MoCI).[1097] This may create problems. First, PAIPED should report to the policymaker, which is the proposed Investment Council; second, the World Bank's proposal would be impractical due to the large number of FZs, complexity and huge responsibility under these entities. For

1092 To be able to influence the Ministerial Council decisions regarding foreign investment issues.

1093 For example, this was one difficulty regarding the approval of 100% ownership as will be discussed later. Diwan of Royal Court (n 722) 3.

1094 Ibid.

1095 Established by Royal Decree 30/2012 on 26 May 2012 see Supreme Council for Planning <https://www.scp.gov.om/en/Page.aspx?I=6> accessed 24 March 2016.

1096 Supreme Council for Planning (n 1095).

1097 World Bank Group (n 665) 6.

example, DSEZ is bigger than Singapore.[1098] Third, the MoCI already has huge responsibilities, having 15 jurisdictions according to Royal Decree 102/2005.[1099] Therefore, Oman should reform and strengthen the function of the FZs and SEZs because of regional competition.[1100] Although each FZ should have its own independence and complete power to decide its affairs, all FZs should have one coherent policy.

Another important issue to be recommended in this regard is the need for a unified policy among all government bodies. Other Omani government bodies' policies and regulations should not conflict with the central foreign investment policy. This challenge of conflict with the protection needed for foreign investment was seen in Chapter Four in relation to certain regulations and policies of the MoM, PACP and Oman Royal Police. Although the regulations of other government bodies exist to maintain national security and ensure social development, it is clear that there must be coherence between maintaining these goals and the goal of attracting foreign investment. Therefore, it is likely that the proposed council will help to establish the needed coordination and a bridge between foreign investment policymakers and the policies of other government's entities, in order to create harmonisation among them.

6.3.2 Making it Easy to do Business in Oman

Oman should make it easy for foreign investors to do business in order to improve its foreign investment environment. This because it is a key element in attracting foreign investment. Administrative measures including approval requirements and screening for foreign investments should be reduced.[1101] Although Oman has made some progress in ease of doing business, moving from 77 in 2015 to 70 in 2016 in the ranking

1098 The size of the DSEZ is over 1745 km² <www.duqm.gov.om/sezad/about-us/welcome-to-duqm> whereas Singapore itself is only 719.1 km² <https://en.wikipedia.org/wiki/Singapore> accessed 25 March 2016.

1099 The Jurisdictions of the Ministry of Commerce and Industry were promulgated under Royal Decree 102/2005 MoCI <https://www.moci.gov.om> accessed 3 April 2016.

1100 There are over twenty well-established FZs in Dubai alone, within just a few hundred kilometres. See Weaver (n 1068) 75.

1101 Mehmet Ogoto, 'Investing in the Middle East and North Africa Region to Promote Development and Modernization an OECD Initiative in the Making' (2004) 5 J. World Investment & Trade 767, 772.

of 189 economies, it is still far behind.[1102] Despite progress in some areas such as getting electricity, trading across borders and resolving insolvency, Oman fell back in other areas such as starting business, dealing with construction permits, registering property, getting credit, and protecting minority investors.[1103]

The factor of ease of doing business is one of the elements that makes Singapore successful in attracting investment to the country.[1104] According to the World Bank 2016 report on ease of doing business, internationally, the UAE ranks as No. 31, and Singapore is No.1.[1105] Within this global context, Oman is ranked at 149 from 189 economies in terms of ease of starting business, whereas the UAE in the same year ranked 60, and Singapore was 10.[1106]

Keong maintains that the problems caused by ineffectual bureaucracy in Singapore have been eliminated by the strong rule of law, one of a number of elements contributing to the success of business there.[1107] Foreign investors in Singapore must register their business according to the Business Registration Act (BRA) and the only reason for which registration may be refused is if the proposed business is unlawful or harmful to public welfare or national security.[1108] Importantly, foreign investors can apply directly to the Registrar of the Accounting and Corporate Regulatory Authority (ACRA), or else online at the business service portal run by ACRA, introduced to facilitate and secure online transactions.[1109] Foreign business owners can benefit from a one-stop service maintained by the Singapore government which helps investors with obtaining licences, and approvals, employment and all the requirements necessary for starting up business.[1110]

1102 World Bank and International Finance Corporation. *Doing Business 2016: Measuring Regulatory Quality and Efficiency* (World Bank Group 2016) 5 DOI: 10.1596/978-1-4648-0667-4.

1103 Ibid.

1104 Open Company Singapore (n 1034).

1105 World Bank and International Finance Corporation (n 1102).

1106 Ibid 19, 11, 232.

1107 The other elements are strong economic fundamentals and socio-political stability. See Low Kah Keong, 'Go east to Singapore', 28 Intl Fin. L Rev 92 2008-2010, 92.

1108 Shan (n 372) 596.

1109 Ibid 597.

1110 *Singapore Business and Investment Opportunities Yearbook* (2011 International Business Publications) 84.

However, there are some similarities between Oman and the UAE, especially when it comes to federal level regulations. For example, to establish a firm in the UAE, the firm and its resident employee must find a local sponsor, either a UAE citizen or a local institution such as a FZ.[1111] In addition, a firm cannot begin business activities until it is licensed by the emirate of domicile.[1112] However, Dubai established a plan to provide 1000 government services including services to business by smart phone in partnership with Google and Apple.[1113] In addition, it allows the establishment of Offshore Companies with no need to even set up an actual office facility.[1114] As noted in Chapter Four, one of the difficulties in Oman FZs is that companies must rent a site in order to be able to invest. Another feature in Dubai is that it has issued Regulation 3/2006 determining areas for absolute ownership of land without restrictions, which specifies an exhaustive list of all 23 areas in the Emirate of Dubai in which foreign investors can hold real estate outright.[1115] As discussed in Chapter Four, although Oman has issued a regulation granting ownership for foreign investors in such areas, numbers are relatively low and there is no comprehensive list of these.

Oman has taken steps to address this challenge by establishing 'Invest Easy' in 2015, an e-service portal for the business community in Oman, intended to minimise paperwork and save costs and time by offering e-services to facilitate setting up and managing companies in Oman.[1116] Such services will benefit USA and GCC investors; however, services for other foreign investors will vary according to the description of each business entity.[1117] It is anticipated that this service will be extended to other nationalities after the promulgation of the new law, if the guarantees in the current draft are maintained. Although the government claims that since the establishment of the online service in 2015 the number

1111 *UAE: Investment and Business Guide*, (Vol 1, Global Investment and Business Center 2015).

1112 Ibid.

1113 Global Smart Grid Federation, 'Dubai's 'one-stop shop' for government services' 9 July 2014 <www.globalsmartgridfederation.org/2014/07/09/dubais-one-stop-shop-for-government-services/>.

1114 UAE Free Zones <www.uaefreezones.com/dubai_company_registration.html>

1115 Regulation 3/2006 Determining Areas for Ownership by Non-UAE Nationals of Real Property in the Emirate of Dubai.

1116 MoCI <https://www.business.gov.om/wps/portal/> accessed 24 March 2016.

1117 Ibid.

of registered companies has risen from 4,000 to 22,000 per year,[1118] the efficiency of the service and its impact on foreign investment need to be examined further. Nevertheless, it should be noted that the increase in the number of companies that have registered for online services is remarkable.

To address the issue of easing foreign investment establishment and entry in Oman, Oman needs to consider the following steps: First; to reduce investor approval requirements, local ownership requirements, minimum capital requirement, Government discretion in all investment-related activities including Omanisation[1119] and minimum capital requirements by using visas and work permits.[1120] Second, to use modern technologies to issue the necessary permissions and licences, eliminating the need for labour to issue licences, by facilitating all procedures necessary on the governmental body websites.[1121] Finally, minimizing the procedures needed to achieve the licence and permissions.[1122] This can be done in three ways: fully implement the One Stop Shop (OSS), fully integrate the notion of OSS with related ministries such as MECA and MoM, and establish a list of sectoral restrictions.[1123] Overall, while the establishment of the 'Invest Easy' service is the first step on a long road, intended to facilitate doing business in Oman, there is still a need to consider the application of these steps.

6.3.3 Training to Gain

It was argued in Chapter Four that the lack of training for some jobs important to foreign investment in Oman, particularly judges and employees, is a challenge. Therefore, providing the necessary training for these jobs is expected to enhance the guarantees of legal protection, making Oman more attractive to foreign investment. It is believed that establishing efficiency, accountability and predictability of the judicial system is one of key the factors to attract foreign investors to any country.[1124] Clearly, the only way to achieve the efficiency and predictability of the Omani judiciary

1118 MoCI 'Invest Easy: One Stop Shop' <https://www.business.gov.om/> accessed 15 April 2016.
1119 Omanisation could be achieved by using visas and work permits.
1120 World Bank Group (n 665) 6.
1121 Ithraa, 'Some challenges faced by investors in establishing business in Oman and solutions recommended', (Unpublished paper, Muscat, 15 July 2015) 7.
1122 Ibid.
1123 World Bank Group (n 665) 6.
1124 Ogoto (n 1101) 772.

is by ensuring that judges dealing with foreign investment-related cases are well qualified and trained.

However, Weaver argues that the most important element in attracting FDI is not an efficient, transparent, and developed judicial or legal system but real business opportunities, as is the case in Dubai.[1125] He maintains that establishing business opportunities through FZs will bring the needed initial FDI for creating a legal framework for long-term FDI, arguing that if the state has promising business opportunities even if it has a poor judicial or legal system, this will not discourage investors from investing in the country.[1126] Weaver cites Saudi Arabia, Abu Dhabi, and Kuwait as examples of states with poor legal systems that are leading the Middle East in attracting foreign investment.[1127] As another example, it is said that the recognition and enforcement of ICSID awards in the UAE are not guaranteed because, although it has signed and ratified the ICSID Convention, it has so far failed to meet its obligation to enact national provisions dealing with recognition and enforcement of ICSID awards, or "to designate a competent Court or authority for that purpose".[1128]

Nonetheless, Weaver acknowledges that although foreign investors deciding whether to invest in a specific country may not be interested in abstract reforms, they are interested in those specific areas of the legal and judicial system that may impact on their investment.[1129] For example, their whole investment might be at risk if judges interpret legislation inconsistently or if bribes are required to obtain permits.[1130] Training for judges would deal with the first but not the second point as it relates to other factors, but ensuring the first is significant for Oman.

In addition, the efficiency of the legal and judicial systems of the countries mentioned needs to be examined more closely. It can be argued that one reason for Dubai's success was its establishment of DIFC Courts modelled on the English commercial court system, which operate

1125 Weaver (n 1068) 67.

1126 Ibid.

1127 Ibid.

1128 King & Wood Mallesons, 'The current status of investment arbitration in the UAE' 5 December 2014 <www.kwm.com/en/ae/knowledge/insights/the-current-status-of-investment-arbitration-in-the-uae-20141205> accessed 25 March 2016.

1129 Weaver (n 1068) 43.

1130 Ibid.

independently from those of Dubai and the UAE.[1131] Judges are well qualified and typically have experience in insurance, commercial, and banking matters, for example, in 2015, the Deputy Chief Justice of the DIFC Courts is a former High Court Judge from the UK, while the Chief Justice formerly held the same position in Singapore.[1132] The DIFC Courts are based on the common law legal system and consist of two levels: a Court of First Instance, and a Court of Appeal.[1133] Carballo argues that the provision of the DIFC Law Courts seeks to persuade foreign investors that DIFC legislation will be applied effectively and independently by neutral foreign judges, without fear of domestic dependence or protectionism.[1134]

Singapore is another example of the significant role the judiciary may play in attracting foreign investment. The judiciary in Singapore is influenced by the People's Action Party's (PAP) vision for economic growth since Lee Kuan Yew[1135] believed that a dependable judiciary is vital to economic development and the government's economic strategy.[1136] In 1995, he stated:

> But when the government, including me, takes a matter to court or when the government is taken by private individuals to court, then the court must adjudicate upon the issues strictly on their merits and in accordance with the law. To have it otherwise is to lose [...] our standing and [...] our status as an investment and financial centre. [...] Our reputation for the rule of law has been and is a valuable economic asset, part of our capital, although an intangible one. It has brought to Singapore good returns from the MNCs, OHQs, the banks, the financial institutions, and the flood of capital to buy up properties in Singapore.[1137]

1131 To set up the DIFC court the UAE issued four Federal Decrees including 35/2005, an amendment to the UAE Constitution, and passed three laws: Federal Law 8/2004, Federal Decree 9/2004, and Dubai Law 12/2004.60 see Griffin Weaver, 'Legal and Institutional Remedies for Middle East states Wishing to Develop and Increase Foreign Direct Investment' (2015) 27 Fla J Intl L 65, 81.

1132 Weaver (n 1131) 81, 82.

1133 Ibid 82.

1134 Alejandro Carballo, 'The Law of the Dubai International Financial Centre: Common Law Oasis or Mirage Within the UAE?' (2007) 21 Arab LQ 91, 97.

1135 First Prime Minister of Singapore (3 June 1959–28 November 1990).

1136 Murugesan (n 1079) 110.

1137 Ibid.

Accordingly, the vision of well-qualified judges meeting Singapore's needs as an investment and financial centre was a target of Singapore's ruler from the outset. Murugesan describes the judiciary in Singapore as part of a corporatist state where everything functions "like a precision Swiss watch, with all parts working efficiently, effectively and collaboratively" to maintain the country's status.[1138] Hence, Omani courts and judges should be prepared to be part of national economic development, helping the state to achieve its goals.

Another area that Oman needs to improve to enhance the guarantees of foreign investment is the provision of well-qualified Omani employees. As argued earlier, in Chapter Four, the real challenge for Omani employment is not Omanisation or minimum wage regulations; rather, it is the lack of skilled Omani labour. In comparison, one of Singapore's strengths is its well-educated and skilled employers, who must meet the national requirement.[1139] If there is any evidence of breaching domestic employment requirements, employers may face sanctions from the Singaporean Ministry of Manpower, benefiting from its sophisticated website.[1140] The emphasis in Singapore seems to be on the skills of foreign employees; it also requires employers to apply for a work permit or employment pass, under the terms of the Employment of Foreign Workers Act (Chapter 91A) and the Immigration Act (Chapter 133).

However, one challenge that the Omani Government needs to consider these days is that cutbacks due to the decline in oil prices in 2015 and 2016, are expected to lead to a reduction in the training budget or in cancellation of training in many governmental bodies.[1141] Therefore, cutbacks need to be carefully targeted to avoid negatively affecting training programmes, as the competence of the national employment market is necessary to attract foreign investment.[1142]

6.3.4 The Need for a National Arbitration Centre in Oman

The availability of arbitration in a country is one of the factors included in 2016 in the World Bank's index for Doing Business under the quality

---

1138 Ibid 110-111.

1139 Shan (n 372) 598.

1140 Ibid.

1141 Saoud Al Shoaili, 'The Spend on Training May Affect the Competency and the Productivity of the State' (in Arabic) *Oman Daily* (Muscat, 9 February 2016) <http://omandaily.om> accessed 13 May 2016.

1142 Ibid.

of judicial processes indicators on enforcing contracts.[1143] Although Oman is a member of the GCC Commercial Arbitration Centre, due to developments in the commercial and industrial sectors in Oman, the country has realised that it needs its own arbitration centre.[1144] Therefore, it is widely believed that in order to encourage greater investor confidence in the Omani legal system and to build a healthy business environment, Oman has made promising progress towards establishing a national arbitration centre.[1145] However, nothing has been done up to date, but if things go well, it is expected that after the establishment of the national arbitration centre, companies will be encouraged to settle their disputes before the centre, and will be free to choose their arbitrator from Oman or from outside the country.[1146]

As an example of such a measure, the Singapore International Arbitration Centre (SIAC) was established in 1991 to provide neutral arbitration services to the global business community.[1147] Although like Singapore and Dubai, Oman has generally adopted the Model Law, Singapore issued two separate pieces of legislation, an International Arbitration Act what contains minor modifications from the Model Law and an Arbitration Act, the latter being provided for domestic arbitration.[1148] Pryles observes that the significance of the International Arbitration Centre in Singapore is mainly due to the support it receives from the country's Supreme Court[1149] as this offers the assistance needed for international arbitration, and also supervises and occasionally intervenes in these processes.[1150] Therefore, the establishment of a national arbitration centre in Oman afterward would require support from the Omani courts.

To take another example, Dubai first established the Centre for Commercial Conciliation and Arbitration in 1994, and then the name was changed to Dubai International Arbitration Centre (DIAC).[1151] In 2008, in

1143 World Bank. and International Finance Corporation (n 1102) 105
1144 Kaushalendra Singh, 'Efforts on to Set Up Arbitration Centre', *Oman Daily Observer* (Muscat, 19 August 2015) <http://omanobserver.om/efforts-on-to-set-up-arbitration-centre/>.
1145 OBFA (n 683) 6.
1146 Ibid.
1147 Singapore International Arbitration Centre (SIAC) <www.siac.org.sg/> accessed 31 January 2016.
1148 Aboul-Enein (n 906) 3; Pryles (n 1017) 37; Weaver (n 1131) 87-88.
1149 Pryles (n 1017) 53.
1150 Ibid.
1151 Dubai International Arbitration Centre (DIAC) <www.diac.ae/idias/aboutus/> accessed 31 January 2016.

conjunction with the London Court of International Arbitration, Dubai established another new arbitration institution called the DIFC-LCIA Arbitration Centre.[1152] The 2008 amendment to Dubai Arbitration Law provided the DIFC Arbitration Centre with a broad jurisdiction, allowing parties to arbitrate regardless of their location once they expressly agree to the jurisdiction of the DIFC Arbitration Tribunals.[1153] For example, in *Al Khorafi v. Bank Sarasin & Co.* the DIFC Court provided that "the Tribunal might claim jurisdiction notwithstanding the parties having a prior agreement to an unambiguous foreign selection clause".[1154] Consequently, as mentioned earlier, it is believed that the establishment of the DIFC-LCIA Arbitration Centre has contributed in increasing the FDI in Dubai and was a key factor in Dubai's ability to overcome the 2008 financial crises quickly. This is because the Arbitration Centre gives foreign investors the added confidence needed to invest in Dubai and as a result, arbitrations in the Emirate have increased.[1155]

Therefore, Oman could benefit from the experiences of both Singapore and Dubai. This could be done by providing the judiciary support needed for arbitration, especially from the Omani High Court. This matter is also connected with the training needed for judges, discussed above. In addition, establishing conjunction with one of the most well-known international arbitration bodies in developed countries will help the Omani arbitration centre to gain the experience and the recognition needed. It can be argued that the FZs and DSEZ in Oman will not achieve their aim of attracting foreign investors unless Oman establishes its own national arbitration centre, close to where foreign companies are based. Thus, it is strongly recommended that the cheap option for Middle East countries wishing to move to the next stage of development and ensure their economic health, is to set up independent arbitration centres within the FZs.[1156]

1152 Weaver (n 1131) 87- 88.

1153 Ibid 88.

1154 *Al Khorafi v Bank Sarasin & Co.*, 30 May 2014 (CFI 026/2009).

1155 Weaver (n 1131) 89.

1156 Ibid 68.

6.4 Conclusion

As a basis of the recommendations for enhancing legal protection for foreign investment in Oman, this chapter summarised the main findings of the arguments put forward in this book. Thus, it is argued that Oman has taken a greater protection approach towards foreign investment on two levels; in its national legislation and in its international agreements. Nevertheless, due to the potential risks involved in this approach, illustrated particularly by the experience of the *Al-Tamimi* case, the contribution of Omani law and practice to the development of international investment law can draw attention to the need to consider a balanced approach between protecting its sovereignty and attracting foreign investment. On the above basis, it was also highlighted that if Oman uses restrictions in its international agreements to safeguard its own national interests, without having efficient national system in foreign investment-related issues, this will negatively affect Oman's ability to attract foreign investment.

While the recommendations focus mainly on national policies, amendment may be required in the relevant Omani regulations to implement the recommended policies. These recommendations further emphasise the need to improve the efficiency of the national investment system, including the need for a specialised foreign investment council with a unified policy, the need to facilitate doing business in Oman, the need for well-qualified judges and employees and the need to establish a national arbitration centre in Oman. All these would be supported by Oman's unique characteristics of external peaceful policy in the region and peaceful coexistence that is expected to enhance foreign investors' trust and maximise Oman's ability to attract foreign investment.

After ensuring the improvement of the efficiency of its national legal and policy system, Oman needs to consider and investigate two issues in depth. First, older treaties need to be revisited and reviewed in order to see whether they need specific amendments to be made that would serve the balanced approach. Second, consideration needs to be given to whether Oman should establish its own model for BITs, following the experience of some of the countries mentioned above.

Although this study was able to examine in depth a number of key aspects of the current legal system in relation to foreign investment in

Oman, these areas will need to be re-visited following the promulgation of the DNFIL since the new legislation provides improved guarantees for foreign investment and its effect needs to be evaluated after its implementation.

Bibliography

1. Primary Sources

1.1 Interviews

Interview with foreign investor 1, (Muscat, Oman, 17 August 2014)
Interview with foreign investor 2, (Muscat, Oman, 28 August 2014)
Interview with foreign investor 3, (Muscat, Oman, 24 August 2014)
Interview with foreign investor 4, (Muscat, Oman, 9 September 2014)
Interview with policymaker 1, (Muscat, Oman, 14 August 2014)
Interview with policymaker 2, minister (Muscat, Oman, 18 August 2014)
Interview with policymaker 3, (Muscat, Oman, 19 August 2014)
Interview with policymaker 4, (Muscat, Oman, 19 August 2014)
Interview with policymaker 5, (Muscat, Oman, 21 August 2014)
Interview with judge 1 and judge 2, (Muscat, Oman, 17 August 2014)
Interview with judge 3, (Muscat, Oman, 18 August 2014)
Interview with lawyer 1, (Muscat, Oman, 20 August 2014)
Interview with lawyer 2, (Muscat, Oman, 5 September 2014)
Interview with lawyer 3, (Muscat, Oman, 27 August 2014)
Interview with lawyer 4, (Muscat, Oman, 30 September 2014)

2. Secondary Sources

2.1 Books and Chapters in Books

Allen J R K and Rigsbee W L, Oman Under Qaboos: From Coup to Constitution, 1970-1996 (Frank Cass, 2000)

Al Sameraie D, Foreign Investment Legal Challenges and Guarantees (1st edn, Center for Arab Unity Studies, 2006)

Anthony J D, 'Oman, the Gulf and the United States', in R Pridham (ed), Oman: Economic, Social and Strategic Developments (Croom Helm 1987)

Ballantyne W M, 'The states of the GCC: Sources of law, the Shari'a and the extent to which it applies' in W M Ballantyne, Essays and addresses on Arab law (reprint, Routledge 2000)

Bazeley P, Qualitative Data Analysis Practical Strategies (SAGE 2013)

Berg B L and Lune H, Qualitative Research Methods for the Social Sciences (8th edn Pearson 2012)

Blaikie N, Analyzing quantitative data: from description to explanation (SAGE 2003)
Bovis C, EC Public Procurement: Case Law and Regulation (1st edn, OUP 2006)
Bovis C, The Liberalisation of Public Procurement and its Effects on the Common Market (Ashgate 1998)
Bjorklund A, Laird I and Ripinsky S (eds), Investment Treaty Law: Current Issues III: Remedies in International Investment Law Emerging Jurisprudence of International investment Law (British Institute of International and Comparative Law 2009)
Cotula L, Foreign Investment, Law and Sustainable Development, A handbook on agriculture and extractive industries (International Institute for Environment and Development 2014)
Crawford J, Brownlie's Principles of Public International Law (8th edn, OUP 2012)
Crawford J and Koskenniemi M (eds), Cambridge Companion to International Law (Cambridge University Press 2012)
Di Blasé A, 'Intellectual Property in Investment agreements and public concerns' in G Sacerdoti Charmaz K, (eds) Constructing Grounded Theory: A Practical Guide through Qualitative Analysis (SAGE 2006)
De Luca A, 'Indirect Expropriation and Regulatory Taking' in G Sacerdoti (ed) General Interests of Host States in International Law (1st edn, Cambridge 2014)
Denzin N and Lincoln Y (eds), The SAGE Handbook of Qualitative Research (4th edn, SAGE 2011)
Dimsey M, The Resolution of International Investment Disputes: Challenges and Solutions (Eleven International Publishing 2008)
Dixon M, McCorquodale R and Williams S, Cases and Materials on International Law (5th edn, OUP 2011)
Dolzer R and Schreuer C, Principles of International Investment Law (1st, OUP 2008)
Dugan C, Wallace D, Rubins N and Sabahi B, Investor-State Arbitration (OUP 2008)
Emery J, Spence M, Wells L, and Buehrer T, Administrative Barriers to Foreign Investment: Reducing Red Tape in Africa (World Bank, 2000)
Federal Research Division, Oman: A Country Study (Kessinger 2010)
Flick U, An Introduction to Qualitative Research (4th edn, SAGE 2009)

Friedmann V, and Pugh R, Legal Aspects of Foreign Investment (Stevens and Sons 1959)
Hackworth G H, Digest of International Law (vol III, US Dept of State 1942)
Harrison J, 'UK National Report' in Wenhua Shan (ed), The Legal Protection of Foreign Investment A Comparative Study (Hart Publishing 2012)
Harten G, Investment Treaty Arbitration and Public Law (OUP 2011)
Ho J, 'Singapore National Report', in Wenhua Shan (ed), The Legal Protection of Foreign Investment A Comparative Study (Hart Publishing 2012) 593
Hoekman B M and Mavroidis P C, The World Trade Organization, Law, economic, and politics (Routledge 2007)
Hughes H and PohSeng Y, Foreign Investment and Industrialisation in Singapore (1st edn, University of Wisconsin Press 1969)
Khaldoun Hassan Al-Naqeeb, Society and State in the Gulf and Arab Peninsula: A Different Perspective (1st edn, Routledge 2012)
Kuokkanen T, International Law and the Environment: Variations on a Theme (Kluwer Law International 2002)
Loibl G and Evans M D (eds), International Law (3rd edn, OUP 2010)
Matsushita M, Schoenbaum T J and Mavroidis P C, The World Trade Organization Law, Practice, and Policy (2nd edn, OUP 2006)
Mavroidis P C, 'Regulation of Investment in the Trade Regime: From ITO to WTO' in Zdenek Drabek and Petros C Mavroidis (eds), Regulation of Foreign Investment: Challenges to International Harmonization (World Scientific Publishing 2013)
Metz M Chapin, 'Oman', in H Chapin Metz (ed), Persian Gulf States: Country Studies (Library of Congress 1993)
Montt S, State Liability in Investment Treaty Arbitration Global Constitutional and Administrative Law in the BIT Generation (Hart Publishing, 2009)
Moses M L, The Principles and Practice of International Commercial Arbitration (2nd edn, Cambridge University Press 2012)
Muchlinski P T, Multinational Enterprises and the Law (2nd edn, Oxford International Law Library, 2007)
Newcombe A and Paradell L, Law and Practice of Investment Treaties, Standards of Treatment (Kluwer Law International 2009)
Nwogugu E, The Legal Problems of Foreign Investment in Developing Countries (Manchester University Press, 1965)

Oman, Investment and Business Guide: Strategic and Practical Information (International Business Publication 2013)
Oxford Business Group, The Report: Oman 2012 (Oxford Business Group 2012)
Rerakyla A and Ruusuvuori J, 'Analysing Talk and Text' in N K Denzin and Y S Lincoln (eds), The SAGE Handbook of Qualitative Research (4th edn, SAGE 2011)
Rubin H J and Rubin I S, Qualitative Interviewing: The Art of Hearing Data (2nd edn, SAGE 2005)
Sarantakos S, Social Research (2nd edn, Palgrave 2005)
Schrijver N, Sovereignty Over Natural Resources, Balncing Rights and Duties (Cambridge University Press 2008)
Shan W (ed), 'General report' in Wenhua Shan (ed) The Legal Protection of Foreign Investment A Comparative Study (Hart Publishing 2012)
Shavarsh T, Legal Aspects of Oil Concessions in the Middle East (Hamaskaine Press 1972)
Shaw M N, International Law (6th edn, Cambridge University Press, 2008)
Singapore Business and Investment Opportunities Yearbook (International Business Publications 2011)
Smith B, Market Orientalism: Cultural Economy and the Arab Gulf States (Syracuse University Press 2015)
Sornarajah M, The International Law on Foreign Investment (3rd edn, Cambridge University Press, 2011)
Subedi S P, International Investment Law: Reconciling Policy and Principle (2nd edn, Hart Publishing 2012)
Subedi S P, International Investment Law: Reconciling Policy and Principle (3rd edn, Hart Publishing 2016)
Toriguian S, Legal aspects of oil concessions in the Middle East (Hamaskaine Press 1972)
UAE, Investment and Business Guide, vol 1 (Global Investment and Business Center 2015)
Vandevelde K J, Bilateral Investment Treaties: History, Policy, and Interpretation (OUP, 2010)
Vaver D, Intellectual Property Law, Copyright. Patent. Trade-Mark (2nd edn, Irwin 2011)
Watson, J K R, The WTO and the Environment: Development of Competence Beyond Trade (Routledge 2013)
Werbicki R J, 'Arbitral Interim Measures: Fact or Fiction?'in AAA (ed) Handbook on International Arbitration and ADR (2nd edn, Juris 2010)

Wigwe C, International Law and Practice, The World Bank, IMF and State Sovereignty (Mountcrest University Press, 2011)
Wilson R, United States Commercial Treaties and International Law (New Orleans: The Hauser Press 1960)

2.2 Journals

Aboul-Enein M I M, 'The Development of International Commercial Arbitration Laws in the Arab World' (1999) Arbitration 1
Afrin Z, 'Foreign Direct Investments and Sustainable Development in the Least-Developed Countries' (2004) 10 Ann Surv Intl & Comp L 215
Agil H and Zeller B, 'Foreign Investments in Saudi Arabia' (2012) 15 Intl Trade & Bus L Rev 60
Al-Azri M, 'The Role of the Omani Judiciary in Supporting Arbitration' (2010) 2 J Arab Arbitration 1
Al-Azri, M, 'Prevention of Non-Compliance with Arbitral Awards: Some Proposals for Efficient Enforcement' (2005) 12 Tilburg LR 348
Alvarez-Jiménez A, 'Minimum Standard of Treatment of Aliens, Fair and Equitable Treatment of Foreign Investors, 'Customary International Law and the Diallo Case before the International Court of Justice' (2008) 9 J World Investment & Trade 51
Al-Siyabi M K A, 'A Legal Analysis of the Development of Arbitration in Oman with Special Reference to the Enforcement of International Arbitral Awards', (PhD thesis, University of Hull, 2008)
Ayad M B, 'International Commercial Arbitration Award Enforcement at the Crossroads of Sharial Law and Ordre Public in the MENA: Paving the Golden Path towards Harmonisation' (2009) 10 J World Investment & Trade 723
Babeiya E, 'Trade Unions and Democratization in Tanzania: End of an Era?' (2011) 4 J Pol & L 123
Ballantyne W M and Monico A R, 'Latest Trends in Corporation Law and Other Developments in Kuwait, Saudi Arabia, Bahrain, Qatar, the United Arab Emirates and Oman' (1978) 6 Intl Bus Law 666
Ballantyne W M, 'Comparative Commercial Law in the Middle East' (1987) 53 Arbitration 51
Borchardt E, 'The 'Minimum Standard' of the Treatment of Aliens' (1939) 38 Mich L Rev 445
Bossdorf, M, Engels C and Weiler S, EU GCC Invest Report 2013: Promotion of Mutual investment opportunities and creation of a virtual European structure in the GCC (2013)

Brewer T L, 'International Investment Dispute Settlement Procedure: The Evolving Regime for Foreign Direct Investment' (1994) 26 Law & Pol'y Intl Bus 633
Brewer T L and Young S, 'Investment Issues at the WTO: the Architecture of Rule and the Settlement of Disputes' (1998) 1 J Intl Econ L 457
Campbell A, 'Insolvent Banks and the Financial Sector Safety Net - Lessons from the Northern Rock Crisis (2008) 20 SACLJ 316
Carballo A, 'The Law of the Dubai International Financial Centre: Common Law Oasis or Mirage Within the UAE?' (2007) 21 Arab L Q 91
Carmody C, 'The Duty to Settle in WTO Dispute Settlement' (2011) 6 Asian J. WTO & Intl Health L & Policy 169
Choudhury B, 'Evolution or Devolution? Defining Fair and Equitable Treatment in International Investment Law' (2005) 6 J World Investment & Trade 297
Crook J R, 'Applicable Law in International Arbitration: the Iran-US Claims Tribunal Experience' (1989) AJIL 278
de Luca A, 'Note on the Yearbook on International Investment Law & Policy 2008–2009: Foreign Investment Promotion and Protection vs Host States' Regulatory Powers (2010) 11 J World Investment & Trade 1115
DiMascio N and Pauwelyn J, 'Nondiscrimination in Trade and Investment Treaties: Worlds Apart or Two Sides of the Same Coin?' (2008) 102 Am J Intl L 48
Dumberry P, 'Are BITs Representing the "New" Customary International Law in International Investment Law?'(2009) 28 Penn St Intl L Rev 675
Dry E K, 'Corporate Governance in the Sultanate of Oman' (2003) 3 Rich J Global L & Bus 45
Elcombe J, 'Regulatory Powers Vs. Investment Protection Under Nafta's Chapter 1110: Metalclad, Methanex, and Glamis Gold' (2010) 68 U Toronto Fac L Rev 71
Elias O, 'The Relationship Between General and Particular Customary International Law' (1996) 8 Afr J Intl & Comp L 67
Ewing-Chow M, 'Thesis, Antithesis and Synthesis: Investor Protection in BITs, WTO and FTAs' (2007) 30 U N S W LJ 548

Falsafi A, 'The International Minimum Standard of Treatment of Foreign Investors' property: A Contingent Standard' (2006) 30 Suffolk Transnational L Rev 317
Fauchald O K, 'The Legal Reasoning of ICSID Tribunals – An Empirical Analysis' (2008) 19 EJIL 301
Garcia-Bolivar O E, 'Past and Present Legal Guarantees for Protection of Foreign Investments in Venezuela', 18 (2012) L & Bus Rev Am 173
Gazzini T, 'The Role of Customary International Law in the Field of Foreign Investment' (2007) 8 J World Investment & Trade 691
Gresh G F, 'Traversing the Persian Gauntlet: U S Naval Projection and the Strait of Hormuz' (2010) 34 Fletcher F World Aff 41
Gutbrod M Hindelang S and Kim Y I, 'Protection against Indirect Expropriation under National and International Legal Systems' (2009) 1 Göttingen J of Int L 291
Hill T W, 'The Commercial Legal System of the Sultanate of Oman' (1983) 17 Intl L 507
Hirst A, 'Contemporary Mercantile Jurisdiction in Oman' (1992) 7 Arab LQ 3
Hsueh C W, 'Direct Effect, WTO Compliance Mechanism and the Protection for Individuals: Lessons Learned from the EC' (2009) 4 Asian J WTO & Intl Health L & Pol'y 521
Hunter R J, Shapiro R E and Ryan L V, 'Legal Considerations in Foreign Direct Investment', 28 (2003) Okla City U L Rev 851
Hurtado H A, 'Is Latin American Taxation Policy Appropriate for Promoting Foreign Direct Investment in the Region?' (2011) 31 New J Intl L & Bus 313
Jones A and Al Sabahi F, 'Recent Changes under Commercial Laws of Oman' (2013) 4 Middle East Business L Rev
Keong C S, 'The Courts and the 'Rule of Law' in Singapore, a Lecture Delivered at the Rule of Law Symposium' (2012) Sing J Legal Stud 209
Keong L K, 'Go East to Singapore'(2008) 28 Intl Fin L Rev 92
Khan A A and Laubach C S, 'Oman: Further Development of Oman's Legal System' (2000) 15 Arab LQ 112
Kohona P T B, 'Some Major Provisions in Modern Investment Protection Agreements' (1987) Third World Legal Stud, 151
Kotuby C T, 'General Principles of Law, International Due Process, and the Modern Role of Private International Law' (2012) 23 Duke J Comp & Intl L 411

Kucera D, 'Core Labour Standards and Foreign Direct Investment'(2002) 141 Intl Lab Rev 31
Kutty A and Chakravarty S, 'A Multilateral Investment Agreement: Poison or Antidote?' (2010) 22 Sri Lanka JiL 89
Lane T and Morton W, 'Enforcing a Foreign Arbitration Award in Oman' (1985) 4 Intl Fin L Rev 33
Leal-Arcas R, 'The Multilateralization of International Investment Law' (2009) 35 NCJ Intl L & Com Reg 33
Lester S, 'Reforming the International Investment Law System' (2015) 30 Md J Intl L 70, 78
Luttrell S R, 'Choosing Dubai: A Comparative Study of Arbitration under the UAE Federal Code of Civil Procedure and the Arbitration Law of the DIFC' (2008) 9 Bus L Intl 254
Malkawi B H, 'Balancing Open Investment with National Security: Review of US and UAE Laws with DP World as a Case Study' (2011) 13 U Notre Dame Austl L Rev 153
Mallat C, 'From Islamic to Middle Eastern Law. A Restatement of the Field (Part II)'(2004) 52 Am J Comp L 209
Maniruzzaman A F M, 'Expropriation of Alien Property and the Principle of non-Discrimination in International Law of Foreign Investment: an Overview' (1998) 8 J Transnational L & Policy 57
Marar A D, 'The Cooperation Council for the Arab States of the Gulf' (2004) 10 Law & Bus Rev Am 475
McHugo J J H A, 'The Practice of Law by Foreign Lawyers in the Sultanate of Oman' (1985) 7 Mich YBI Legal Stud 89
McHugo J, 'Joint Ventures in the Sultanate of Oman' (1987) 2 Arab LQ 130
McKinney B, 'Privatisation: Oman and Egypt' (1997) 25 Intl Bus Law 126
McKinney B, 'Economic Reform Legislation in Oman' (1995) Intl Bus Lawyer 131
McRae D, 'Measuring the Effectiveness of the WTO Dispute Settlement System' (2008) 3 Asian J WTO & Intl Health L & Policy 1
Mellahi K, Guermat C, Frynas J G and Al-Bortmani H, 'Motives for Foreign Direct Investment in Oman' (2003) 45 Thunderbird Intl Bus Rev 431
Menalco J and Solifs R, 'Creation and Enforcement of a Minimum Standard of Treatment Applicable to Foreign and Domestic Juristic Persons' (1962) 37 Tul L Rev 205

Miles K, 'International Investment Law: Origins, Imperialism and Conceptualizing the Environment' (2010) 21 Colo J Intl Envtl L& Policy 1
Mishra A and Mishra A, 'Fair and Equitable Treatment Standard in International Investment Law: an Analysis Vis-A-Vis Public International Law' (2012) 11 Kor U L Rev 107
Mistelis L A, 'Regulatory Aspects: Globalization, Harmonization, Legal Transplants, and Law Reform-Some Fundamental Observations' (2000) 34 Intl L 1055
Mosoti V, 'Bilateral Investment Treaties and the Possibility of a Multilateral Framework on Investment at the WTO: Are Poor Economies Caught in Between?' (2005) 26 Nw J Intl L & Bus 95
Murugesan S, 'Judicial Independence in a Corporatist State: Singapore - a case study' (2012) Lawasia J 99
Nawafleh A, 'Development of Intellectual Property Laws and Foreign Direct Investment in Jordan' (2010) 5 J Intl Com L & Tech 142
Ocran T M, 'International Investment Guarantee Agreements and Related Administrative Schemes' (1988) 10 J Intl L 341
Ogoto M, 'Investing in the Middle East and North Africa Region to Promote Development and Modernization An OECD Initiative in the Making' (2004) 5 J World Investment & Trade 767
Olynyk S, 'A Balanced Approach to Distinguishing Between Legitimate Regulation and Indirect Expropriation in Investor-State Arbitration' (2012) 15 Intl Trade & Bus L Rev 254
Pepper W F, 'Foreign Capital Investment in Member States of the Gulf Cooperation Council Considerations, Issues and Concerns for Investors' (1991) 6 Arab LQ 331
Porterfield M C, 'State Practice and the (Purported) Obligation under Customary International Law to Provide Compensation for Regulatory Expropriations' (2011) 37, NCJ Intl L &Com Reg 159
Primo Braga C A and Fink C, 'The Relationship between Intellectual Property Rights and Foreign Direct Investment' (1998) 9 Duke J Comp & Intl L 163
Pryles M, 'Recent Singapore Decisions on International Arbitration' 24 (2012) Nat'l L Sch India Rev 35
Radulescu R and Robson M, 'Trade Unions, Wage Bargaining Co-ordination and Foreign Direct Investment' (2008) 22 Labour 661
Root E, 'The Basis of Protection to Citizens Residing Abroad' (1910) 4 AJIL 517

Ryan C M, 'Meeting Expectations: Assessing the Long-Term Legitimacy and Stability of International Investment Law' (2007) 29 U Pa J Intl L 725
Salacuse J W, 'The Emerging Global Regime for Investment' (2010) 51 Harv Intl LJ 427
Salacuse J W, 'TheTreatification of International Investment Law' (2007) 8 Stud Intl Fin Econ & Tech L 241
Saleem H, 'Comments of Professor Hadi Saleem' (2016) 29 J of Arab Arbitration 819
Saroosh D, 'Investment Treaty Arbitration and the World Trade Organization: What Role for Systemic Values in the Resolution of International Economic Disputes?' (2014) 49 Tex Intl L J 445
Sattorova M, 'Investment Treaty Breach as Internationally Proscribed Conduct: Shifting Scope, Evolving Objectives, Recalibrated Remedies?' (2012) 4 Trade L & Dev 315
Sauvé P, 'Multilateral rules on Investment: is Forward Movement Possible?' (2006) 9 J Intl Econ L 325
Schill S W, 'Enhancing International Investment Law's Legitimacy: Conceptual and Methodological Foundations of a New Public Law Approach' (2011) 52 Va J Intl L 57
Schlemmer E C, 'A New International Law on Foreign Investment' (2005) J S Afr L 531
Shan W, 'Is Calvo Dead?' (2007) 55 Am J Comp L 123
Shanmugam K, 'The Rule of Law in Singapore' (2012) Sing J Legal Stud 357
Siegfried N A, 'Legislation and Legitimation in Oman: the Basic Law' (2000) 7 Islamic L & Soc'y 359
Sornarajah M, 'Protection and Guarantees of Investment' (2000) 26 Commw L Bull 1290
Spain A,'Examining the International Judicial Function: International Courts as Dispute Resolvers' (2011) 34 Loy LA Intl & Comp L Rev 5
Spoliansky L G R, 'Modern Business Law in the Sultanate of Oman' (1979) 13 Intl L 101
Stovall H L, Tinawi E, Katz Y, and Uliman H, 'Middle East Commercial Law Developments', (1998) 32 Intl L 411
Subedi S P, 'The Challenge of Reconciling the Competing Principles within the Law of Foreign Investment with Special Reference to the Recent Trend in the Interpretation of the Term "Expropriation"'(2006) 40 Intl Law121

Subedi S P, 'India's New 'Bilateral Investment Promotion and Protection Treaty with Nepal: A New Trend in State Practice' (2013) 28 ICSID Rev 384
Sun TT, 'Investor-State Dispute Settlement Provision in the Cross-Strait BIT: Possible Enhancement in its Operation' (2014) 7 Contemp Asia Arb J 195
Sutton S D, 'Emilio Augustin Maffezin v Kingdom of Spain and the ICSID Secretary-General's Screening Power' (2005) 21 Arbitration Intl 113
Swenson D L, 'Why Do Developing Countries Sign BITs?' (2005) 12 UC Davis J Intl L & Policy 131
Tanzi A,'On Balancing Foreign Investment Interests with Public Interests in Recent Arbitration Case Law in the Public Utilities Sector' (2012) 11 Law & Prac Intl Cts & Tribunals 47
Tweeddale A G, 'Enforcing Arbitration Awards Contrary to Public Policy in England' (2000) 17Intl Construction LRev 159
Vadi V S, 'When Cultures Collide: Foreign Direct Investment, Natural Resources, and Indigenous Heritage in International Investment Law' (2010) 42 Colum Hum Rts L Rev 797
Vandevelde K J, 'A Brief History of International Investment Agreements' (2005) 12 UC Davis J Intl L & Policy, 157
Vandevelde K J, 'The Political Economy of a Bilateral Investment Treaty' (1998) 92 Am J Intl L 621
Vannieuwenhuyse G, 'Bringing a Dispute Concerning ICSID Cases and the ICSID Convention before the International Court of Justice' (2009) 8 L & Prac Intl Cts & Tribunals 115
Villalta Puig G and A1-Haddab B, 'The Constitutionalisation of Free Trade in the Gulf Cooperation Council' (2011) 25 Arab LQ 311
Voon T, 'Eliminating Trade Remedies from the WTO: Lessons from Regional Trade Agreements' (2010) 59 Intl & Comp LQ 625
Waelde T, 'International Law of Foreign Investment: Toward Regulation by Multilateral Treaties' (1999) Bus L Intl 50
Wang G, 'International Investment Law: An Appraisal from the Perspective of the New Haven School of International Law' (2010) 18 Asia Pac L Rev 19
Wang W, 'National Treatment in Financial Services in the Context of the GATS/WTO' (2003) 6 Stud Intl Fin Econ & Tech L 149
Weaver G, 'Legal and Institutional Remedies for Middle East states Wishing to Develop and Increase Foreign Direct Investment' (2015) 27 Fla J Intl L 65

Weaver G, 'The Underutilized Foreign Investor' (2013) 5 Creighton Intl & Comp LJ 29
Westcott T J, 'International Investment Dispute Settlement Procedure: The Evolving Regime For Foreign Direct Investment' Recent Practice on Fair and Equitable Treatment (2007), 8 J World Investment & Trade 409
Wick D M, 'The Counter-Productivity of ICSID Denunciation and Proposals for Change' (2012) 11 J Intl Bus & L 239
Wouters J and Man P de and Chanet L, 'The Long and Winding Road of International Investment Agreements: Toward a Coherent Framework for Reconciling the Interests of Developed and Developing Countries?' (2009) 3 Hum Rts & Intl Legal Discourse 263
Yackee J W, 'Do We Really Need BITs? Toward A Return To Contract In International Investment Law' (2008) 3 Asian J WTO & Intl Health L & Policy 121
Yackee J W, 'Do Bilateral Investment Treaties Promote Foreign Direct Investment? Some Hints from Alternative Evidence' (2010) 51 Va J Intl L 397
Yackee J W, 'Political Risk and International Investment Law' (2013) 24 Duke J Comp & Intl L 477
Yuh G G J, 'The Law of Recognition and Enforcement of Arbitration Awards in Singapore' (1993) 14 Sing L Rev 220

2.3 Internet Resources

Abdallah A, 'Arbitration in Administrative Disputes in Oman' (ICCA) <www.youngicca-blog.com/arbitration-in-administrative-disputes-in-oman/> accessed 2 December 2015
Al-Duqm Special Economic Zone, 'About us' <www.duqm.gov.om/sezad/about-us/welcome-to-duqm> accessed 20 May 2015
Al Ghadani F, 'Oman expat labour law: No plan to defer two-year ban on expatriate return', Times of Oman (Muscat, 15 June 2014)
Al Kiyumi B, 'Report' Oman Daily Observer (Muscat, 7 May 2012) accessed 15 June 2014)
Al Lawati H, 'GCC countries need to address expat remittances' Oman Daily Observer (Muscat, 14 July 2015) <http://omanobserver.om/> accessed 11 May 2016
Almutawa A M and Maniruzzaman A F M, 'Problems of enforcement of foreign arbitral awards in the Gulf Cooperation Council states

and the prospect of a uniform GCC arbitration law: an empirical study' (3 February 2015), 24 <http://ssrn.com/abstract=2559590> accessed 22 February 2016

Al Shoaili S, 'Time Spent on Training may Affect the Competency and the Productivity of the State' (in Arabic) Oman Daily (Muscat, 9 February 2016) <http://omandaily.om> accessed 13 May 2016.

Anderson R, 'Majid Al Futtaim plans $1.3bn investment in Oman malls', 2 May 2016 <www.gulfbusiness.com> accessed 4 May 2016

Azamn Newspaper Thursday 26 July 2016, available at <www.azamn.com> accessed 05 August 2016.

Bossdorf M, Engels C and Weiler S, EU GCC Invest Report 2013 (April 2013) <www.eurochambres.eu/custom/EU_GCC_ INVEST_REPORT_2013-2014-00273-01.pdf>

Braun V and Clarke V (2006) Using thematic analysis in psychology. Qualitative Research in Psychology, 3 (2) 77-101. <http://eprints.uwe.ac.uk/11735> accessed 16 June 2016

BTI Project, BTI 2014 Oman Country Report, 9 <www.bti-project.org/reports/country-reports/mena/omn/index nc#chap3> accessed 24 November 2015

Bureau of Economic and Business Affairs, 'Investment Climate Statement – Oman' (May 2015) <www.state.gov/> accessed 5 May 2016

Bureau of Economic and Business Affairs, '2012 Investment Climate Statement-Oman' (ICS 2012) <www.state.gov/e/eb/rls/othr/ics/2012/191213.htm> accessed 2 March 2015

CAAJ, 'The judiciary power' <www.caaj.gov.om/word_sultaneng.aspx> accessed 19 November 2015

Carnegie Endowment/FRIDE, 'Arab Political Systems: Baseline Information and Reforms-Oman', March 6 2008 <http://carnegieendowment.org/2008/03/06/arab-political-systems-baseline-information-and-reforms> accessed 2 July 2015

Deloitte, 'International Tax: Oman Highlights 2014' <www.deloitte.com/content/dam/Deloitte/ global/Documents/Tax/dttl-tax-omanhighlights-2014.pdf> accessed 29 June 2014

Diwan of Royal Court, 'Barriers to Foreign Investment in Oman' (Muscat 20 January 2014) <www.mola.gov.om/eng/index.aspx> accessed 29 April 2016

Doing Business in Singapore (4 October 2010) <www.legal500.com/assets/images/stories/firmdevs/asia_doing_business_publication_-_singapore_4 10 10.pdf> accessed 2 July 2015

Drabek Z and Mavroidis P C, 'Regulation of Foreign Investment: Challenges to International Harmonization' (Dubai FDI) <www.dubaifdi.gov.ae> accessed 29 March 2016

Dubai. 'Obtaining one-stop shop services from free zones' (11 November 2013) <www.dubai.ae/en/Lists/Articles/DispForm.aspx?ID=127&category=Businesses> accessed 27 March 2016

Dubai International Arbitration Centre (DIAC) <www.diac.ae/idias/aboutus/> accessed 31 January 2016

Ernst & Young, 'Doing business in Oman. An executive's guide to doing business in Oman' (January 2011) <http://vae.ahk.de/fileadmin/ahk_vae/Startseite_Oman/Doing_ business_in_Oman_Final_.pdf> accessed 6 March 2015

Ernst & Young, 'Oman proposes new foreign capital investment law' (Tax Insights, 25 January 2016) <http://taxinsights.ey.com/archive/archive-news/oman-proposes-new-foreign-capital-investment-law.aspx> accessed 3 March 2016

Filaifel J, 'Conference on Intellectual Property Rights in Oman' <I:\ORGARAB\SHARED\TINA\New_docs\Muscat_February_13_and_14_05\feb_15 & 16\ar\wipo_ipr_mct_05_5 doc> (NA)WIPO/IPR/MCT/05/5 accessed 20 March 2015

FTB, 'The FDI Report 2012: Global Greenfield Investment Trends' <http://ftbsitessvr01 ft.com/forms/fDi/report2012/files/The_fDi_Report_2012.pdf> accessed 25 April 2016

Gallagher K P and Shrestha E, 'Investment Treaty Arbitration and Developing Countries: A Re-Appraisal' (2011) Global Development and Environment Institute Working Paper 11/01, 1 <http://ase tufts edu/gdae> accessed 3 May 2016

Global Smart Grid Federation, 'Dubai's 'one-stop shop' for government services' 9 July 2014 <www.globalsmartgridfederation.org/2014/07/09/dubais-one-stop-shop-for-government-services/> accessed 3 May 2015

Gordon K, 'Investment Guarantees and Political Risk Insurance: Institutions, Incentives and Development' in OECD Investment Policy Perspectives (OECD 2008) 92, <www.oecd.org/finance/insurance/44230805.pdf> accessed 29 June 2015

Gulf Business, 'Majid Al Futtaim plans $1.3bn investment in Oman malls' (2 May 2016) <www.gulfbusiness.com> accessed 4 May 2016

GCC Arbitration, 'Arbitration in Oman' (GCC Arbitration, 21 August 2010) <https://gccarbitration.wordpress.com/2012/08/21/arbitration-in-oman/> accessed 2 December 2015

Healy Consultants, 'Oman Free Zones' <www.healyconsultants.com/oman-company-registration/free-zones/> accessed 12 June 2015

Healy Consultants, 'Disadvantages of Oman company registration' <www.healyconsultants.com/oman-company-registration/#disadvantages> accessed 12 June 2015

Herbert Smith Freehills, 'South Africa terminates its bilateral investment treaty with Spain: Second BIT terminated, as part of South Africa's planned review of its investment treaties', 21 August 2013, <http://hsfnotes.com/arbitration/> accessed 15 April 2016

International Centre for Settlement of Investment Disputes (ICSID), 'Member States' <http://web worldbank.org/apps/ICSIDWEB/about/pages/Member-States.aspx> accessed 4 December 2014

International Monetary Fund (IMF), 'Members of IMF' <www.imf.org/external/about/members.htm> accessed 22 December 2014

International Monetary Fund, 'Oman-2013 Article IV Consultation Concluding Statement of the IMF Mission' (14 May 2013) <www.imf.org/external/np/ms/2013/051413.htm> accessed 28 April 2016

International Trade Union Confederation (ITUC), 'Oman: A New Trade Union Centre is Born' (19 February 2010) <www.ituc-csi.org/oman-a-new-trade-union-centre-is.html?lang=en> accessed 17 June 2015

ITUC, 'Internationally-recognised core labour standards in the Sultanate of Oman: Report for the WTO General Council review of trade policies of the Sultanate of Oman' <www.ituc-csi.org/IMG/pdf/TPR_Oman Final.pdf> accessed 18 June 2015

Invest Easy, 'One Stop Shop' <https://www.business.gov.om/> accessed 15 April 2016

Ithraa, 'Some challenges faced by investors in establishing business in Oman and solutions recommended', <www.ithraa.om> accessed (15 July 2015)

Ithraa, 'Report of challenges facing investor to establish projects in the Sultanate' <www.ncsi.gov.om./NCSI_website/N_media_ar aspx> accessed 21 May 2016

Jahn H, 'Omani Labour Law – Recent Changes and Amendments' (Lex Arabiae, January 2012) <http://lexarabiae meyer-reumann.com/issues/2012-2/vol-xvi-january-2012-1st-issue/omani-labour-law-recent-changes-and-amendments/> accessed 9 March 2015

Just Landed, 'Currency: The Omani Riyal and international transfers' <https://www.justlanded.com/english/Oman/Oman-Guide/Money/Currency> accessed 30 June 2015

King & Wood Mallesons, 'The current status of investment arbitration in the UAE' (5 December 2014) <www.kwm.com/en/ae/knowledge/insights/the-current-status-of-investment-arbitration-in-the-uae-5.December.2014.20141205> accessed 25 March 2016

KOM, 'About KOM' <www.kom.om/About-KOM> accessed 11 October 2015

KOM, <www.kom om/Incentives-Services/Incentives> accessed 12 October 2015

Majlis Alshura, 'Official website of the Majlis Alshura' <www.shura.om/en/preface.new.asp> accessed 29 April 2016

Malik M and Singh R, 'Taxation in Oman'<www.amjoman.com/docs/MEED> accessed 18 March 2015

Mann H, 'The Final Decision in Methanex v United States Some New Wine in Some New Bottles' (2005) 1 <www.iisd.org/pdf/2005/commentary_methanex.pdf> accessed 7 May 2016

Mcchantaf K, 'The Legal System and Research in the Sultanate of Oman' (July 2010) <www.nyulawglobal.org/globalex/oman.htm> 12 accessed 6 March 2015

Mellahi K and Guermat C, 'What Motivates Foreign Direct Investment? The Case of Oman' (2002) 3 Exeter Business School (Working Paper 02/01) <http://business-school.exeter.ac.uk/documents/papers/management/2002/0201> accessed 28 April 2016

Mellahi K Guermat C Frynas G and Al Bortamani H, 'Motives for Foreign Direct Investment in Gulf Cooperation Countries: The Case of Oman', 4, <http://www.mafhoum.com/press6/173E13.pdf> accessed 6 March 2015

MENA-OECD Investment Programme, 'Assessing Investment Policies of GCC Countries: Translating economic diversification strategies into sound international investment policies' <www.oecd.org/mena/investment/Preliminary%20assessment %20GCC%20invt%20policies.pdf> accessed 16 October 2014

Ministry of Commerce and Industry (MoCI), 'The Jurisdictions of the Ministry of Commerce and Industry promulgated under Royal Decree 102/2005' <https://www.moci.gov.om> accessed 3 April 2016

MoCI, 'WTO Agreement' <www.mocioman.gov.om/Main-Menu/Agreements/wto/wto-agreement> accessed 13 October 2014

MoCI, 'Highlights of the Free Trade Agreement (FTA) between the Sultanate of Oman and the United States of America' <www.mocioman.gov.om/> accessed 16 September 2014

MoCI, <https://www.business.gov.om/wps/portal/> accessed 24 March 2016

MoCI, 'Invest Easy: One Stop Shop' <https://www.business.gov.om/> accessed 15 April 2016

Multilateral Investment Guarantee Agency (World Bank Group), 'Investment Guarantees' <https://www.miga.org/investment-gurantees> accessed 14 March 2015

National Centre for Statistics and Information <https://www.ncsi.gov.om/Pages/NCSI.aspx> accessed 5 June 2016

Newton Martin H, 'What Oman's legal system needs today' (LinkedIn, 29 June 2014) <https://www.linkedin.com/pulse/20140629144025-66699887-what-oman-legal-system-needs-today> accessed 24 November 2015

OECD, 'Investment Policy Perspectives 2008' <www.oecd.org/finance/insurance/44230805.pdf> accessed 29 June 2015

Oman Law Blog, Restructuring an Entity: The Right to Transfer Employees from a Group of Entities under Omani Law'

(December 2014) <http://omanlawblog.curtis.com/2014/12/restructuring-entity-right-to-transfer.html> accessed 2 March 2015

Oman Law Blog, 'Corporate Tax Matters in Oman' (November 12 2013) <http://omanlawblog curtis.com/2013/11/corporate-tax-matters-in-oman.html> accessed 5 June 2015

Oman News Agency <http://omannews.gov.om>

Omani British Friendship Association, 'Barriers to Trade and Foreign Investment in Oman' (Joint Working Group, 10 February 2013)

'Oman's Foreign Policy, A country apart, A tiny Sultanate that not afraid to stand alone', The Economist (London, 30 May 2015) <www.economist.com/news/middle-east-and-africa/21652308-tiny-sultanate-not-afraid-stand-alone-country-apart> accessed 10 September 2015

ONA, 'Foreign investment law to create jobs, woo investors to Oman', Times of Oman (Muscat, 25 January 2016) <http://timesofoman.com/article/76202/Oman/ Government/Foreign-investment-law-to-create-jobs-woo-investors-to-Oman> accessed 3 March 2016

Open Company Singapore, 'Why Is Singapore Attractive for Foreign Investors?' (1 September 2015) <www.opencompanysingapore.com/why-is-singapore-attractive-for-foreign-investors> accessed 17 February 2016

Oxford Business Group, 'Free zones and special economic zone to boost investment', <www.oxfordbusinessgroup.com/analysis/incentivising-growth-free-zones-and-special-economic-zone-boost-investment> accessed 9 June 2015

PKF, Oman Tax Guide 2013 (May 2013) 12 <www.pkf.com/media/1958939/oman%20pkf%20tax%20guide%202013.pdf> 12 accessed 7 January 2015

Qatar Chamber of Commerce, <http://qatarchamber.com/1505> accessed 9 February 2016

Rejimon K '100% ownership for foreign investors in Oman?' Times of Oman, (Muscat, 27 January 2016) <http://timesofoman.com/article/76347/Oman/Government> accessed 4 May 2016

Schill S W, 'Investment Treaties: Instruments of Bilateralism or Elements of an Evolving Multilateral System' (The 4th Global Administrative Law Seminar, Viterbo, June 13-14 2008) <www.iilj.org/gal/documents/schill.pdf> accessed 16 January 2015

Secretariat General for Taxation (Ministry of Finance), 'Tax system in Oman' <www.taxoman.gov.om/tax%20 system_inoman_features.html> accessed 24 May 2016

Singapore International Arbitration Centre <www.siac.org.sg/> accessed 31 January 2016

Singh K, 'Efforts on to Set Up Arbitration Centre', Oman Daily Observer (Muscat, 19 August 2015) <http://omanobserver.om/efforts-on-to-set-up-arbitration-centre/> accessed 4 May 2016

Sohar Port and Free Zone, 'Incentives for setting up business' <www.soharportandfreezone.com/en/setting-up-business/incentives> accessed 13 June 2015

Supreme Council for Planning, 'Agreements' <https://www.scp.gov.om/en/Agreements.aspx> accessed 7 June 2016

Swiss Business Hub, 'The Sultanate of Oman Legal Provisions, GCC/Saudi Arabia, Riyadh' (July 2014) 8 <www.s-ge.com/schweiz/

export/de/filefield-private/files/784/field_blog_public_files/53243> accessed 4 March 2015

Tax Insights, 'Global Tax Alert' (Tax Insights, 25 January 2016) <http://taxinsights.ey.com/archive/archive-news/oman-proposes-new-foreign-capital-investment-law.aspx> accessed 3 March 2016

Tax Office Oman, 'The Legal Problems of Foreign Investment in Developing Countries' <www.taxoman.gov.om> accessed 1 October 2015

Times News Service, 'Oman's Ministry of Manpower signs pact to issue expat labour permits in five days' Times of Oman (Muscat, June 29 2015) <http://timesofoman.com/article/62230/Oman/Government/Omans-Ministry-of-Manpower-signs-pact-to-issue-expatriate-labour-permits> accessed 30 June 2015

Times News Service, 'Oman expatriate labour ban: Two-year ban to end poaching of foreign workers' Times of Oman (Muscat, 11 May 2014) <http://timesofoman.com/article/34219/Oman/Oman-expatriate-labour-ban-Two-year-ban-to-end-poaching-of-foreign-workers> accessed 22 June 2015

Townsend S, 'Oman: where to now?' (Arabian Business, 29 January 2016) <www.arabianbusiness.com/oman-where-now--620154.html> accessed 22 March 2016

UAE Free Zones, <www.uaefreezones.com/dubai_company_registration.html>

UAE Federal Ministry of Economy, <www.economy.gov.ae/English> accessed 29 March 2016

United Nations, 'Member States' <www.un.org/en/members/index.shtml> accessed 19 November 2014

United Nations Conference on Trade and Development (UNCTAD), World Investment Report 2004: The Shift Towards Services <www.unctad.org/en/docs/wir2004.en.pdf> accessed 4 May 2016

United Nations Conference on Trade and Development (UNCTAD), World Investment Report 2013; Global Value Chains: Investment and Trade for development <http://unctad.org/en/PublicationsLibrary/wir2013_en.pdf> accessed 3 May 2016

UNCTAD, World Investment Report 2015: Reforming International Investment Governance, 52 <http://unctad.org/en/PublicationsLibrary/wir2015_en.pdf> accessed 3 March 2016

UNCTAD, World Investment Report 2015: Country Fact Sheet Oman <http://unctad.org/sections/dite_dir/docs/wir2015/wir15_fs_om_en.pdf> accessed 3 March 2016

US Department of State, Diplomacy in Action <www.state.gov/documents/organization/227428.pdf> accessed 10 March 2015

US Trade Representative (USTR), 'Bahrain FTA' <https://ustr.gov/trade-agreements> accessed 5 May 2016

USTR, 'Statement of Why the United States–Oman Free Trade Agreement is in the Interest of U S Commerce' <www.ustr.gov/webfm_send/2650> accessed 13 December 2014

USTR, 'United States–Oman Free Trade Agreement Summary of the Agreement' <www.ustr.gov/webfm_send/2648> accessed 3 January 2015

USTR, 'Oman Free Trade Agreement' <www.ustr.gov/trade-agreements/free-trade-agreements/oman-fta> accessed 25 April 2016

Vaidya S K, 'Oman makes judiciary independent of executive Council reconstituted to eliminate interference', Gulf News (Dubai, 2 March 2012)

World Intellectual Property Organization (WIPO), 'Member States' <www.Wipo.int/members/en/> accessed 9 October 2015

World Bank and International Finance Corporation, Doing Business 2014, Economy Profile: Oman (2013) 5 <www.doingbusiness.org/data/exploreeconomies/oman/~/ media/giawb/doing%20business/documents/profiles/country/OMN.pdf> accessed 2 August 2014

World Bank, Doing Business 2015: Going Beyond Efficiency, Economy Profile 2015 Oman <www.doingbusiness.org/data/exploreeconomies/oman/> accessed 28 March 2016

World Bank Group, 'Economy Profile 2015 Oman' in Doing Business 2015: Going Beyond Efficiency (12th edn, World Bank 2014) 56 <www. doingbusiness.org//~/media/giawb/doing%20business/documents/profiles/country/OMN.pdf> accessed 29 December 2015

World Bank, Doing Business 2016: Measuring Regulatory Quality and Efficiency, Economy Profile 2016 Oman (World Bank) <www.doingbusiness.org/data/exploreeconomies/oman/> accessed 14 April 2016

World Bank, 'FDI: net inflows' <http://data.worldbank.org/indicator> accessed 14 April 2016

World Bank, 'Foreign Investment Net Inflow' <http://search.worldbank.org/all> accessed 13April 2016
World Economic Forum, Global Competitiveness Report 2009 Doing Business in Singapore (4 October 2010) <www.legal500.com/assets/images/stories/firmdevs/ asia_doing_business_publication_-_singapore_4.10.10.pdf> accessed 2 July 2015
WTO, 'Oman and the WTO' < https://www.wto.org/english/thewto_e/countries_e /oman_e.htm> accessed 5 May 2016
WTO 'Principles of the trading system: trade without discrimination' <www.wto.org/english/thewto_e/whatis_e/tif_e/fact2_e.htm#nondiscrimination> accessed 24 November 2014
WTO, Trade Policy Review: Report by the Secretariat: Oman (2008) 65, <www.wto.org/english/tratop_e/tpr_e/s201-02_e.doc> accessed 6 January 2015
World Trade Organization (WTO), Trade Policy Review Report by the Secretariat: Oman (2013) WT/TPR/S/295, 23, <www.wto.org/english/tratop_e/tpr_e/s295_e.pdf> accessed 8 January 2015
WTO, Trade Policy Review Report by the Secretariat: Oman (2014) 10 <www.wto.org/english/tratop_e/tpr_e/g295_e.pdf> accessed 24/09/2014
WTO, 'TRIPS' <www.wto.org/english/tratop_e/trips_e/intel2_e.htm> accessed 26 January 2014
WTO, 'Understanding the WTO: Who we are' <www.wto.org/english/thewto_e/whatis_e/who_we_are_e.htm> accessed 3 May 2016

List of Abbreviations

ACRA	Accounting and Corporate Regulatory Authority
ASCD	Authority for the Settlement of Commercial Disputes
BIPPA	Bilateral Investment Promotion and Protection Agreement
BITs	Bilateral Investment Treaties
BRA	Business Registration Act
CFCI	Committee for Foreign Capital Investment (Oman)
CSCD	Committee for the Settlement of Commercial Disputes (Oman)
DIAC	Dubai International Arbitration Centre
DNFIL	Draft of New Foreign Investment Law
DSB	Dispute Settlement Body
DSEZ	Duqm Special Economic Zone
DSU	Dispute Settlement Understanding
EDB	Economic Development Board
EFTA	European Free Trade Association
ESSL	Faculty of Education, Social Sciences and Law
EU	European Union
FACB	Freedom of Association and Collective Bargaining
FBIL	Foreign Business and Investment Law 1974
FCIL	Foreign Capital Investment Law 1994
FCN	Friendship, Commerce and Navigation
FDI	Foreign Direct Investment
FTA	Free Trade Agreement
FZ	Free Zone
GATS	General Agreement on Trade in Services
GATT	General Agreement on Tariffs and Trade
GCC	Gulf Cooperation Council
GDP	Gross Domestic Product
GFOTU	General Federation of Oman Trade Unions
ICC	International Chamber of Commerce
ICJ	International Court of Justice
ICSID	International Centre for Settlement of Investment Disputes
IE	Industrial Estate
IIA	International Investment Agreement
IISD	International Institute of Sustainable Development
ILC	International Law Commission
ILO	International Labour Organisation
IMF	International Monetary Fund

IP	Intellectual Property
ISDS	Investor-State Dispute Settlement Mechanism
ITC	Integrated Tourism Complex
ITUC	International Trade Union Confederation
KOM	Knowledge Oasis Muscat
KPI	Key Performance Indicator
MAI	Multilateral Agreement on Investment
MFN	Most-Favoured-Nation
MIGA	Multilateral Investment Guarantee Agency (World Bank Group)
MoCI	Ministry of Commerce and Industry
MoH	Ministry of Housing
MoM	Ministry of Manpower
NAFTA	North American Free Trade Agreement
NGO	Non-Governmental Organisation
OBFA	Omani British Friendship Association
OCIPED	Omani Centre for Investment Promotion and Export Development
OECD	Organization for Economic Cooperation and Development
OGSO	Official Gazette of the Sultanate of Oman
OMR	Omani Riyal
OSS	One-Stop Shop
PACP	Public Authority for Consumer Protection (Oman)
PAIPED	Public Authority for Investment Promotion & Export Development (Oman)
PAP	People's Action Party (Singapore)
PEIE	Public Establishment for Industrial Estate (Oman)
QICCA	Qatar International Centre for Conciliation and Arbitration
RTA	Regional Trade Agreement
SCP	Supreme Council for Planning (Oman)
SEZ	Special Economic Zone
SIAC	Singapore International Arbitration Centre
TNC	Trans-National Corporation
TRIMS	Agreement on Trade Related Investment Measures
TRIPS	Agreement on Trade-Related Aspects of Intellectual Property Rights
TTIP	Transatlantic Trade and Investment Partnership
UAE	United Arab Emirates
UN	United Nations
UNCITRAL	United Nations Commission on International Trade Law
UNCTAD	United Nations Conference on Trade and Development

VCLT	Vienna Convention on the Law of Treaties
WIPO	World Intellectual Property Organisation
WTO	World Trade Organization

Table of Cases

ADF v United States, ICSID Case No ARB (AF)/00/1 (NAFTA) (Award) 9 January 2003

Adel A Hamadi Al-Tamimi v Sultanate of Oman (Award) 27 October 2015 ICSID Case No ARB/11/33

Al Khorafi v Bank Sarasin & Co., 30 May 2014 (CFI 026/2009)

Alqudra Holding Company v Registrar of Trademarks (MoCI) case 628/2014, Commercial Circuit (Court of Appeal - Muscat) Judgment, 24 March 2016 Oman

Anglo-American Oil Company (1952) ICJ Reports 93

Argentina/Spain BIT 1991

Barcelona Traction Light and Power Company Limited (Belgium v Spain) (Judgment) 5 February 1970 (ICJ Reports 1970,4)

Bank Melli Iran v Pahlavi 58 F 3d 1406 (9th Cir 1995)

Case No 9/1996 Supreme Court Decision, 13 July 1996 Dubai

Case No 127/2000 High Court Decision, Appeal 10/2000 Oman

Case No 1/2002 High Court Decision 92, 28 May 2002 Oman

Case No 23/2003 High Court Decision 171, 19 November 2003 Oman

Case No 24/2004 High Court Decision 39, 26 May 2004 Oman

Case No 57/2005 Commercial Court, Commercial Objection Oman

Case No 164/2005 Administrative Court (Primary Court, First Circuit) Judgment, 27 December 2005 Oman

Administrative Court (Appeal Circuit) 5 January 2009 Oman

Case No 197/2010 Primary Court (Commercial Circit) Oman

Case No 177/2013 High Court (Commercial Circuit) Judgment 2 January 2013 Oman

Case No 301/2013 Administrative Court (Appeal Circuit - Muscat) Judgment, 30 April 2013 Oman

Case No 510/2014 Administrative Court (Appeal Circuit- Muscat) Judgment, 29 April 2014 Oman

Case No 628/2014 Administrative Court Decision, 24 March 2016 Oman

Compañía del Desarrollo de Santa Elena S.A. v Costa Rica, ICSID Case No ARB/96/1

Concrete Pipe & Products of California v Construction Laborers Pension Trust for Southern California (Judgment) US 602 (1993)

Elettronica Sicula S.p.A (ELSI) (United States of America v Italy) (Judgment) ICJ Reports 1989

Emilio Agustin Maffezini v Kingdom of Spain (Decision on Jurisdiction) 25 January 2000 (ICSID Case No ARB/97/7)
EnCana v Ecuador (Award) 3 February 2006 LCIA Case No UN3481, UNCITRAL
Enron v Argentina Award of 22 May 2007
Factory at Chorzów, Germany v Poland (Judgment) No 13, 1928 PCIJ (ser A) No 17
Fisheries Jurisdiction (United Kingdom of Great Britain and Northern Ireland v Iceland) ICJ Reports 1974
Generation Ukraine, Inc v Ukraine (Award) 16 September 2003 (ICSID Case No ARB(AF)/00/9)
Hopkins (US) v Mexico (Award) March 1926, Mexican-US General Claims Commission IV RIAA 41
Marvin Roy Feldman Karpa v United States of Mexico (Award) (ICSID Case No ARB(AF)/99/1)
McKesson Corp v Iran 116 F-Supp 2d 13 41 (DDC 2000)
Metalclad Corp v United Mexican States (Award) 30 August 2000 (ICSID Case No ARB(AF)/97/1)
Methanex Corporation v USA (Final Award on Jurisdiction and Merits) 3 August 2005 NAFTA, ICSID
Mondev International Ltd v United States of America (Award) 11 October 2002 (ICSID Case No ARB (AF)/99/2)
Noble Ventures v Romania, ICSID Case No ARB/01/11
Parsons & Whittemore Overseas Co Inc v Societe General de l'Industrie du Papier (RAKTA) 508 F 2d 969 (2d Cir 1974)
Roberts (US) v Mexico, I Op COMM (2 November 1926)
Ronald S Lauder v The Czech Republic (Final Award) 3 September 2001 UNCITRAL Arbitration
Salem (U.S.) v Egypt, 2 RIAA 1161, 1202 (1932)
Saluka Investments BV v the Czech Republic, (Partial Award) 17 March 2006 UNCITRAL Arbitration
SD Myer, Inc. v Government of Canada (Partial Award) 13 November 2000 NAFTA Arbitration 40 ILM 1408
Society of Lloyd's v Ashenden 233 F3d 473 477 (7th Cir 2000)
Southern Pacific Properties (Middle East) Ltd v Arab Republic of Egypt ICSID case No ARB/84/3
United States - Import Prohibition of Certain Shrimp and Shrimp Products Appellate Body Report T 122 WT/DS58/AB/RW (22 October 2001)
Waste Management v United Mexico States (Final Award) (Dismissing on Jurisdiction) 2 June 2000 (ICSID Additional Facility Case No ARB(AF)/00/3)

Table of Legislation

Administrative Court Law (1999) Oman
Banking Law (1974) Oman
Banking Law (2000) Oman
Basic Law of the State (1996) Oman
Civil Law (2013) Oman
Commercial Agencies Law (1977) Oman
Commercial Companies Law (1974) Oman
Commercial Register Law (1974) Oman
Law on Copyright and Related Rights 2008 Oman
Criminal Law (1974) Oman
Customs Management Law (1978) Oman
Federal Decree 35/2005 UAE
Federal Decree 9/2004 UAE
Federal Law 8/2004 UAE
Finance Law (1998) Oman
Foreign Business and Investment Law (1974)
Foreign Capital Investment Law (1994)
Foreign Investment Guidelines 1992 Oman
Foreigners' Residence Law (1995) Oman
Free Zones Law (2002) Oman
Income Tax Law on Companies (1981) Oman
Income Tax Law (2009) Oman
Industrial Property Law (2008) Oman
Insurance Companies Law (1979) Oman
Interpretation of Certain Terms and General Provisions (1973) Oman
Labour Law (2003) (amended 2006) Oman
Labour Law (2011) Oman
Law 12/2004 Dubai
Law for the Organization and Encouragement of Industry (1979) Oman
Law for the Protection of Copyright and Neighbouring Rights (2008) Oman
Law for the Protection of Developing Industries (1974) Oman
Law of Arbitration in Civil and Commercial Disputes (1997) Oman
Law of Foreign Investment 1994 Oman
Law of Intellectual Property (2000) Oman
Law of Judiciary Power (1999) Oman
Law of Money Laundering (2002) Oman
Law on Civil and Commercial Procedures 2002 Oman

Law on Industrial Property Rights (2008) Oman
Law on the Protection of Consumers (2002) Oman
Law Regulating the Administrative Apparatus of the State (1975 amended by Royal Decree 13/1976) Oman
Ministry of Finance Executive Regulation 30/2012 Oman
Ministry of Manpower Ministerial Decision 321/2009 Oman
Ministry of Manpower Ministerial Decision 550/2013 Oman
Ministry of Manpower Ministerial Decision 617/2013 Oman
Ministry of Manpower Ministerial Decision 618/2013 Oman
Patents Law (2000) Oman
Privatization Law (2004) Oman
Profit Tax Law for Establishments (1989) Oman
Royal Decree 14/1994 Oman
Royal Decree 29/2002 Oman
Royal Decree 67/2003 Oman
Royal Decree 119/2011 Oman
Royal Decree 9/2012 Oman
Royal Decree 30/2012 Oman
Royal Decree 79/2013 Oman

Table of Conventions, Treaties, and Agreements

Agreement Establishing the World Trade Organisation 1994
Agreement on Economic and Technical Cooperation 1980
Agreement on Trade-Related Investment Measures (TRIMs) 1994
Articles on State Responsibility 2001
Berne Convention 1971
Charter of Economic Rights and Duties of States 1974
Convention on the Protection of Foreign Property 1967
Convention on the Settlement of Investment Disputes between States and Nationals of Other States 1965
Draft Articles on Diplomatic Protection with Commentaries 2006
Draft Convention on the International Responsibility of States for Injuries to Aliens (1961 Harvard Draft)
Draft Convention on the Protection of Foreign Property 1967
Draft Statutes of the Arbitral Tribunal for Foreign Investment 1948
Unified Economic Agreement between the GCC States 2001 (GCC Economic Agreement)

GCC-Singapore FTA 2008
General Agreement on Trade in Services (GATS) 1995
General Agreement on Tariffs and Trade (GATT) 1994
Guidelines for International Investments 1972
Havana Charter for an international trade organization 1947
ICC proposal for an International Code of Fair Treatment for Foreign Investment (ICC Code) 1949
ICSID Convention 1966
ICSID Additional Facility Rules 1978
ILC Draft Articles on responsibility of states for internationally wrongful acts 2001
International Arbitration Act Model Law for International Arbitration 1985
International Law Association's Draft Statutes of the Arbitral Tribunal for Foreign Investment and the Foreign Investment Court (ILA Statute) 1948
Investment Protection Agreement 1976
Protocol relating to the Madrid Agreement 1989
Memorandum of Understanding between Special Economic Zone Authority of Al Duqm and the Ministry of Manpower 29 June 2015
Memorandum of Understanding Regarding the Continuation of Limited Services 1996
Model International Agreement on Investment for Sustainable Development 2005
Montevideo Convention on the Rights and Duties of States 1933
New York Convention on the Recognition and Enforcement of Foreign Arbitral Awards 1999
Oman-USA Free Trade Agreement 2009
Paris Convention 1967
Patent Cooperation Treaty 2001
Responsibility of States for Internationally Wrongful Acts 2001
Singapore Industrial Relations Act 1960
Trade and Investment Framework Agreement 2004
Treaty between Switzerland and the United States1850
Oman- USA Treaty of Amity and Commerce 1833
United Nations Charter 1945
USA-Bahrain FTA 2006
US Model BIT 2012
Vienna Convention on the Law of Treaties 1969
WIPO Copyright Treaty 2005
WTO Custom Valuation Agreement 1994

Appendix A: Oman's BITs

COUNTRY	SIGNED	ENTERED INTO FORCE
Algeria	9 April 2000	22 June 2002
Austria	1 April 2001	1 February 2003
Belarus	10 May 2004	18 January 2005
Belgium and Luxembourg	16 December 2008	
Brunei Darussalam	8 June 1998	
Bulgaria	2 February 2007	
China	18 March 1995	1 August 1995
Croatia	4 May 2004	
Egypt	25 March 1998	3 May 2000
Finland	27 September 1997	20 February 1999
France	17 October 94	4 July 1996
Germany	30 May 2007	4 April 2010
India	2 April 1997	13 October 2000
Iran	2 December 2001	8 April 2003
Italy	23 June 1993	23 January1997
Jordan	9 April 2007	
Korea	8 October 2003	10 February 2004
Lebanon	11 April 2006	20 October 2008
Morocco	8 May 2001	30 March 2003
Netherlands	17 January 2009	
Pakistan	9 November 1997	14 May 1998
Singapore	10 December 2007	12 October 2008
Sweden	13 July 1995	6 June 1996
Switzerland	17 August 2004	18 January 2005
Syria	14 September 2005	
Tanzania	16 October 2012	
Tunisia	19 October 1991	1 March 1992
Turkey	4 February 2007	15 March 2010
Ukraine	1 January 2002	
United Kingdom	25 November 1995	21 May 1996
Uzbekistan	30 March 2009	20 August 2009
Vietnam	10 January 2011	
Yemen	20 September 1998	1 April 2000

Source: UNCTAD <http: //unctad.org/Sections/dite_pcbb/ docs/bits_oman.pdf> accessed on 28 September 2014

Appendix B: Sultanate of Oman Investment Reform Map

GOVERNMENT ENTITY	AUTHORITY/BOARD
Supreme Council for Planning (SCP)	Chaired by the Sultan; Deputy Chair is Minister of MoCI
Foreign Investment Committee	MoCI
One Stop Shop	MoCI
Free Zones Committee	Chaired by Minister of MoCI
Public Establishment for Industrial Estates (PEIE)	CEO but Board chaired by Minister of MoCI
Ithraa	Board chaired by a Minister/Salim Al Ismaily
Sohar Free Zone	Board chaired by Secretary General of SCP
Sohar Port	Board chaired by Secretary General of SCP
Salalah Free Zone	Board chaired by the Minister of Tourism
Salalah Port	Board chaired by the Minister of Tourism
Al Mazunah Free Zone	Board chaired by CEO of PEIE
Duqm Special Economic Zone	Chairman (Ministerial rank) reports to Ministerial Council

Source: World Bank Group, 'Investment Reform Map – Sultanate of Oman' (unpublished paper, 25 April 2015) 8

Hussain S. Alsalmi

Oman's Basic Statute and Human Rights

Protections and Restrictions – with a Focus on Nationality, Shura, and Freedom of Association

Hardcover / 347 pp. / ISBN 978-3-87997-423-8

Recent developments in several Arab states in 2011 in what is now dubbed the 'Arab Spring', have refocused and placed human rights and freedoms norms at the forefront of many Arab states' agenda. Over the last two decades or so there have been some developments in Gulf States in the areas of human rights and developments. However, substantial oil and gas revenues have served as a basis for social and economic development and Government largesse in providing basic needs has generally kept at bay demands for political freedoms in comparison to other parts of the world.

This book seeks to answer the main question: To what extent is the application of human rights and freedoms set forth in the Oman Basic Statute compatible with international conventions?

Muhammad Zafer Alhazmi

Maritime Terminology of the Saudi Arabian Red Sea Coast

A Lexical Semantic Study

Paperback / 228 pp. / ISBN 978-3-87997-455-9

Arabic lexicographers concentrated their efforts mainly to document Classical Arabic, at the same time, they ignored a substantial body of words including material cultural terminology. This book aims to understand this phenomenon by examining a sample of Red Sea maritime terminology to prove the lack of such terms in Arabic lexica. The author creates a model of approach to help modern researchers to understand the meanings of such non-documented terms. Investigating spoken maritime terms gives this book the strength of synchronic and diachronic studies because terms were analysed against Arabic lexica from the classical ages until modern times.

Bei Fragen zur Produktsicherheit wenden Sie sich bitte an:
If you have any questions regarding product safety, please contact:

Walter de Gruyter GmbH
Genthiner Straße 13
10785 Berlin
productsafety@degruyterbrill.com